INSIDE THE NATIONAL ENQUIRER...

CONFESSIONS OF AN UNDERCOVER REPORTER

INSIDE THE NATIONAL ENQUIRER...

CONFESSIONS OF AN UNDERCOVER REPORTER

by George Bernard

Ashley Books, Inc.
Port Washington, N. Y. 11050

INSIDE THE NATIONAL ENQUIRER . . . CONFESSIONS
OF AN UNDERCOVER REPORTER
© Copyright 1977 by George Bernard

Library of Congress Number: 76-44613
ISBN: 0-87949-089-6

First Edition
9 8 7 6 5 4 3 2 1

Published by Ashley Books, Inc.
Manufactured in the United States of America

Published simultaneously in Canada by
George J. McLeod, Limited, 73 Bathurst Street,
Toronto, Ontario M5V 2P8

Address information to Ashley Books, Inc.,
Box 768, Port Washington, New York 11050

To the memory and dignity of my dad, his goodness and greatness. In a tragic death, he was cheated of seeing his last living son's book in print.

Over the years, his pride in my accomplishments was my propellent. If it were Godly possible, I would have willingly forfeited my life for his.

Photo Cover Composite By:
RON GALELLA

CHAPTER I

The *Enquirer*: What's It All About?

During five totally unforgettable years in the nostalgic sixties, I was a reporter for the *National Enquirer*. Beginning in '64, my baptismal year at the *Enquirer*, grisly gore, grime and gossip were considered great. Bravery was beautiful! Mutilation, murder and the macabre—magnificent! It was all part of a decadent decade when expose and sensationalism flourished in a sinister, sadistic style that would have caused cardiac arrest for even Jack the Ripper, and might have roused executed criminals from their graves.

"MAN EATS DOGS—He Hammers Pooches to Death, Chops Them Up And Boils Them ... He used his own dog to lure other dogs ..." Does this shock or startle you? How about, "MAN SCALDS SON TO DEATH WITH TEA" or even "DOG DRIVES CAR"? And what about "CHEN JUI LIVES AS MALE NUN for 17 YEARS"? Three of the last four mentioned here I covered as a reporter for the *National Enquirer*.

On the personality put-down ledger, I recorded the following scoops, among others: "I WAS JFK'S PROBLEM CHILD" says Judy Garland; "TWIGGY HATES AMERICANS, BUT LOVES THEIR MONEY!"; "I'M NO FAT SLOB LIKE GEORGIE GIRL" says Lynn Redgrave.

In those great gore-gossip years of the sixties, such was the steady diet of more than a million blood-starved *Enquirer* addicts. *Smut, sensationalism and sadism* was the special formula employed by publisher Generoso Pope, Jr. Using this triple threat, Pope built the circulation from 17,000, when he purchased the tottering tabloid in '52, to over a million shortly thereafter. Spellbinding his readers with stomach-turners, maintained his "SSS" policy into '68 when he discovered he had reached the point of "no additional sales."

Today, through a revamped game plan, the *Enquirer* has surpassed the five-million weekly reader mark; is sold in supermarkets; is considered a "family-type" publication and has been read, at times, by U.S. Presidents Ford, Nixon and Johnson. It had an "estimated average circulation of 4,600,000 weekly readers for the first six months of '76," the *Enquirer's* New York sales office revealed to me. And one particular issue in April '75 devoted to the funeral of Aristotle Onassis hit the jackpot: 4,800,000, their sales director claimed. But the *Enquirer's* biggest bonanza occurred on January 6, '75 when the mushrooming magazine expanded from forty-eight to sixty-four pages —"one-third *more* pages" — and recorded an unheralded 5,300,000 readership for that edition, their sales office reported. The following week, the *Enquirer,* in its new, trimmed half-inch smaller size, but still sixty-four pages, also went over five million. Currently, however, the *Enquirer* is a fifty-six page tabloid.

The *Enquirer's* '74 gross was at a whopping $41 million versus $17 million for '73, according to a recent *Newsweek* report, in which Pope is quoted as saying, "A Pulitzer Prize ain't going to win us two readers." So much for Generoso Pope, nicknamed "Gene" by those who dare refer to him on a first name basis. More in detail on "G.P." throughout the book, including a special chapter aptly titled "The High Priest of Low Brow." After all, he *is the Enquirer!*

But for this reporter, bringing in the stories of the bizarre and the beastial became a 24-hour-a-day occupation. The analogy of a bounty hunter who painstakingly and methodically pursues his man, operating at great odds and adversity, is totally repulsive to me. But that's how it really was at the *Enquirer,* or *"The Inc.,"* as it was sometimes called.

On occasion, there were disappointments, defeats. When I attempted to interview the debonaire Billy Daniels in November '64, as to why so many beautiful women had put him on a pedestal, Pierette, his beautiful French-Canadian blonde wife who was sitting between us, wouldn't budge from her seat. And when I tried to delve into his reported "other" relationships of the past, I was sure she'd claw my eyes out if I didn't either change the subject or leave the table. Daniels, who had sold over 6,000,000 copies of "That Ol' Black Magic," the song he immortalized, was Eddie Satin in Sammy Davis's "Golden Boy" on Broadway—the forty-nine year-old Billy's first play. But what I really wanted to verify, from Daniels' own mouth, was his reported "friendship" with Lana Turner in those "good old days." While Daniels was a black man, his hair still gleamed with a platinum-gold luster that only matched Pierette's. The two blonds looked so stunning together. And everytime a young girl passed our table, and stared at the debonaire Daniels, his wife would almost explode.

There were other stories that didn't pan out either. And many of these I pursued directly or in concert with one of my secret agents, reporters, correspondents or "stringers," the latter being a term for a journalist who is usually on the staff of a newspaper, magazine or broadcast station and is commissioned to moonlight. But for the most part, I succeeded. And at a mock ceremony, I was christened by the *Enquirer's* executive editor, "Goldmine George—The Man With the Midas Touch!"

Of the several hundred unusual stories the *En-*

quirer assigned to me, only two I rejected unequivocally. One involved securing a written murder confession from a man dying in a heavily-guarded New York hospital. I chalked that one up to "pangs of conscience" and not to any other considerations—especially the presence of armed guards. If a man is on his way to his Maker, he should not be disturbed enroute, by anyone, especially an *Enquirer* reporter.

The other assignment I turned down involved jumping out of a plane—free falling—and writing about the sensation with pad and pen while falling—as a professional took my picture as I plummeted to earth more than 10,000 feet below. Doing the insane was my bag, but in this case my assignment followed a terrifying story of September 26, '65 that made me bail out of the project: "MY PAL WAS SO BUSY SHOOTING PICTURES OF ME TANGLED IN MY PARACHUTE THAT HE FELL TO HIS DEATH ... Because His Chute Had Failed."

Can you believe that two editions earlier, the *Enquirer* reported: "DOCTOR TELLS PATIENT—GO JUMP OUT OF A PLANE ... To Cure Jitters, Heart Trouble and Ulcers!"

Then in the *Enquirer's* July 17, '66 edition: "SKY DIVING—CHASING ADVENTURE ... OR CHASING DEATH ... Every 2 weeks, on the average, a sky diver falls to his death somewhere in the U.S. What makes men and women gamble with their lives all over the country while pursuing this dangerous sport?" Certainly, I was not going to find out to satisfy a publisher's wretched whim.

In three giant ads that ran in the *New York Times, Chicago Tribune* and the *Detroit Free Press* in '74, Gene Pope risked the lives of thirty-five people to prove a point. The ad stated, in part: "Here at the *National Enquirer* we've got the country's highest-paid journalists working double-time to report on all the lively, entertaining news they can find.

"But—if things get a bit quiet—we'll occasionally set out to make a little news of our own. According to the *Guinness Book of Records* the world's record for skydivers-linked-up-in-a-circle was twenty-four jumpers. 'Duck soup,' we said. And organized the *Enquirer* team. We got thirty-five jumpers, three pilots, a specially-modified DC-3, and a photographer with enough nerve to put on a parachute.

"We waited three days at a Florida airport for the weather to be just right. Then, on March 25th of this year, our team went up to 13,500 feet and then careened out of one small door in twelve seconds. (That may be a record in itself—matched only by New Yorkers exiting the IRT subway at Grand Central.)

"It took six of these jumps to set the record. On that sixth leap, twenty-nine of our jumpers managed to grab hands for the required minimum of three seconds. We're presently awaiting official certification of the world's record.

"Maybe all of this doesn't quite jibe with what you've thought of the *Enquirer*. Well, here are some facts that may help you jibe more accurately:—With a 31% *jump* in circulation over the last twelve months, we're the fastest growing major weekly in America . . ."

Just to justify the word "jump" in a sales pitch, Pope commissioned thirty-five human lives to play daredevil. And like a movie director who calls the shots and reshoots the scene over until satisfaction is achieved, Pope did six retakes—even after his tabloid told of the taboos of skydiving, over and over again. What men won't do to make a buck in this business!

The "insane" I speak of includes crawling, very cautiously, into an animal cage to photograph a real live lion said to have partially-paralyzed

front paws. Nothing was said, however, about his
menacing roar that rattled the bars of his cage
and shook the shit out of me. And what about his
razor-sharp dentures, powerful jaws and the
agility the *Enquirer* assured me " wasn't there.
He's a cripple!" And how would you like to crawl
through the muck and scum of a typical New
York City sewer tunnel—just for the *Enquirer*
experience? Believe me, all refuse canals are
alike—in Chicago, San Francisco, or any other
big city. They're real shitty!

I've even been attacked by a pack of ferocious
dogs, while in a deserted cemetery, no less, with
no one about but the dead. A former prize fighter,
who spars with his pet hawk, presented problems
when the winged wonder almost gashed my eyes
out. A character billed as "the tallest man in the
world" at a quarter-inch short of nine feet, in
anger lifted me over his head and threatened to
throw me out a hall window fourteen stories
above Broadway. Reason: I could not assure him
in writing that the *Enquirer* would run his
story—and pay him for it! And if that's not
enough, three muggers jumped me on a deserted
street of Manhattan's West Side while I was
making my way home from an interview with a
psychiatrist. Subject of interview: the ways of
reducing crime in America.

While my journalistic skills were established,
my expertise as a photographer was also required by the *Enquirer*. The more gory and gruesome the photos and the more vivid the captions
describing the terror—the more money this reporter received. So, pictures were an absolute
must, and in most instances, were as vital, if not
more so, than the text itself.

If a family perished in a head-on crash and
their heads were cut off in the process, it was a
good bet that the *Enquirer* photo editor would
want the death scene pictures for centerfold dis-

play. Mutilated animals—dogs, birds and especially horses—were on priority status. I recall one particular picture spread of a stallion's head lying in a pool of its own blood. While the thoroughbred was being transported by open trailer, the animal stuck his head out for a better view of the countryside. The horse tragically didn't see the tunnel approaching and, on impact, lost his head.

Often the dead had to be resurrected, temporarily, by raiding morgues in the middle of the night. Imagine the anguish, the despair and the hatred generated towards the *Enquirer* by the family and friends of the deceased when they saw their loved ones plastered through the pages of what was then the most terrifying tabloid in the country.

When you "raid a morgue," you pull the corpse out of a special drawer, photograph the deceased, then return the body to where you found it. Not a very pleasant business. Yet again, who ever said covering stories for the *Enquirer* was utopian?

It was not uncommon to receive disturbing phone calls from crying and vindictive mourners. Some of the questions they would invariably ask included: "How could you? How much did they pay you? Are you able to sleep at night? Why couldn't you let him rest in peace? He was such a good man, why?" Over the years, and even today, these questions plague me, over and over again. "Why?"

This book is not totally about one George Bernard and how through a strange series of circumstances he came to be a reporter for the *National Enquirer*. It is not restricted to this journalist's vivid accounts of "true" stories that, for the most part, often were stranger than fiction.

Certainly my focus will not be a rehash of old *Enquirer* articles. In part, it will be the story behind the story. It will also be a highly graphic insight into the people behind the scene at the publication. And, most significantly, a focus on Generoso (Gene) Pope Jr., the illustrious publisher of the *National Enquirer,* which today boasts on its masthead: "The Largest Circulation of Any Paper In America."

Pope, now forty-nine, a towering, rugged man of six feet, four inches and steel-gray hair, looks like a movie star who could have played the lead in one of Hollywood's super-westerns. Soft-spoken, whenever you can get close enough to hear him speak, he could be mistaken for a former Washington Redskins defensive tackle. But there is no mistaking that he is the sole guiding genius behind the paper's overwhelming success.

"My articles editors kid me, 'You should do a rags-to-riches-story about yourself," Pope once told William R. Amlong, an extremely competent staff reporter for the *Miami Herald.* "I'll try and stay in the background. The average *Enquirer* reader never heard of me," Pope modestly adds.

True, Gene! The average *Enquirer* reader was so mesmerized by your hypnotic headline-grabbers that he never bothered to inquire, or never cared, who you were. Frankly, I'll bet you never knew too much, if anything, about George Bernard. If you did, I wasn't aware. One thing for sure, however—you know of me now!

For five years we exchanged glances and hellos over our infrequent meetings. I knew well what was in your head—what you liked and what you disdained. And the information came to me from your own employees, who nine-out-of-ten times, were extremely accurate. It was in this way that the feedback allowed me to survive. Other dedicated reporters for you, Gene, did not subscribe to this service and accordingly perished.

And for all you might have known, I could even have been a spy for the competition—*Midnight* or the *Insider*. Or, I might have been a paid assassin for the respected *Time* and *Newsweek*—to knock you off, editorially, in the cold and calculated manner I character-tainted, exposed and derided the scores of innocent people and personalities you placed on the *Enquirer's* "most wanted" list.

Can you believe that in five years I was never invited even once to join the *Enquirer's* chief executive for lunch? Yet, I was the *Inc's* ace reporter — "Goldmine George" — who brought in a treasure of "exclusive" front-page pieces that obliterated the competition.

It is said by those who work for you, and those you've canned—and there have been so many— that you eat, live and sleep the *Enquirer*, seven days a week, or is it eight? It is said that if the *Enquirer* was taken away from you tomorrow, you would jump off the Empire State Building. But before you took your life, you'd leave instructions with the new publisher, exactly how to cover the plunge, and what layout to use.

Until now the inner doings of the *Enquirer* were a tight-lip secret. Just wait until you wade deeper into this book, especially the chapter devoted to you. For the first time you will learn about the *Enquirer* what you never knew before, and surely, what you never dreamed existed.

There is considerably more to relate about Gene Pope. Unfortunately, he has no interest in publishing his own rags-to-riches story, but his constant quest for scoops and authenticity in reporting the facts—to the most minute detail— has become a full-time and very lucrative occupation. Others, which include psychiatrists, psychologists, sociologists, might describe Pope's compulsive behavior as "monomania"—an apt term Herman Melville used to characterize Captain Ahab's frenzied pursuit of the white whale in *Moby Dick*.

For those who call Pope's page-one exclusives "bunk" and a "lot of garbage without a shred of truth", I can only speak for myself. Never have I fabricated an article in my life. I have always been able to discern fact from fallacy, and was never tricked into writing a feature story for Pope that was bullshit!

Pope also strove diligently for accuracy in reporting. On occasion, he was known to have spent more money verifying a reporter's facts than the fee he was paying for the story. And old Gene was known to have gone as high as $25,000 for a particular story he had to have!

But while Gene's editorial gang never changed the facts, they often toyed with—and altered—quotes. This harsh fact came to light recently when a resourceful reporter from the *Palm Beach Post* rummaged through Pope's garbage and came up with the evidence.

On most occasions, my articles were published with a fictitious byline—to protect George Bernard from the wrath of the disgruntled and vengeful. Certainly, Gene Pope would hardly pay the expense of stationing a 24-hour bodyguard outside my office. So, Paul Mazzelli, Jack Collins, Kenneth Dorn, Philip Ashton became some of the pseudonyms I attached to my articles. In each instance I always introduced myself on *Enquirer* assignments as George Bernard. And it would take three weeks to a month to get the story in print after being approved for publication. By that time, connecting the interview to George Bernard when the byline read Paul Mazzelli became quite difficult. Today, however, Pope has streamlined his entire production operation and it takes only one week to get his paper on the street and into the supermarkets.

The *Enquirer* became the dread of almost every press agent in America—at least, the competent ones who gave a darn about their clients. Many flacks were on salary just to keep their accounts out of papers like the old *Enquirer*.

Only God could help me if my cover was ever exposed to a vindictive press agent. In such an event, my effectiveness as an undercover reporter would have been seriously impaired and I would have had one of two choices open: resign, or play a game of Russian roulette with myself. Certainly, I would have been barred, banned and blackballed—which are all one and the same—from most of the celebrity affairs, which for this undercover reporter became the greatest source of unsuspecting personality prey.

From time to time, articles did appear under the byline of George Bernard. These were of the "pussy cat" variety, mostly human interest stories where nobody got hurt editorially, and where there was absolutely no fear of recrimination. Usually these byline pieces were psychiatric-oriented.

But to succeed as an effective *Enquirer* reporter, it was necessary to establish at least one dependable front, or cover. If you had two covers going for you, you were way ahead of the game. For the mere mention of the *National Enquirer* sent shivers down one's spine and became the instant kiss of death: "Interview over. Unless you leave, I'm calling the police," one starlet was known to have barked. Strange, though. Gene Pope would believe the *Enquirer* rang the same responsive chord as *The New York Times*.

I recall vividly stalking Tony Randall and Shelley Winters, who were at the same Sunday afternoon benefit cocktail party, in a congested room overlooking Broadway. Tony complained of a migraine and begged me to leave him alone. My eyes then followed Shelley carefully around the room for some twenty minutes as I waited for a propitious moment to ask her why she didn't consider herself a sex symbol—assuming she considered herself anything but a screen siren. There were two effective openings I would use: either flatter a person and allow the interview to slowly evolve; or openly accuse them of being or doing something outrageous, and force them to defend themselves. But when accusing, I would be sure the statement was framed like, *"others have said that . . ."* or, "It was reported that . . ."

Before I could rattle off the question, Shirley Schrift, born in St. Louis on August 18, '22, otherwise known as Shelley Winters, blurted out: "Why are you . . . you following me? What are you anyway, some reporter for the *National Enquirer?*"

I turned red, then white . . . and then the blues set in patriotically. She was too quick for me. I couldn't think fast enough, and so I thought it best to exit.

When I spoke with Jimmy Stewart in Yuma, Arizona on the movie set of *Flight of the Phoenix,* I never would have gained the confidence of the drawling, Oscar-winning actor if I had said, "Pleased to meet you. I'm George Bernard of the *National Enquirer.*" Instead of hearing Stewart tell me how he became charged being around young, attractive girls on the set, I would have been shown the gate. But as there weren't any women in *Flight of the Phoenix,* Stewart, who had made movies with film beauties Jean Harlow, Maureen O'Hara, Lee Remick, among others, said that though he was happily married, he was glum. At age fifty-seven, Jimmy said young women kept him feeling younger, the main reason he refused to quit making movies.

And I might not have received cooperation a year earlier in Mexico City when a baby was born in a phone booth, if the name *Enquirer* was bandied about. Even in Mexico they knew of the tenacious tabloid.

This again brings me to the absolute necessity

of establishing covers—which for George Bernard would later include an international news agency headquartered on Broadway in New York City complete with stringers on call at any moment of the day . . . anywhere in the world.

I also set up and incorporated an entertainment organization as another cover. And as yet another front, I employed two "pirate" stations called Radio Caroline which were broadcasting "illegally" to more than thirty-nine million people. The stations were aboard two reconstructed World War II merchant ships moored in separate locations three and a half miles off the coast of Great Britain. This clandestine broadcast network, through my direction as a front for obtaining stories for the *Enquirer,* was later to precipitate a major controversy with Senator Robert F. Kennedy. Contained in a separate chapter is his "spirited" speech that has never been printed anywhere in America.

My memoirs also focus on the Kennedy beat —all of them. While writing for the *Enquirer,* I came to know their comings and goings; the people they associated with, their friends, their antagonists.

Jackie, Robert and Ted were high on *The Inc's* "most wanted" list. Stories of the late J.F.K. were in great demand, too. If you couldn't get an interview with the Kennedys, and they were almost impossible to come by, then speculation on the clan from *leading* psychiatrists was second-best and highly valued by Pope.

There are those political pundits who would wager their last dollar that Ted Kennedy will run for the highest office in the land someday and will become President of the United States. But what do we really know about Edward, except what we read in the newspapers? Are the stories of his "other" life true? And is he any different in this respect to his late brothers John and

Robert? What of Ted's "friendship" with an exotic dragon lady . . . and his fondness for rum cokes? Were you aware that there once existed a growing rift between Bobby and Teddy?

Speaking of rifts between brothers, what about the one between co-anchormen of the historic "Huntley-Brinkley Report?"

You'll also learn the truly fascinating story of my man Chu in China and some of the most bizarre murders and mulitations ever to come out of Southeast Asia.

While the pen, pad and camera were indispensable, I also maintained an arsenal of sophisticated taping and other bugging equipment. One recorder, the size of an eyeglass case, weighed only eleven ounces and retailed for $700. The intricate instrument featured twin stereo microphones that were taped to my chest and recorded in stereo—at a radius of seventy-five feet. The promotional literature that accompanied the sale of the recorder stated: " Each word—all intonations and inflections—even whispers—unmistakably captured on tape . . . used extensively by law-enforcement agencies . . . " The manager of their New York office showed me two orders for the pocket recorder: one was from the F.B.I.—the other from the Kremlin!

Political in-fighting existed at the *Enquirer,* where the ax fell often, and hard. Articles editors, layout men and special reporters came and went. At times, it was like one revolving door. I was one of the three or four reporters "permitted" to write for *The Inc.* out of the New York base—which was considered the highest honor. Silly grudges, on occasion, kept perfectly good articles from ever appearing in print. So one could not afford the luxury of having any enemies.

Then there were the silly shrinks—psychiatrists and psychologists—who played God to *Enquirer* readers. What flowed from their mouths to the printed page was tantamount to an edict from the Pope. Many of the shrinks were emotionally disturbed, were tottering on playful perversions and on the brink of suicide.

The lore of this literary legacy would be incomplete if I failed to include Ron Galella. Today, thanks to Jacqueline Onassis, almost everyone in America knows him. They had a falling out which was only resolved after their day in court—which lasted twenty-six days. As a result, the *paparazzo* is restricted in his shooting of the former first lady to beyond an invisible barricade of twenty-five feet. But ten years ago, he was just another unknown, fighting for recognition as a free-lance photographer. Together, as a team on many assignments, we brought in the exclusives, often facing bolted doors and hostile hosts.

There was the story I mentioned of a leading actress who insisted she wasn't a fat slob . . . and a well-known actor who claimed he *was* one. The latter, at the time, was "too hot to print." Another that smacked of libel, and appears here for the first time, involved my taking a death confession from the late Tallulah Bankhead.

I have likened myself to a relentless bounty hunter. But after one particular assignment at which I miserably failed, I slept considerably easier. The *Enquirer* wanted a hatchet-job done on Inger Stevens, best known for her long-running TV series, "The Farmer's Daughter." And so, while on the set of a movie she was making, I tried reaching her by phone. Whether out of intuition, or just simple fright of reporters, the bright-eyed Inger would not accept my calls at the Hollywood studio. "Thank God!" I said to myself. "Hasn't she had enough trouble in her life?" Others could better withstand the piercing *Enquirer* blade, so I put my ax back in my coat

pocket and reported the "good" news to *The Inc.*
Known for her despondency, Inger must have
been off-guard when she later appeared in the
Enquirer. Later, she took her own life. Fragile,
fearful and so delicately beautiful, she will always be remembered.

Other personalities were also terrified of the
Enquirer. Many became infuriated at seeing
themselves in *The Inc.* and would write deadly
poison-pen letters to the publisher. On December
20, '64, the *Enquirer's* cover story accused Anne
Bancroft of admitting: "I BURP AND SLURP
IN PUBLIC." If you want to know what the
award-winning actress did about it, write her
agent.

Preying and prying on the innocent, the guilty,
those whose only desire was to be left alone, was
part and parcel of the job. I was twenty-four-
years old when I first began servicing the *Enquirer.* When I left at twenty-eight, I felt like a
man of eighty-two. I was wrecked.

Sleep was a scarce commodity. I lived off pots
of black coffee which sickened me. But it was better than konking out. Many times I asked myself
if it was all worth it. I was on a treadmill. I
couldn't get off. The money was fantastic and I
didn't have to battle with my greatest enemy—
boredom.

Always performing with professionalism, in
retrospect I have little to be ashamed of. Still,
there are many ex-*Enquirer* executives in top
levels of communications and publishing today,
who constantly cringe in fear at the prospect of
being identified with the gore-gossip phase of the
Enquirer.

Some of these former *Enquirer* generals secretly consider themselves to be fugitives from
ethical justice. I recently met with some and
have given my solemn word not to expose their
cover in any way—in exchange for their coopera-

tion in providing important data to be contained
in this "unauthorized, first time ever" account of
the *National Enquirer*.

Debonair Billy Daniels, who immortalized "That Ol
Black Magic", with blonde wife, Pierette, who sat be-
tween me and a juicy story I was trying to worm out of
Billy. (*Ben McCall*)

Joyful Joey Heatherton says a few words to me at the opening of a New York-TV station in '64.

Saying "hello der" to Marty Allen (right) and Steve Rossi before they said "goodbye der" to each other.

CHAPTER II

Mitchum's Madness, The Wild Party, And
The "New" Leak-Proof Cars Leak!

Robert Mitchum clenched a ferocious fist and dared me to move from my spot, or blink an eye. The actor with the battered, belligerent face, who has gone on record as saying — "I agree with the guy who wrote that I look like a shark with a broken nose" — placed me in imminent peril of losing my fine-featured face.

Becoming more plastered and incoherent by the passing seconds, my interview with rugged Robert was becoming increasingly distasteful. If there's one step I would never stoop to, that is taking advantage of an intoxicated individual.

So, as I attempted to cut the interview session short and flick off the record button on my Wollensak, glassy-eyed Mitchum rose half-way from his seat, tightened his grip on my right hand, and directed: "Sit down!"

A gent sitting alongside, who earlier had presented himself as the performer's press agent, nodded his head, leaned over the table and whispered that I leave the machine running and go along with it.

I sat back in my seat.

"Now, where were we?" Mitchum queried me, burped, then again.

"We're at Danny's Hideaway, Mr. Mitchum," I responded with a distinct tremor in my faltering voice.

"Now, who are ya with . . . and what's this for?"

"I'm with Trans-Atlantic Features . . . and the article is going to be syndicated," I replied.

"That's good. Now, what do you want to know?"

"Well," I nervously continued, "you're considered top box office ... one of the most accomplished actors in Hollywood today ... "

"Wait one minute. There is no Hollywood. It's just a small square in the ground that once was ... " He continued to feed from his drink.

My close friend, photographer Ben McCall, was also seated at the table. Ben knew just when and where a celebrity could be found and was an excellent door-opener for this *Enquirer* reporter.

"Mr. Mitchum. What's your image? How do you see yourself?" I politely asked, hoping that I would get a short answer, thank him for his time and be off.

Instead, my seemingly innocuous question struck an unpleasant chord. Mitchum regained his grasp of my right hand and applied excruciating pressure as he responded:

"What's my image? What are you, some sort of juvenile masturbator, or something? What do I have to do — stand before a mirror and compare my cock to yours?"

Ben sensed the impending danger. But even this most clever of free-lance photographers was not aware of my *Enquirer* intentions. Had he been, it is likely he would have abandoned me on the spot and I surely would have been bait for the shark.

"Hey, George is a good guy," pleaded Ben. "Why, he meant nothing by it, you old son of a gun," Ben laughed.

Mitchum's grasp loosened. I pulled my hand away and tested for circulation. And as I removed the recorder plug from the restaurant's wall outlet, Mitchum's face broke into a pleasantly warm smile.

"A pleasure to meet you. Maybe we can do a follow-up later," I said.

Mitchum rose and shook my hand.

"You've got some grip," I said.

"Sorry if I hurt you," he apologized, seeming now to grow more sober.

"If you want to reach me, call me ... Ya got a pencil?"

"Sure."

"Well, call me at 301 area code ... Greenfield 6-3127. That's Maryland. I'll be there in three days ..."

"Right!"

My associate did just that, and the *Enquirer* had a story. But I was still in shell shock from the shark.

Several months after my encounter with Mitchum, Gene Carter, in his *Enquirer* HOLLYWOOD KEYHOLE column of September 12, '65 headlined: "MITCHUM KO'S TWO BULLIES WITHOUT THROWING A PUNCH — Robert Mitchum Knocked Out Two Thugs The Other Night Outside a Sunset Strip Spot ... Mitchum knocked the bullies' heads together."

If you believe Mitchum's not one to be seriously reckoned with, and the bully beat-up was just an isolated instance, I refer you to Carter's January 2, '66 *Enquirer* report: "MITCHUM & WAYNE TEAM UP TO KNOCK DOWN FIVE HOODLUMS." Want more? July 2, '67, also by Carter: "MITCHUM BEATS UP A BUNCH OF FLAG BURNERS."

How lucky I was to escape the explosive short fuse of Robert Charles Duran Mitchum.

One of my associates, an affable British chap whom we will know as Reggie Crawford, assured me that lady luck was watching over me.

It was through Reggie that I became an unrelenting reporter for the *Enquirer*. And oddly enough, my first contact with the *Enquirer* came at a party, and at the time, I didn't even know it.

It was the summer of '64. My boss had just been canned and I was promoted from writer-producer to acting general manager, a post I would hold at a local TV station until a replacement could be found. On a Monday morning in August, a friend tipped me off about an all-night party. The big bash was to be held that same evening in a posh apartment on Manhattan's East Side. Wild girls and a wild live band were on the double bill, which, this friend insisted, also featured John Lennon.

As my cab pulled in front of the building, I saw throngs of young people in their early to mid-twenties, of all descriptions — long hair, bearded, others clean-shaven and many young girls, some very sharp. All were lined up, three or four abreast, and maybe one hundred deep. Most appeared irate that they couldn't get into the party.

I paid the driver and pushed my way to the front of the line past three ferocious-looking guys who were trying desperately to maintain a semblance of order. I flashed a station press card, entered the building and made my way towards the blaring music. I rapped several times on the door with my fist, then the heel of my shoe. Between record changes somebody came to the door.

A beat-looking young man of average height, a three o'clock shadow in a green pastel shirt and blue jeans greeted me in a hostile manner: "Can't you see there's no more room, chum?" he said in a dripping British accent.

"May I come in?" I asked, ignoring his rudeness.

"Are you a little deaf?" he said, annoyed at my attutude.

I quickly pulled out my press card and mentioned the name of the TV station I headed. His eyes lit up. Instantly, the situation was turned around. Impressed, for reasons I was to learn later, he invited me in.

About ten guests left after I was in the party some ten or fifteen minutes and I finally had some breathing room.

My host, Reggie Crawford, told me to make myself a drink, "and have a good time."

My friend's guarantee that *everything* would be *wild* was true — the music, the girls, and even John Lennon performed *all* evening — on a 45rpm with George, Paul and Ringo.

Unless you sported a British accent, or could fake it reasonably well, you couldn't get to first base with any of the gals there — all of whom were very high on the British. Americans were not on their menu, which featured explicit sex in the far bedroom and love-making in the bathroom shower stall.

The night seemed destined for a total loss when Reggie brought an alluring dark-haired, green-eyed girl of twenty, or so, over to me.

"Mr. George Bernard Shaw, meet Miss Carla Warren. She's . . . What are you, honey?"

"I'm an actress" she replied, fluttering her false eyelashes.

"George is the grandson of Britain's greatest writer, if not the world's," Reggie laid it on. "Look, I've got to run. Stay here as long as you wish, but just give me your business card, if you have one. I'll be contacting you."

I gave Reggie my card and he was off. Can you imagine — he left his own party?

Carla really believed Reggie's bull, and who was I to contradict anyone? Carla and I spent the next three days in bed together.

About a week later, Reggie called me at the TV station and invited me to lunch.

"Look, you're at the TV station, and you can probably accomplish a few things with greater efficiency than I can. You've got a great cover that I can use," he stressed over a prime ribs lunch at Gallagher's Steak House.

"I write for the *National Enquirer*," he confessed, "and . . ."

"Did I hear you correctly?"

"Yes. The *National Enquirer*. But why so shocked?"

I nodded my head and said nothing.

Reggie was wearing a Christian Dior suit. Glistening gold cufflinks matched his pocket lighter which rested by the side of the ash tray that was already brimming with five or six half-smoked cigarettes.

Reggie looked as if he hadn't slept for a week. He offered me a Wing's from his cigarette case that was also fashioned in gold.

With a snapping of the fingers, he summoned a waiter. "Double scotch on the rocks and my friend will have ..."

"A Heineken" I said.

"To get to the point," Reggie continued, "each year the *Enquirer* secures and publishes photos of America's *new* cars, *before* the automobile corporations actually release the pictures to the newspapers and magazines. This year the *Enquirer* is having problems."

"What can I do about it?" I asked.

"As I said," he began to explain, now missing the ash tray, and crushing his cigarette into the tablecloth. "Your TV station is a great cover ... and you appear to be a bright guy who I'm sure could *always* use some more bread ..."

The constant reference to the *National Enquirer* sent shrill pains to my stomach. Suddenly, I had lost my appetite. For many years I would cringe at the mere thought of being discovered reading the *Enquirer* concealed between the pages of the *New York Times* — especially in the City College library or cafeteria. But I had never met anyone who had anything to do with such a publication, no less write for it!

Reggie promised me an even split of $1600. Looking me straight in the eye, he assured me the figure he quoted was the *Enquirer's* top fee for this particular annual assignment. Frankly, even if Reggie was lying and he was getting $3200, or even $4800 on the successful completion of the assignment, I couldn't have cared less. As far as I was concerned, this was found money.

"You'll have $800 — cash — in your hand, and thousands more will follow. You'll make more through me and the *Enquirer* than you've ever dreamed of making at your TV station, mate," Reggie assured me.

"General Motors, Ford, American Motors, Chrysler and their Dodge Division — photos and captions. Now, remember, they're carefully guarded," he cautioned.

Working an average of sixty, or more, thankless, grueling hours each week at the station, underpaid and understimulated, I agreed to consider the offer.

"When would I start, and when do you need the pictures?" I asked.

"You start right NOW. You have *two* weeks, no more! *Do not,* I repeat, *Do not,* under any circumstances in securing this material, ever mention the names Reggie Crawford or the *National Enquirer.* If for any reason one of the automobile companies nabs you — and it shouldn't happen — I will say, and so will the paper, that we don't know you. Get it?"

"Yes, I get it. But, where's my instructions?"

"Your instructions are to use your ingenuity and *successfully* complete the assignment. Now, if you feel you're not up to it ..."

Although I had reservations about his boast of great wealth, I was intrigued enough to accept. "I'll do it," I said with new conviction. I felt like agent 007, and the feeling was exhilarating!

Before we left the restaurant, Reggie briefly filled me in on the logistics. The photos, he said, would be kept "in vaults, locked in impenetrable safes, and in tightly secured storage cabinets."

Reggie explained that the car companies normally release, through their press departments, photos and information about their new models sometime in late September or October. But when the pictures appear in the *Enquirer* in late August or early September, the concerned and impulsive consumer who was comtemplating buying "this year's model" might decide to wait until the *new* models went on sale to the general public. "It's the old saying," Reggie noted. "What you don't know, you won't miss. But once you know it. ..."

Consequently, through an early break in the *Enquirer*, automotive dealers throughout the country would wind up with large inventories and be "forced to eat 'em" — an American expression Reggie had picked up, which aptly described the mess that would be created.

In essence, Reggie pointed out, the auto dealers would take a financial bath. But that didn't worry the *Enquirer* which was not in the market to sell cars, but newspapers.

Reggie said that *after* I delivered the goods — and he was now talking as if it would be a snap for me — the paper would totally sell out that car issue, even with a large extra run. Those who never purchased the *Enquirer*, and those who weren't steady readers, would buy it just for the car exclusives. For Pope, it meant an immediate circulation jump over the previous editions, and the chance to capture new readers who otherwise might not spend 15 cents for the paper— that was the price the 32-page tabloid was selling for in 1964, at *every* newsstand in the United States and Canada.

Several months later, when I was firmly entrenched as a *National Enquirer* reporter, I would query some of the staff about the paper's excellent distribution, and the fact that it was prominently displayed, even next to the *New York*

Times, on *every* newsstand.

"It wasn't always that way," a staffer confided. "When our boss took over the paper, there were those newsstand people who said they had no room for the *Enquirer,* and practically told us to get lost. Then, suddenly, those uncooperative newsstands mysteriously were blown up in the middle of the night. You know, the mob works in strange, and quick ways," he said.

"Preposterous," I said to myself.

At the time I believed — and still do today — that the newsstands were *forced* to carry the *National Enquirer* and prominently display the tabloid for one very good reason: "The public ate it up!" The insinuation that pressures from the underworld influenced the news dealers, in my opinion, is truly preposterous!

Reggie had picked up the check and dropped me off at the station while he continued on to the *Enquirer,* where he was going to report that I had accepted my first assignment for the paper.

CHAPTER III

The Goliaths and
My Sling Of Ingenuity

That night was spent restlessly in bed, pondering the problem of securing the car pictures.

My first thoughts were to offer a bribe, but with all the car companies I had to reach, and the $800 I had to work with, if this plan were possible, I'd wind up probably losing on the deal—and nobody likes to take an unnecessary loss. So, the pay-off was out!

I considered posing as an out-of-town automotive buyer who was looking to pick up two hundred *new* cars. Or even as an oil tycoon with millions who might demand hysterically to see the '65 models.

A year later I would learn that this exact millionaire approach had actually been put into operation by the *Enquirer* in the past—and had failed. The man portraying the eccentric oil executive was an actor. The performer, a virtual unknown—the *Enquirer* wanted it that way—got to see a short twenty-minute color film of the new cars at a private screening set up for him by one of the automotive giants. During the showing, the actor inconspicuously clicked off twelve shots through a hole he had cut in his pants that concealed a miniature spy camera. Unfortunately, he used slow film and the prints were blurred and unusable.

But this determined actor didn't give up, just as I couldn't either. He next posed as an automotive dealer at a private showing of the cars at a New York exposition center. A major problem arose: the hood of the car he was about to photograph was open for dealer inspection of the engine and other parts. So, the actor closed the hood, stepped back ten feet and through the same hole in his pants pocket, started clicking. Suddenly, a security guard collared the chap and threw him out bodily, ignoring the actor's admittance pin that featured a miniature U.S. flag the *Enquirer* had paid for under the table. How unpatriotic the guard! Again, the actor's shots, that were rushed, were unusable. The *Enquirer,* did, however, arrange to replace his torn pants with a new set of trousers.

I was still wide awake when my alarm went off at 7:30. Through the night my imagination had run the gamut, which even included thoughts of flying out to Detroit over the weekend and trying my luck there. Surely, I thought, I might be able to photograph some of the models as they were being transported to the East and other sections of the country that might be holding dealer demonstrations. But, I reasoned, there would probably be as many guards there as here. So, that took care of that idea.

As I showered and dressed I recalled a cooperative, conscientious secretary to a vice-president at General Motors. The girl, whom we will know as Angela, was extremely helpful in putting my sales manager together with her boss and the media people who buy TV spots.

Angela, whose big blue eyes were anything but angelic-looking, had a crush on me. I wondered if her naughty appearance was skin deep. If so, my *Enquirer* assignment, at least at G.M., would be completed in short time.

I met Angela for cocktails at the Palm Court of the Plaza that evening after she finished work. She assumed our meeting was social.

"Well, it's about time we got together," Angela scolded me.

"It would have been sooner, but I've been so busy at the station. There isn't a day that I . . ."

"Oh, you poor dear," she leaned over and kissed me.

"Angela," I said, bracing myself for what was to come next. "How would you like to make some quick spending money?"

Her face stiffened. She drew her hands back and they dropped like petrified wood in her lap.

"What? Are you propositioning me? I'm no hooker, you know. Hey, I thought you cared for me!"

"Nobody's asking you to do anything like that ... and I *do* care for you," I assured her.

I now felt uncomfortable telling her my true intentions, but I blurted them out anyway: "I need photos of G.M.'s full line for '65!"

"You son of a bitch!" her tirade began. "You got me here because you wanted car pictures. I could have told you right off the bat it can't be done. Look, nobody can get their hands on them—not me, not my boss. There's an embargo on them, you know."

"Yes, I know."

"And even if I could get them—which I can't—I wouldn't risk my job for some 'quick spending money.' You really have some fuckin' nerve. Where's the powder room?"

"That way," I pointed, dumbfounded by her volatile reaction to my offer.

It seemed she was away a good half hour before I got up from my seat and attempted to inquire through a matron what had detained Angela in the powder room. Just then the *maitre d'* informed me that "the young lady left the restaurant some time ago, with a scowl on her face."

Anyone else, after Angela's frustrating antagonism, might have abandoned the project. Instead, the challenge, the desire to overcome and succeed in the face of adversity, spurred me on.

Angela's rejection was an affront to my ego. In college, I proved that I was worthy of my schol-

arship; in the U.S. Army, that I was better than
the next guy.

The next morning, a half-hour before coming
into the station, I dropped by a local Ford showroom.

"Now here's a fine model. Has the most modern
features," the salesman began his patented
pitch.

"I don't think so," I cut him short. "I want a
1965 model."

"Really, I think you should pick this model up,"
pointing to a blue sedan. "It's a steal," he per-
sisted.

"How do I get to see one of the *new* models?" I
pressed.

"You'll get to see it on television in the fall, and
only then," he said sarcastically, and began to
walk away, conceding a no-sale.

On the way back to the station, the solution
came to me in the taxi cab: "You'll get to see it on
television . . ."

I instructed my secretary not to put any calls
through to me. I didn't want to be disturbed by
anyone.

"Sir, I understand your office has a set of sharp
prints of the '65 cars," I said to the head of
Chrysler Motor Corporation's press information
department, who, to protect his present job in
Detroit, I'll refer to as Mr. M.

"Yes, we do, Mr. Bernard. But they're not for
release right now." Mr. M. told me what I had
already known.

"In any event, Mr. Bernard, what can we do for
you?"

"I think it's more what we can do for each
other," I responded, taking a firm position of confidence.

"How's that?" he came back, growing more
curious.

"My station is putting together a special half-hour documentary called 'What New York will Offer in 1965' and I'd like to include the '65 Chrysler Corporation cars."

"Will there be other automotive companies in this documentary, or will it just be Chrysler?" he asked.

"I'm glad you asked. It will be *all* the car companies. And it will be free exposure. There will be absolutely no charge to Chrysler for this public service. And there is a possibility that the program will be repeated on the station. Mr. M., if you know anything about the demographics of this station, you'll realize that our audience buys cars, particularly the medium-priced ones, like Chrysler cars. Can we have Chrysler's participation in this documentary?"

"Sounds like something Chrysler would like to be part of," M. said with conviction. "But as far as releasing them to you now, I'm afraid that might be difficult. If we give to one station, or newspaper, we have to give to the rest at the same time. We don't play favorites here."

"I don't blame you, sir. We don't play favorites here, either. But my problem is a production one. We need a good three months', possibly four, advance time to be in a position to put the ingredients of this broadcast into professional shape. So, since this is a special situation, I'm going to ask you to make *the* exception."

"Your point is well taken, Mr. Bernard. But let me call you back in, say, twenty minutes."

"Fine," I said, which was the only thing I could say.

Twenty increasingly long minutes later, to the minute, he called.

"Mr. Bernard," he opened, my pressure rising as the blood flushed in my face. "Can you come over *now* to my office?"

"Now?" I said, perplexed at the immediacy.

"Yes, *now*," he emphasized.

"Yes, I'll come over now. I had a meeting planned, but the car photos have a *special* priority," I said, thinking: If he only knew just how *special*. "See you in fifteen minutes!"

I didn't really know what to make of the situation. I had hoped that he was not going to shove legal documents in front of me. I imagined him saying: "Look here, Bernard. You appear to be an honest guy, but sometimes looks are deceiving. I can't afford to take any chances. Once I let the pictures go—and they find their way to the *National Enquirer*—I'll have to pack my bags. The only way I'll release these pictures is if you sign a sworn affidavit. Then, if I ever find out you deceived me, I'll have you by the balls."

I was frightened beyond belief at the thought of going to jail. I resolved that under no circumstances would I sign anything. Before I'd do that, I'd scrap the whole project.

When I arrived at Chrysler, a pretty receptionist asked me to have a seat while she buzzed M.'s secretary, who didn't answer.

The receptionist looked up at me in a peculiar way.

"Are you sure you have an appointment with Mr. M.?" she interrogated me.

"Yes, I do," I said assuringly.

"I don't know where his secretary is. I didn't see her go out. I'm afraid you'll just have to wait until she gets back from wherever she is.

"Is Mr. M. here?"

"You'll have to wait until his secretary gets back," the receptionist insisted.

Something didn't smell right. I was getting cold feet. Maybe they were having second thoughts.

"Could you please buzz her again?" I asked politely.

This time, a young girl came out to greet me, and I was directed into his office. I had imagined

M. to be short and comical-looking. Instead, he was tall and ruggedly handsome, and conveyed authority.

But he wasn't smiling as I would have hoped, which bothered me.

"Mr. Bernard," he said, as he placed a small key into the lower drawer of his desk. "I had these pictures put aside for you. But one thing bothers me. How do I know the photos won't break today, or tomorrow on the station?"

"I give you my word they won't," I said.

He was silent as he pulled out a series of printed white sheets from another drawer he had opened with another key. Were these the affidavit forms I would be required to sign my life away for?

"These are press releases. Same applies. No mention of the cars' specifications, either."

"Agreed," I said.

"Good luck with your documentary. I hope it sells many cars, especially Chrysler cars," he laughed.

I laughed—at M., though he didn't know it. For sure it would certainly sell a lot of *National Enquirers*, though I couldn't vouch for the inventoried '64 cars that were still standing in dealer showrooms.

What a cover the station was! My loot carefully locked in my attache case, I knew I had developed the secret formula.

The next morning I called General Motors—not Angela.

"Yes," I said. "I picked up the Chrysler pictures yesterday. Yeah, thanks to Mr. M. Oh, you know him. Yes, great guy . . . "

This was my approach with American Motors and Ford. It is called the "snowball effect," where one builds from the other. When you get one, they all want to jump on the bandwagon. But it's the damn toughest getting that first one.

I had learned that the direct approach is usually the best approach. But I could laugh at the antics of one auto V.P.

"Don't let them out of your sight. Take care of them. If there's a leak, it could be disastrous," he warned.

In all probability, it was disastrous.

But I wasn't totally heartless. I did protect their jobs. Nobody ever knew, until now, that is, that I duped them. I made sure that the background of each car, whether it was the countryside, or a showroom, was carefully airbrushed. Any other distinguishing marks were also removed chemically. Then, the duplication of the originals was done in an hour at a slick, speedy midtown photo lab.

So, Mr. V.P., your concern was for naught. They weren't really out of my sight—for too long. But while they were at the lab don't think I didn't worry that one of the automotive press guys might drop by, or call, checking to see if I still had the photos in my possession.

When the photos came back from the lab, I had slides made of them and started work on the documentary I was now committed to, which ultimately ran on the station.

Four days after I had placed the last of the car pictures in the hands of the *Enquirer*, an envelope arrived for me by special messenger at the station. Enclosed was a check for $800, which, to me, represented a major coup. I had seduced and conquered the great giants of industry—General Motors, American Motors, Ford and Chrysler, including their Dodge Division. They were my Goliath and I slew them with the sling of my ingenuity. I had tried, and I had succeeded.

Three weeks later the '65 car pictures broke on the *Enquirer's* front page and two centerfolds. I could hardly contain my excitement, especially when Reggie told me that Gene Pope literally did a dance for joy around his desk at the paper's 655 Madison Avenue headquarters. Later, Pope's "exclusives" would build circulation to the point that he felt crowded in his quarters, and destined for bigger and better facilities to hang out his *Enquirer* shingle. These included Englewood Cliffs, New Jersey, followed by Lanatana, Florida.

From the moment I did the impossible for *The Inc.,* I became known as "Goldmine George — the man with the Midas Touch." I came through for the more than one million readers who would purchase that scoop edition.

The car photos behind me, at least for another year, I expanded the use of the station as a cover. I began to supply *The Inc.* with "exclusive" interviews—of celebrities such as Phyllis Diller and Polly Bergen, among others, who were taped at the station for *later* airing—much later . . . after the stories first appeared in the *Enquirer.* And when the celebrity neglected to say something inviting, shocking, or revealing, I would follow up in the star's dressing room, or innocently over a cup of coffee—without exposing my true Enquiring intentions.

Even earlier, the TV station had provided me with countless invaluable opportunities to learn the art of interviewing. I had covered the star-spangled cinema and Broadway premieres and held the mike to entertainment's notables. Gregory Peck, when asked "What's your image?" responded in his deepest resonance, "I wasn't aware I had an image!" Joyful Joey Heatherton posed with me for a studio photo and so did Gretchen Wyler, and the hot comedy team of Marty Allen and Steve Rossi, who have since gone their own ways in the style of Martin and Lewis.

But amid all the plotting and the added pressures of avoiding detection by my own staff as an

Enquirer agent, there were moments of tensionless pleasure and hilarity. The pleasure came when feasting my eyes on the beauty of precious Polly who, even today, appears not to have aged a day in the last decade. And Phyllis provided the unexpected laughs. She was even funnier off camera.

In the control room, I had remarked to Phyllis that the sack dress she was wearing looked comfortably cool.

"You think that's cool?" she screeched. "What do you think now?" Before my startled, disbelieving eyes, and those of the three engineers on duty, she pulled her dress completely over her frizzy hair, exposing her devastatingly shapeless torso. Then, she allowed the sack to drop back gently over her body, as if she were playing professional stripper.

That day I met beauty and the beast. I will say, however, that since that entertaining episode, Phyllis has had a complete face lift that has done the very most . . . for the very worst.

For all my *extra* enterprising activities, there was added remuneration. The special messenger would deliver a check to me at the station. And, as before, the story fee would be split with Reggie—"right down the middle."

It was still warm in October when Reggie and I took our dates to the beach for the day. When we were alone for a moment from our two chatterboxes, I informed Reggie that the owners of the station had now found a permanent general manager. In a few days the new manager would report for work and I would be reduced in position and salary to my old job of writer-producer. I was anything but thrilled.

Reggie sympathized with me, and offered a viable alternative. "You've been killing yourself at the station, and for what?" he asked. "Is it to make some bloke rich who couldn't care if you fell over dead with a heart attack? Listen, we've been working extremely well together and the *Enquirer* is more than pleased with your work. You're one hell of a writer. Let's form a news agency of our own just to service the *Enquirer*. And, as a back-up cover, we'll form an entertainment corporation so we can represent ourselves as press agents, or show-biz managers. What do you think, mate?"

My mind was made up. We shook hands in agreement. I gave the station two weeks' notice. Reggie and I were now partners in developing accounts of the sublime for the *Enquirer*.

Good-bye mediocrity. Hello, Trans-Atlantic Features. Welcome, Trans-Atlantic Entertainment Corporation—T.A.F. and T.A.E.C., for short, and for sure!

CHAPTER IV

Weirdos and Weapons—They're Both Dangerous

One of the most unlikely deadly duos I encountered as an *Enquirer* reporter was a pugilist and his pet hawk. Together, they maintained temporary residence in a roach-infested one-room apartment of a rundown tenement that had been boarded up and condemned by the city.

John Roland was a sturdy, semi-professional prize fighter from New England who was in New York to plead the cause of neglected zoo animals and to draw attention to the plight of wild birds, which he felt were threatened with extinction. Roland's crusade was brought to my attention by press agent Richard H. Roffman, a fellow City College alumnus, who thought I could give his client exposure in *The Inc.*

Roffman, who had a penchant for taking on a clientele of the absurd and the bizarre, was one of the very few I entrusted with my *Enquirer* cover, and the burly publicist never betrayed that confidence.

R.H.R., as he continues to be known in the industry today, was bored by the prestigious accounts he maintained, which had included Jacob Javits and Senator Robert F. Wagner, Sr.

Bill, an articles editor for the *Enquirer* (they're the guys who process the stories and are responsible to Pope for the story, before and after it leaves my hands) gave me the official go-ahead.

On January 31, '65, the *Enquirer* had run a story of a wild bird that relished living in captivity: "BUZZARD DUCKS THE WILD LIFE TO BE A PET" The article stated that "buzzards are known as vicious birds of prey, but not Jelly Bean

George. The only preying George does is at a church. He's a pet buzzard, and could be the only such in the world."

Pope considered such stories precious. In fact, they would lay a golden egg with the readers, who according to special *Enquirer* research studies, loved capers of dogs, horses and any other pet, especially the unusual — and the unnatural!

"Get real close with your camera," Bill instructed me. "I want to see the glare of ferocity in his eyes. Also, get pictures of the fighter sparring with the bird."

"Are you kidding?" I asked.

"That will make the story."

But Bill said nothing about being careful.

As I gingerly took my first step into Roland's one-room apartment, the nauseating stench of rotting flesh became apparent. For in the corner, a hawk in his cage, resting on the sink above the radiator, was ripping apart the remains of a snake. Its razor-sharp teeth and treacherous talons were working methodically well for this bird of prey.

Roland, though fearless, was not stupid. Before he took the hawk out of the cage, he slipped his hands into giant, protective gloves fashioned out of durable buffalo hide. Then he carried his "best friend" out of the cage, and allowed the bird to perch atop—his favorite spot. Then his master changed his gloves, and began shadow boxing at imaginary opponents and figures of his past.

I clicked the "on" button of my flash, stepped back a few feet and took my first picture of the bird and the boxer. Suddenly, the hawk dropped the snake and flew directly at my head. Luckily, the monster missed and landed on top of the door.

Robust Roland was deeply concerned that I had frightened his baby. Some baby! He cautioned that I should show the camera to the hawk first, let him get accustomed to seeing a few flashes go off. Then, take a *few* shots, but not too many. I did just that.

"Could I get a few pictures of you and the hawk together, Roland? Could you spar with your friend?"

Oddly enough, he didn't oppose the idea. But the flash startled the bird again and he took off to the other part of the room, thankfully, not after me.

Roland grew rattled and picked up where he had left off with his shadow boxing. Suddenly, the punches grew closer and closer to my face and I found myself slowly retreating towards the door. I reached behind me, grabbed the knob and pulled hard. The door opened and I closed out the interview. I figured what I didn't have, Roffman could fill me in on. That's what press agents are for.

My copy was crisp and the photos were sharp and explicit. But the story never ran. Gene Pope killed it, and for the most idiotic of all reasons: they had a better bird story in the house. Which is another way of saying that another feathered friend article tickled Pope's fancy stronger than mine. It was the *Enquirer* article of April 11, '65: "WATCHDOG WITH WINGS ... OWNER KEEPS AN EAGLE TO GUARD HOME." The story emanated out of Pwllhelli, Wales and Pope contended that the eagle was superior to the hawk, and *Enquirer* readers should not get a hawkish second best!

Who was I to argue with Gene Pope? And even if I wanted to gripe, it was highly unlikely that the Pope would give me an audience. But I was raging like a roaring inferno.

Reggie and I had established Trans-Atlantic Features as a news front and Trans-Atlantic Entertainment Corporation as another cover. Our office overlooked the hallucinating neon lights of

Broadway, which seemed a proper location for our crazy and clandestine operations.

We were to continue as partners in prying and preying for about a year. Then, Reggie would leave to enter the music business, and I would continue alone, undercover, as a reporter for the *Enquirer*.

There were times when an *Enquirer* assignment required both of us. Reggie was out covering a British rock group's stormy New York arrival one afternoon and I wished that he would have been back when Ed Carmel dropped by the office.

Dick Roffman represented Eddie, and Mr. Carmel was not the average Joe. He was about *nine* feet tall, had attended City College, and it was out of his campus affiliation and my friendship with Roffman that I agreed to interview the big boy from the Bronx.

The *Enquirer* was not overly ecstatic about the story suggestion I had delivered to them in the form of a brief memo. Two editors did not see the angle, but suggested I should speak to him anyway—"on spec"—which is short for speculation. If the story did not pan out, there would be no fee—and no expense reimbursement either.

I was typing a murder story on the sturdy keys of my trusty 110 SCM electric when I heard a loud thumping noise at the front door. My secretary was out to lunch and because of robberies in the building, I had securely locked the door.

By the time I reached the noise, Eddie had almost ripped the door from its hinges.

I showed Mr. Carmel into my office and asked him to take a seat, which he declined, explaining that if he sat in one of the expensive fiberglass contour chairs, it would instantly crumble. I took his word. So, Eddie stood while I took some of the facts down on my typewriter.

Eddie's resume read like a checkerboard. He

had sold mutual funds, had been a sales promotional executive, and had even worked for the Ringling Bros. Circus. But what distinguished Eddie from others, irrespective of his massive presence, was his deep and articulate speaking voice which he used to full advantage as a part-time disc jockey.

I knew his beautiful voice could not be translated effectively into the pages of the *Enquirer*, unless, of course, the paper knew a scientific way I wasn't aware of. As for Eddie's unusual height, it was only significant if he did something with it—like painting ceilings without a step ladder for a living, or truly being "the tallest man in the world," which the *Enquirer* didn't buy.

Editors at *The Inc.* would tell me that Pope considered midgets and giants to be freaks—a dime a dozen. So, to get into *The Inc.*, they had to be "special freaks!"

Eddie told me that his weight fluctuated around the four hundred-pound mark, and that he consumed more food in one day than the average person could eat in half a week. Further, his parents were average height!

I was curious to learn if he had a normal sex life. But looking at his monstrous frame, I knew the answer. How could he find a mate that he wouldn't kill in the sack? Further, Gene Pope stayed away from sex, one reason he continued to stay in business.

My feeling was that I had a weak freak story in comparison to another article that had just run in the *Enquirer's* December 27, '64 edition: "NINE-YEAR-OLD GIRL BARRED FROM SCHOOL BECAUSE SHE'S TOO UGLY."

I was convinced the only chance I would have of getting Eddie into the paper would be via a pictorial layout. So, I took my camera with me as I walked the giant to the elevator.

I posed Eddie before the elevator doors and

asked him to play King Kong for my camera. Instinctively, he grabbed the clock-like floor indicator that was boldly facing him—eye level. The photo was right. It gave the impression that Eddie's brute strength was preventing the elevator from moving to another floor.

I made the almost mortal mistake of telling Eddie my misgivings, that a lengthy feature had less chance of making the *Enquirer* than President Johnson doing an ad for a nudist colony. The best I could do, I leveled with him, was a photo piece, and I couldn't even guarantee that. "It's not my publication," I said.

My candor was not well received by Eddie, who reasoned that he had unselfishly given me his valuable time, and was entitled to half of the story fee I was to get. He couldn't conceive that he was not a story. It was an attack on his ego, and what was to ensue in the next few moments was psychologically—and physically—the only course of action he knew.

The gargantuan lifted me high over his head to the point where I was almost scraping the ceiling with my head. He walked over to an open hall window and threatened to throw me out of it if I did not assure him—in writing—that he would get paid for the interview, and that the *Enquirer* would run it.

"Anything you say, Eddie," I assured him as he slowly lowered me to a standing position.

I took two ten-dollar bills out of my pocket and stuffed them in his hand. Mildly pleased with my offering, he temporarily forgot about the signed promise, which even if I complied with, was not binding.

For the next fifteen minutes, I nervously snapped pictures of Eddie next to any prop that looked half-way decent: cramped in a phone booth, looking at his gorgeous mug in a vestibule mirror, and even walking alongside two tots in the street.

Tranquilized by the few dollars I gave him, Eddie never bothered to come back to my office. I was thankful. After what seemed like a long period of time, Eddie Carmel finally made the *National Enquirer.*

Shortly after that eerie episode, I was almost banned from the *Enquirer.* I had turned in the story of a man who called himself an artist. John J. Fischer, another Roffman client, made art objects from bread that he chemically treated with a transparent protective coating, and then he put them on sale.

I made the unpardonable mistake of photographing a doughy penis and a vagina on the same roll of film I had shot guns, knives and other related items he had molded out of bread.

It's true that art is in the eyes of the beholder. And what's art to one can be trash to another. And so it was that the *Enquirer* considered Fischer's work a pornographic rip-off and advised me that whoever gave me the lead should be hung by a rope made of hardened bread, or be buried alive in a vat of butter.

"Don't use that contact again," Bill instructed.

Roffman and I still talked to each other, but after that I never interviewed any of his clients for the *Enquirer.*

I felt compelled to atone to the *Enquirer* for my temporary lapse in editorial judgment. And the rising crime rate in New York and throughout the nation afforded an excellent opportunity.

Pope was deeply and honestly concerned about the welfare of the country. Though he printed mutilation masterpieces, he always hoped that in the process of effecting circulation jumps, he would bring about reform. He wanted then, and still does today, to rehabilitate the nation from the scourge of mental depression and murder. If you read beyond the *Enquirer* headlines and between the lines, you'll note that many of the paper's articles deliver a moral or other uplifting message.

And so my chance to redeem myself in the *Enquirer's* eyes came on October 14, '64 when two Florida boys, ages fifteen and sixteen, entered a weapons shop off Times Square on West 42nd Street and purchased a submachine gun and four hundred rounds of ammunition. Then, they left the store and promptly held up a cab driver who was ordered to drive around New York—at gunpoint—before the thrill-seeking youths forced him to drive to New Jersey.

There they robbed him of $15. And it was extremely fortunate for the taxi driver that the teenagers took only his money and not his life. Shortly after the crime, the two were apprehended by the New Jersey Highway Patrol.

The *Enquirer* wanted to know how two teenage youths could get their hands on a machine gun in New York City with no apparent difficulty. Reggie and I were assigned to find out the answer.

So, before we entered Kaufman's Surplus and Arms, Inc., the very same store that sold the gun and ammunition to the Florida boys, I photographed the shop's exterior. A sign read: "Everything Military—Rifles, Swords, Ammo." A real cannon was also on sale by the entrance.

When we entered, Reggie and I were greeted by a salesman who asked us to call him Benny. "Yes, sir. That's a popular model," Benny said after we wanted to buy the same weapon, and ammunition, that had been sold to those reckless teenagers.

Benny showed no remorse for selling a submachine gun to the kids, noting that he was in business solely to make a profit: "I'm not breaking the law, and I can't be responsible for what people do with guns I sell them."

We purchased the same machine gun model that the boys had bought—plus four hundred rounds of ammunition for slightly over $100. And the transaction was carried out before a New York City police officer who happened to be there at that moment because he was making the rounds of shops in the neighborhood that were constantly being held up by prostitutes, drunks, and two-bit thieves out for kicks.

I couldn't believe that no registration of the weapon was requested, but I did become nervous as the officer watched Reggie pick up the machine gun that weighed nine pounds and came with a clip that took thirty rounds. For an extra $34, we could have purchased an attachment that would have made the weapon fully automatic.

Reggie carried the gun to the car while I took the ammo. We had enough firepower to cut down scores of people in the crowded streets with one burst of the deadly weapon.

But suddenly, the same officer motioned us over to our car parked at the curb.

"It's overtime parking, Jack," he said roughly. "This time we'll let you off—but not again."

We stood there respecting his position—with the machine gun and rounds of bullets—as he preached on parking violations. When he had finished, we politely put the gun and ammo in the car and drove off.

We loaded the clips at the office. Then we took the elevator, which was thankfully empty, to the street. A cab stopped at the red light and we hopped in.

Looking through his rear-view mirror, the cabbie observed the gun. "You fellas aren't going to do anything foolish, are you?" He seemed to be pleading for his life.

"Nah," Reggie laughed. "All we're going to do is spray some people with hot lead."

"Look, fellas. Maybe you should think this over," he said, becoming more frantic.

"We're reporters doing a gun story," I had to inform him. "Reggie, put the gun on the floor, please ... before you frighten poor Alex to death"—the name of our cabbie I picked off the dashboard I.D.

I don't think Alex totally believed that we were reporters. Most of the respectable publications referred to us not as journalists, but as *Enquirer* hatchetmen — those who destroy others with their pen and photos! In any event, Alex now realized that he personally was not in any danger.

But just to make sure that he wouldn't abandon us, Reggie and I alternated staying in the cab—with the meter running—while Alex stopped at Radio City Music Hall, the Empire State Building, and the front of Grand Central Station. Preoccupied with themselves, as most New Yorkers are known to be, only a few looked curiously at us—but no one screeched, screamed or scattered. Had we pointed the gun at some of these unconcerned, the reaction, I'm sure, would have been drastically different!

Our last stop was Reggie's apartment building, but we had Alex drop us off two blocks away. We didn't want anxious Alex bringing the F.B.I., Secret Service and New York's Finest down on us. After we paid him, we waited until his cab was out of sight before we walked to the building and took the elevator to the roof.

My partner trained his deadly weapon on some innocent bystanders below as I, with my camera, captured the occasion for posterity, and for the *Enquirer.*

I didn't think it strange when Reggie admitted a compelling urge to pull the trigger. A loaded weapon can bring out the killer instinct in the most meek of human beings.

We interviewed a police official who went on record stating that, under New York's antiquated gun law, "we can't arrest someone using a lethal weapon, until he uses it!" Strange, wasn't it?

Our article ran a page and a half, and was replete with my photos. The entire office was buzzing with excitement: Pope was pleased! We had conclusively dramatized the dangers of a gun law that was failing to meet the needs of society—and needed drastic overhauling. We had planted the seeds of awareness and all anyone could do was give it time to bloom into action.

Pope was dancing in delirium. Reader-response letters expressing overwhelming support for stronger gun-control legislation filled Gene's mailroom. And when he was informed that an even more terrifying weapons expose was in the works, Pope, it is said, lit up like a sparkler.

One of Trans-Atlantic Features' new stringers, a staff reporter for the *Detroit Free Press*, who was hired to furnish our news agency with story leads, tipped me off about another American city—Detroit—where *anyone* could buy a cannon with a four-mile range. Our agent might have turned the cannon on us if he knew, in advance, that it could "only" go in the *National Enquirer*.

Reggie and I hopped the first jet out to "the Motor City." It was actually easier, we found out, to purchase a death-dealing antitank cannon in Detroit, than a firecracker. That's a fact. We tried both!

Ironically, the sale of firecrackers was outlawed there. They probably could have been purchased under the counter—but we weren't even sure. We couldn't even pick up a box of sparklers.

But for $150, just about $50 more than we had earlier paid for a submachine gun and ammo in New York, we picked up an antitank cannon.

Maybe "picked up" is wrong, since the monster weighed 683 pounds and was mounted on automobile-type wheels which made our assignment easier. For we could then tow it easily—and safely—behind our car.

It was a twenty-five-millimeter French Hotchkiss weapon with a firing range of at least four miles, and fired powerful armor-piercing shells. The ammo was made available to us by a salesman at Detroit's Lincoln Park gun shop, with no questions asked—for $1 a shell.

I needed no special permit, or permission—no I.D. papers, no proof of age, name or address, and no explanation. All that was required was money and a name and address—any name and address—for the saleman's file. Since the end of World War II, the owner of the store had sold five hundred of them.

When we called the *Enquirer* in New York to say that we had secured the cannon and ammo, Bill insisted that we also get, "by hook or crook," a mug shot of the boss who was not present when we bought the monster.

Walter Hood, the owner, was concerned that any articles printed in the United States condemning gun and weapons dealers would only add more heat to what was already becoming an uncomfortable, incendiary issue. The last thing Hood wanted was his mug plastered in a U.S. publication, but that wasn't the concern of the *Enquirer*.

At the time, a U.S. Senate subcommittee, investigating the international traffic in surplus arms, estimated that 2,300,000 weapons were shipped into the U.S. in the previous two years from five European countries.

After thoroughly photographing the cannon, it was dumped into Lake Erie. What a tremendous splash it made there . . . and in the *Enquirer!*

But the story did not end there.

Using the letterhead stationery of the *Detroit Free Press,* my agent wrote to me. This was his first, and *last* assignment for Trans-Atlantic Features. His letter of August 5, '65, reads, in part: "Dear Mr. Bernard: The piece on cannons in Detroit that appeared in the July 25 issue of the *National Enquirer* is really appalling. It sounded bad enough when described to me over the telephone by Mr. Walter Hood, who is understandably upset. It looks even worse in print . . . What I am mainly concerned about is your repeated promise, both to me and Mr. Hood, that the picture of him would under no circumstances appear in any publication issued in the United States. It's a pretty shabby deal, if you ask me, to go ahead and give it to the *National Enquirer*—of all papers! And frankly, I find it hard to believe that the picture could have fallen into their hands through some other source and unbeknownst to you . . . I don't think that you should be completely unmindful of your reputation here in Detroit. After all, you might want something more some day. Anyway, whatever the explanation for this is, why don't you drop Mr. Hood a line and let him have it?"

I knew two people in Detroit, and one was Hood, who would really have liked to let me have it—right in the gut with a deadly cannon blast!

When I popped a flash at John Roland's pet hawk, the bird of prey—with talons flashing—flew towards my head! (*George Bernard*)

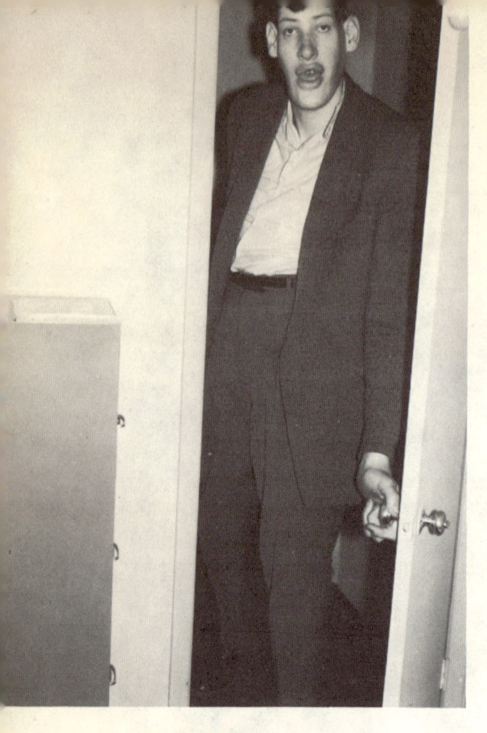

The nine-foot giant Eddie Carmel once threatened to throw me out of a window unless I ran his story in the *Enquirer*. (George Bernard)

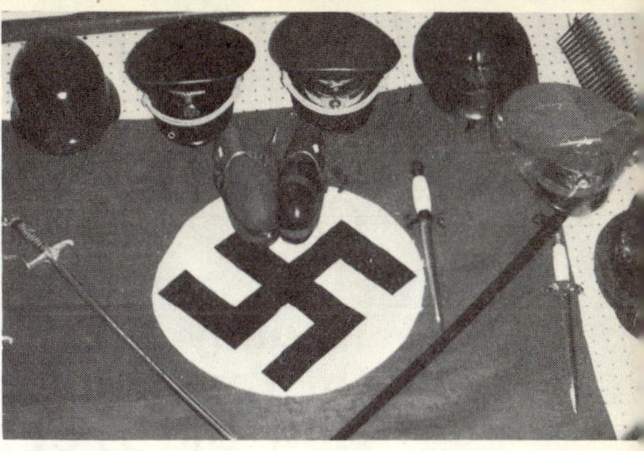

Some murderous memorabilia at Kaufman's.

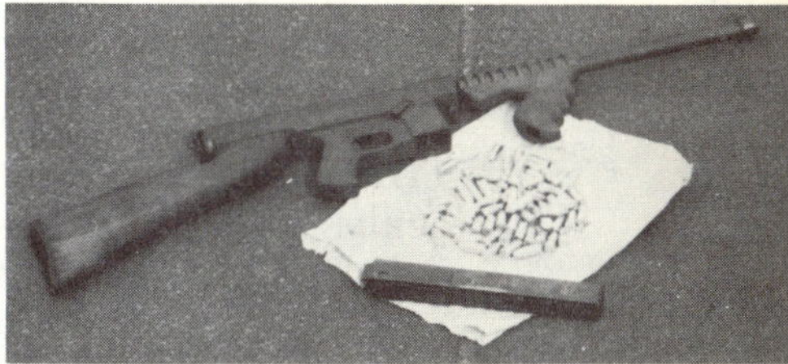

Submachine gun and ammo on sidewalk.

Benny (upper left), a salesman for Kaufman's Surplus and Arms, Inc. stands before an arsenal of death he was peddling to anyone for the right price. After years of bad press, Kaufman's is still at the same Times Square spot—but they no longer sell guns.

The outside view of Kaufman's (left). Inside, they dealt in death. (George Bernard)

CHAPTER V

Huntley & Brinkley
On Top of Ratings—But
How Did They Rate Each Other?

While the wheels of a jumbo jet were finally touching ground after circling for some twenty minutes over a congested airport in Washington, D.C., my cab in New York was trying to break through a massive traffic jam.

Here were a plane and a cab, in two separate locales, racing to the same destination—Huntley and Brinkley, the hottest TV news team in America.

I was desperately trying to be on time for a 12:30 luncheon appointment with Chet Huntley who co-anchored, from New York, the "Huntley-Brinkley Report"—the most talked about, most successful network news half-hour in the history of television.

In Washington, D.C., the plane now landed, Victoria, a young, pretty British journalist in my employ, was now also in a cab racing to meet for lunch the other half of the dynamic duo, David Brinkley.

Chet and David were NBC's top stars. They were truly riding the TV rating crest. Walter Cronkite at CBS was living up to the English translation of his Germanic name, which means a type of sickness. And ABC was a far third in the ratings game.

The *Enquirer* wanted to know how the two men atop the ratings race actually rated each other. So, I wisely scheduled separate *simultaneous* interviews with the two TV titans. In this way, neither could prime, alert, or even discourage the other, if one would develop second thoughts about being interviewed.

My cab stalled, the traffic bumper-to-bumper. The driver turned and said to me: "Buddy, we ain't going nowhere. So, just sit back and be prepared for a long wait!"

That was all I had to hear. It was 12:20 and I had twelve blocks to go. I decided to hoof it.

My confidence was strong that Victoria would get darling David to open up and tell what he really thought of his partner 230 miles away.

It was decided to send a girl instead of Reggie or myself. We were tipped off that David would be more receptive to a female. Victoria was vibrant-looking. She had charm and British sophistication, and was sure to appeal to a cultured American correspondent, like Brinkley. Victoria, to get the interview, was using the same cover I had employed to entice Huntley to the restaurant. But there would be no interview if I didn't get there—fast!

The Wollensak recorder I was dragging through the streets seemed to grow heavier with each labored step.

"Only three more blocks to go," I said to myself. "I'm almost there!" I wished.

Finally, I arrived at Marsh's Steak Place on Central Park South which was one of the restaurants we used for celebrity interviews. The owner, grateful to us for brightening up his establishment with stars, picked up our tabs.

Chet Huntley was already waiting for me. He was seated at a choice table near the rear, reserved for this occasion.

"Mr. Huntley. George Bernard, Radio Caroline. I'm honored you could make it," I said.

Radio Caroline was the name of Great Britain's first commercial station—it was established in March '64 and named after the late President Kennedy's daughter. Radio Caroline comprised a network of two floating radio stations aboard two reconstructed World War II merchant vessel ships that were moored three and one half miles off the coast of Great Britain. Radio Caroline South and North reached an audited listening audience of thirty-nine million listeners, and it was no wonder. The BBC was transmitting programs to sleep by, while Caroline filled the great gap for the discotheque-minded Europeans who wanted to hear the big beat. The only problem was that Radio Caroline was broadcasting illegally, according to the government. Thus, it came to be known commonly as "pirate," a label that intrigued me immensely. So, when Reggie, who hadn't seen his parents in six months, decided to pay a visit in November '64, I asked him to look into the British operation while he was there, as an additional cover for me to secure scoops for the *Enquirer.*

In January '65, we secured a contract from Caroline to provide the station with recorded news and entertainment features. This front came just in time for the Huntley-Brinkley *Enquirer* assignment. Trans-Atlantic Features would have been suspect as a legitimate news agency to a professional newsman. And our entertainment corporation would have been laughed at. But a British commercial radio station requesting an interview with a fellow broadcaster appealed to Huntley. In fact, when I called him at NBC, he agreed immediately. I had been frightened that the NBC press department red tape might stand in the way.

My interview with Chet began with the newscaster's evaluation of the British political system. We then discussed the Common Market.

Huntley thought that Caroline was innovative, especially for using an American to interview personalities for the United Kingdom, and in introducing a "Miss Radio Caroline" to Madison Avenue's ad agencies and the news media.

"In developing and packaging a concept or product, nothing supersedes American know-how," said Huntley, gazing affectionately at a photo of Denina Fiore, a lovely, leading New York model who became our "pirate" girl. Though not wishing to personally offer a recorded testimonial to the clandestine operation that threatened to impose heavy fines, even imprisonment, for aiding and abetting the station, he spoke of the ships with a gleam in his eye.

Frankly, I was not concerned what Huntley thought of Radio Caroline, British politics or the virtues of the Common Market. If he would have admitted being a peeping tom, or Marilyn Monroe's last lover before she left earth, it wouldn't have been the information I wanted. My assignment was to uncover what Huntley thought of Brinkley.

Chet was chatting on, hardly making any headway with a two-inch-thick sirloin steak he had ordered. Finally, after I couldn't help but observe that the take-up reel was half-way filled with unusable material, I broke through the gibberish:

"Mr. Huntley, both you and Mr. Brinkley are on top of the ratings in America. May I ask you, for our listeners, how you rate David?"

Huntley nervously sipped a glass of ice water, then coughed twice. Chet began by giving David a boost, but followed abruptly with a knock that became a knockout headline—"He gets under my skin!"

That was what I had waited for and wanted to hear.

"What do you mean—you don't see eye-to-eye on matters?" I prodded him.

"Well, yes. That's part of it," he said. "My feelings bottle up inside me so much that I finally explode."

Huntley told me that more often than not, his

partner got the brutal brunt of his volcanic eruptions, and that on the tube, it was made to appear that they were the perfect partners.

"But we do fight," said Huntley. "I really must admit that I lose my head and get snappy. David does the same," he went on, providing me with one of the most candid interviews I would ever conduct.

"It pays us to keep apart. It's really best that way," he went on, attempting with his fork to draw four snow peas to his mouth. Instead, his tense hand released the precarious grasp he had on the peas, sending them against his suit jacket and into his lap.

The newsman laughed at his own awkwardness.

Chet was still steeped in serious thought as our interview continued. But it was becoming increasingly obvious that there was an unresolved rift in Huntley's relationship with Brinkley. I had the feeling that though they might both respect each other as journalists, they were in constant conflict. "Mr. Huntley, from what you've told me, it does appear that you really are not fond of your job," I ventured, waiting for his reply.

"I can't honestly say I enjoy being a television personality," he went on, explaining that all he wanted was to be left alone—quietly and privately. He admitted his total disdain with autograph hounds who would pester him for his John Hancock in restaurants, on the street, and even in the hallway at NBC outside his own office.

Huntley revealed his preference for staying in the background—the reason he didn't fly into a temper tantrum if David received more exposure in their nightly news report.

"But don't get me wrong," Huntley added. "Though I don't want to hog the TV screen, at the same time I have to protect myself from becoming a subliminal image that you're not quite sure you saw. I have to fight for my time on the screen—every second I can get."

It seemed inconceivable that the seeming inseparables only saw each other twice a year. The reason, Chet explained, was that David "hated" coming into Manhattan, and only did so when it was absolutely necessary.

When David and his family visited Chet the April before at his western New Jersey cattle ranch, "he brought his three boys over and sort of turned them loose in the acreage," Huntley recounted.

"They stayed for the *entire* weekend and created quite an uproar," Chet added, noting that the visit, in spite of the ranch ruckus, presented an opportunity for them to get to know each other in a social setting—"instead of just arguing over our television program."

At that moment, Reggie popped in on us. He had completed an assignment nearby. After I introduced him to the noted newsman, the waiter took Reggie's order.

More than anything else, Chet Huntley wanted to get out of Manhattan and ramble through the sprawling Jersey ranch land he now called "home sweet home."

The unmistakable lines of strain and tension were etched in his tired face from daily facing the nightly newscast, and he admitted the overwhelming need to relax, which was of paramount concern.

I was puzzled how he ever managed to keep in touch with his news partner when they hardly met.

"We have board meetings by telephone," he explained.

Huntley reported that he began in the afternoon, checking with David, and they tested a few ideas on each other. Then David told Chet what time he wanted him to finish with his stories.

From there, Chet pointed out, it meant going to the studio and praying that all would work according to schedule.

The New York co-anchorman admitted that in spite of all seeming difficulties, "somehow we get on the air—and get off. It's always a relief to get off!"

"And what about an impasse?" I asked. "Suppose you see black and David sees white, which I'm sure does crop up. I'm sure you don't flip a coin."

"David and I made an agreement that the producer should be chairman if we ever got deadlocked over whether we should, or should not, handle a particular story.

"And as far as disagreements go," Huntley added, "arguments don't come up too often, but occasionally, when they do — we have it out hot and heavy. And you wouldn't want to be close by when it happens."

Huntley said that when things started popping in Washinton, at the White House, on Capitol Hill, or in the Pentagon, for example, he had to ask his producer if he was on the thirty-minute newscast at all.

"But as I said," Huntley continued, "I don't particularly like the limelight and I seldom argue because David is getting all the work to do."

I had on tape the blockbuster interview of all time, from someone I had believed to be the most mild, unflappable professional in news reporting — the man who was stingy with emotion.

"Could you please turn the recorder off?" Huntley now politely requested.

I complied.

"Thank you," he said.

I had visions of Huntley regretting what he had said about his partner and the even deeper rift that was sure to develop when Brinkley was made aware. I was sure that Huntley was thinking about Reuters News Service and the British press that were sure to pick the broadcast up and relay the caustic contents to the U.S. newspapers. But how could I tell Chet that Radio Caroline would only receive that which was not destined for the *National Enquirer*—and that was everything nasty about dear David? I couldn't.

"I don't want to go on record with this," Huntley began as I waited for the bomb. "But just thinking about going back to my office and having to prepare for the newscast has given me an upset stomach. As you can see, I hardly touched my lunch, which I thank you for.

"I would like to go to my ranch this very moment, and never have to do another news broadcast. If only I had the gut determination to get out of this tension-packed business—right now!" he ranted.

"I'm sure what I'm doing is draining years from my life. What do I really need it for? I've got more than enough money to live the rest of my life in inner contentment."

Here was Chet Huntley, a newscaster's newscaster. He was the recipient of countless awards for his sober, straightforward reporting through the years, who once went on record describing himself as merely "a solemn horse-faced guy that some people seem to like."

I had instant admiration for Chet. He told me the way it was—even if he didn't have the courage of his convictions that day to chuck broadcasting—before it did him in.

Huntley walked back to NBC which was half-a-mile away. Reggie and I packed up the recorder and returned to the office.

Fifty percent of the assignment was completed. Now if only Victoria was as fortunate.

Ted, one of the *Enquirer's* editorial chieftains,

ordered that we get *both* interviews. In the event that Victoria was unsuccessful, my bet was that the *National Enquirer* would probably go solo with Huntley and wait for Brinkley's reaction—if he would have one, or give one. In any event, a lot was riding on Victoria's victory. At stake was prestige at the paper, and a sizable pay check on the *successful* completion of the assignment.

I carefully transcribed the tape, not trusting anyone else, for the *Enquirer's* edition of February 14, '65.

I had specifically instructed Victoria to call us at the office after the interview. But our secretary said she hadn't called.

We were worried. It was now 6:00. How long does it take to fly back from Washington? The least she could have done was to be decent about the whole thing. She could have called to say, "I've tried, and I've failed. I'm truly sorry."

Restless Reggie was biting his nails to release his anxiety. It was now 6:20. We heard the elevator door open. "Finally, she's arrived," so I thought. False alarm: it was the cleaning lady.

About three minutes later, the sound of the elevator door opening greeted our eager ears. We heard Victoria's unmistakable footsteps.

A sullen-faced Victoria walked slowly into my office, said nothing and plopped down in my white contour ceramic chair. I read doom and gloom in her face.

"Well," I said. "Did you get the interview?"

"No!"

Though we had anticipated defeat the last few hours, we were still shocked.

"I didn't *just* get the interview," she paused. "I've got what you call here," pausing again, "a blockbuster! David Brinkley's blooming happy he works 230 miles away from Chet Huntley. They're not exactly on each other's 'most preferred list'."

"Is there any more?" Reggie yelled.

"Much more. Much," Victoria vowed.

David told Victoria that he wouldn't want to be in Chet's position for all the dollars in the NBC vaults, and all the rice in Rangoon.

David told Victoria that he gets out far more than Chet does. "We never go anywhere together—thank heavens," he let go at Huntley.

Brinkley, our reporter observed, looked as calm, cool and collected in person as he came across on the TV screen. Our London lassie noted that if there was a bomb scare at NBC in Washington, Brinkley would have been unfazed. He probably would have been typing his newscast while the rescue squad searched under his desk.

David, however, admitted that he glued himself to the nation's capitol not out of any profound pleasure, or proximity to the Pentagon, but out of distaste for New York—a point Huntley had confirmed in my interview. David said that it was beyond his mental capacity to be able to figure out why Chet did stay in New York.

"He bubbles all the time like a seltzer tablet being dropped in a glass of water. I prefer being a dud to a fizz," David declared.

Valiant Victoria had come back with venomous invectives on tape that would become dynamite in print.

Brinkley was now firmly on the brink of dropping another verbal bomb. He conceded that Chet always did a first-class job in New York— and hoped he would remain there. "It would be terrible if we had to work together," sharing the sentiment Huntley had expressed for Brinkley.

Listening to Victoria's interview, an eerie feeling came over me. It was as if the two newsmen were being interviewed together, or had telepathic powers. For each was echoing the other's sentiments exactly.

"I don't want to make it sound more important than it is. But I can say that I'm glad, for the sake of us both, that Chet and I work 230 miles apart."

That was the headline grabber. Victoria had done an exceptional job.

Brinkley was spewing forth journalistic gems of dislike for his teammate. He was so deliberate and dogmatic in his ridicule, one might have thought he was composing a story of frantic feuding—and hate—for the *National Enquirer,* which he was. But nobody who knew had told him.

David Brinkley said that he was convinced if he and Chet worked out of the same studio, there would have been terrible arguments, "and the directors would have to pull us apart."

I learned from Victoria's interview that Brinkley, as well as Huntley, was not enamored with being a TV personality. "I would rather be a newspaperman than a television star," said David. "Almost everyone knows our faces—and it doesn't make for a private life."

He confessed that there were many problems that constantly faced anchormen of a top-rated TV broadcast. But he said that, so far, he and Huntley had managed to cope with the problems.

The portion of the two interviews covering the vocal slug fest went to the *Enquirer,* while that which remained, went BOAC to Radio Caroline. This was the policy my partner and I adopted which gave the "eager-for-exclusives" *Enquirer* the cream of the interview crop at all times. Is that any way to treat a pirate? You bet your sweet life, I opined.

"You aren't going to use my real name, are you?" Victoria was concerned.

"Nah, we'll use a male alias, and you can always deny the story came from you. But, why all this concern?" Reggie inquired.

"I just don't want to be remembered as a

female Brutus," she responded.

"Is that all?" I wanted to know.

"If you must know, I found him charming and real super. We got along fabulously!"

"Sounds like you'd adore sleeping with him," I said.

"I would. I most certainly would," she said, flatly and honestly, helping to explain her long delay in returning from Washington. Her head was probably floating high above the clouds looking down upon the District of Columbia—and one David Brinkley. And I'll bet she walked to the airport in rapturous reverie.

Both knockout interviews ran side-by-side in the *Enquirer*. The front page was split evenly down the middle with pictures of the two newsmen, and in comic-book style, Huntley was reporting: "DAVID GETS UNDER MY SKIN," while Brinkley was saying—"I'M GLAD CHET AND I WORK MILES APART."

The check from the *Enquirer* was a whopping one. The day it arrived, the office celebrated over champagne and imported caviar. We had earned our feast.

Undoubtedly, there were those, as there always are, who questioned the credibility of the *Enquirer*, especially the Huntley-Brinkley expose.

To those I offer this fitting epilogue to that story of two dynamic men who worked distances apart, yet considered themselves to be hapless victims of living too close to each other in a goldfish bowl.

On Friday, July 31, '70, Chet Huntley said his final "Good Night, David" to TV-partner Brinkley and ended a partnership that, during their fourteen years on the air together, ranked as the hottest team in broadcasting history since Amos n' Andy.

The two distinguished news correspondents

were teamed up by NBC for the '56 political conventions and they made such impact on the ratings that the network decided to unleash the deadly duo on the nightly news that fall. It was the perfect symbiotic marriage. The two complemented each other so perfectly that one time, when Brinkley was asked, "Are you Huntley or Brinkley?" he answered, "I'm not sure. Sometimes it's hard even for me to keep us straight."

While the Washington spokesman of NBC's nightly "Huntley-Brinkley Report" would quip modestly he was just "the other half of a hyphen," some twenty million viewers took him more seriously. His inimitable style — wry, dry and cynical, laced with heavy strokes of irony and brass — refreshingly altered the staid and stolid stereotype of the newsman in broadcasting.

When Chet left the show in 1970, he was undoubtedly proud of himself. It was five years since my interview, and finally he had the courage to care about what Chet Huntley wanted out of life—not NBC, not the untold people behind the scenes, or even the twenty million dedicated viewers who found his brand of news uniquely entertaining.

Though only conjecture, with no shred of supportive evidence or substantiation, I've always felt to this day that Chet Huntley wanted me to print his total disdain for newscasting in a paper like the *National Enquirer,* if not the *Enquirer* itself.

When he asked me to turn the recorder off, and he was supposedly speaking "off the record," I believe he knew what he was doing. I don't believe he felt I wouldn't print his scathing attack on how he couldn't finish a lunch that brought on nausea when he thought of returning to the office.

Chet Huntley found it difficult to resign. I contend he wanted that decision made for him—by others.

After departing from NBC, though, Huntley headed off for the Big Sky country of Montana to engage in land development, returning to the tube in 1972. This time, however, it was not in a newsroom or on the other end of the phone with David. He was on TV commercials as the "official spokesman" for American Airlines.

Many of Huntley's former friends and peers took exception to the one-time newsman "cashing in," so to speak, on his professional news background. But Huntley was doing what he liked best. He wasn't accountable to anyone, and he didn't have to make any concessions to David Brinkley, or to his producer.

It is probable that Huntley knew he had to make the break—that the job he so disliked was trimming years off his life, a life that was loaded with pressure and dissatisfaction.

On March 20, 1974, Chester Robert Huntley, who had been born December 10, 1911 on a farm in Caldwell, Montana, died of cancer.

When Chet departed NBC in 1970, Brinkley continued on the nightly news show for a year as co-anchorman, and has been unhyphenated since the fall of 1971, with his own segment entitled "David Brinkley's Journal."

Then, on June 7, '76, following Brinkley's teaming with John Chancellor in anchoring a series of special primary reports, whose ratings blitzed CBS and ABC, NBC promptly restored David to the co-anchor seat of the nightly news opposite John, the regular host. The reappointment, NBC announced, was for the remainder of the political year, and possibly extending through the inauguration on January 20. Obviously, NBC was testing and planning: Could the fourteen year successful magic show formula be right now with a two-man team, with David as an "equal partner?" Also, could the NBC news team chip off Walter Cronkite's healthy Nielsen rating while neutralizing the effect of Barbara Walters joining Harry Reasoner in the fall as the first permanent female co-anchorwoman in network news?

But half a decade earlier, NBC's top brass *knew,* and so did the industry, that without Huntley, Brinkley was not effective as an anchorman. Though they had problems of personality, they were professionals and their differences escaped viewer detection. Theirs was the perfect marriage. In the divorce of his resignation, and in his death, Chet Huntley was conspicuous by his absence. He will always be remembered fondly, possibly even by David.

The not-so-grand opening of my office which I used in '64
to conceal my identity as a *National Enquirer* reporter . . .

. . . and the letterhead of that illustrious organization.

Miss Radio Caroline, my pretty "pirate" representative, whose job it was to interest Madison Avenue media men in the British stations. (*George Bernard*)

Chet Huntley revealed to me that he had no great love for his co-anchorman, David Brinkley. "He gets under my skin," the candid Chet confessed.

CHAPTER VI

How I Duped RFK... And Turned The Camera On Allen Funt!

Robert F. Kennedy was nobody's fool, or was he? With the most carefully selected staff of political tacticians, strategists and other highly accredited advisors less than a breath away, the chances of RFK "screwing up" might have drawn odds from Jimmy "The Greek" Snyder of ten-thousand-to-one.

He was a Kennedy. Accordingly, greatness was expected. Though LBJ, another Democrat, was on brother JFK's White House throne, Robert was visibly emerging as a viable, practical Presidential alternative for '68.

Thus, Bobby could ill afford the luxury of error. Yet, the brutal blunder occurred. And I was responsible!

When it happened, the shock was heard—and read—around the world. In New York, on Thursday, March 18, 1965, the *Herald Tribune's* front page read: "KENNEDY VOICE ON PIRATE RADIO."

I had provoked an international incident with my unique cover. And, in the process, I almost crushed the Senator's credibility and altered the course of his "manifest destiny."

In Washington, D.C., one day after the controversial radiocast, a spokesman for rattled Robert said he doubted his boss realized that Caroline was forbidden to broadcast inside Great Britain. "What the station was had nothing to do with it," the official emphasized.

The growing anxiety for Robert Kennedy was initially precipitated by a phone call to me from Ronan O'Rahilly, Caroline's managing director in London. O'Rahilly was no less than the grandson of the Irish patriot who led the ill-fated Easter Uprising against the British in 1916.

"George," he began. "I would like Senator Kennedy to deliver a special five-minute St. Patrick's Day greeting. It will be aired on Radio Caroline, and will be heard simultaneously by Prime Minister Harold Wilson and the Irish Ambassador while they dine at a special dinner held at the London Hilton. I would also like Senator Kennedy to personally address me in his message," Ronan added. "Can you do it?"

This was a request I truly couldn't afford to refuse. Caroline was a fabulous front for my *Inc.* stories. Further, the thought readily occurred to me that the *Enquirer* could become a benefactor. But no one would prosper, if Robert knew the exact illicit nature of the station. I was sure of that.

On Monday, March 15, just two days before the Irish dinner, I tracked down Robert F. in New York.

With little difficulty, I got through to the New York Senator. He came right to the phone. I carefully explained that the British station named after his niece, would be deeply honored to have him speak before an Irish Association dinner in London that would be attended by Harold Wilson, the Irish Ambassador, and others. What appealed to Senator Kennedy was that he wouldn't have to fly to the United Kingdom to be heard.

"I'm prepared to take your comments *now* over the phone," I said to the Senator. "I can hook up an induction coil to the phone and my tape recorder."

"You aren't taping me now, I hope? Are you?"

"No!" I assured him, his voice growing more high-pitched.

"You can't expect me to do it *now,* off the cuff. No, I can't do it like that. I'm not prepared. I would like to have some time to make a prepared statement," Kennedy said.

In other words, I surmised, he would be putting one of his professional, potent writers on it.

Senator Kennedy gave me his word that he would call me the following day—just one day before the dinner—"eight to ten minutes" before he went into the Senate session, at approximately noon.

The Senator would be phoning me from a booth, just outside the Senate. And in case something went wrong, Kennedy gave me the number of the booth.

At 12:20, not hearing from him, I called the number. After ten or eleven rings, a page picked it up.

I put Reggie on the phone. In his best cockney, Reg instructed the page that "London was calling Senator Kennedy," and it was "urgent" he come to the phone. Further, that "the matter concerned Harold Wilson."

In three minutes' time, Senator Kennedy came to the phone, apologizing for the delay, but not explaining why there was one.

"I want to first thank Ronan O'Rahilly, the managing director of Radio Caroline, for the opportunity to extend my greetings to the Honorable Harold Wilson, the Prime Minister, to tell you what an honor it is this evening to have an opportunity to say a few words to you."

If he had stopped there, O'Rahilly would have been ecstatic. Wilson, an arch-enemy of the "pirate" stations, would be furious at Kennedy. And the Irish Ambassador would feel slighted by the error of omission.

Kennedy's speech was garbled. And although the theme was universal brotherhood, if you weren't Irish, you might have mistaken his words for a dull lullaby. Further complicating matters, cable interference developed on the line, causing a noisy connection. But rather than interrupt the Senator and have the call redialed, we continued. I was afraid I wouldn't get him back on the line, for one reason or another.

"As a son of St. Patrick myself, I know just how important this day is, " he went on. "I think of this day as one of the bonds of common kinship that Irish everywhere feel on St. Patrick's Day. This is a day, as legend has it, that three requests were granted by an angel of the Lord, in order to bring happiness and hope to the Irish ... So, I pray that we are all joined together, whether we are of Irish background, English or whatever our heritage, as we are all joined together by a common interest of liberty and a common interest of freedom. ..."

Kennedy praised Owen O'Neill, the great liberator, and described him as "one of the greatest figures of Irish history." But as Robert went on, I detected an underlying rallying call for the Irish at the dinner to become inspired, rise up and slaughter their oppressor-hosts, the British, or so it seemed to me.

At 7:39 a.m., the Kennedy tape arrived at Heathrow Airport in London, but was either held up, or confiscated, and never reached the Caroline pick-up car.

When word reached me of the snag, I had to break through a congested St. Patrick's Day Fifth Avenue parade with a duplicate copy of the tape, and hope I could get to Radio Press International in time.

Fortunately, R.P.I.'s circuits to Britain were open. The tape was transmitted fifty minutes before it was due, being heard at the Hilton at 7:30 p.m., E.S.T., and throughout the United Kingdom, parts of Germany, France, Holland and Spain.

In the ballroom, however, the taped Kennedy message was fed through a faculty "low," loudspeaker system that had to compete with a noisy, festive assemblage. So to make absolutely sure that Harold Wilson was aware of every word of the broadcast, O'Rahilly instructed two assistants to deliver a duplicate tape to 10 Downing Street . . . but not without some unexpected difficulty. When the Caroline couriers, who had Irish brogues you could slice through, approached Wilson's residence, one bobby screamed to his partner—"Watch out, they're revolutionaries! They've got a bomb in the box." The couriers were wrestled to the ground, on the spot.

In essence, the British police were correct. It was an explosive—a verbal one. Later, however, the two buccaneer boys received a formal apology and the tape was accepted for the Prime Minister's attention.

Totally unlike my straightforward approach to Huntley and Brinkley where Caroline's clandestine career was highlighted, Robert Kennedy could not be informed of the station's "skull and cross bones" banner image in the British Parliament.

Chet and David were humored by, and admired, the competitive spirit. Huntley especially praised my American participation in the "Jolly Roger" operation on the high seas.

As certain as one can be, Robert Francis Kennedy would not have become involved, had he known. Kennedy had too much to lose—particularly if he became President in '68 and Harold Wilson was still in office.

Wilson condemned Kennedy's lack of judicious consideration and I, George Bernard, was banned from Britain, under penalty of imprisonment, along with all the others who were secretly providing food, fuel and even water to the pirate people.

Joseph Kaselow, a reporter from the *Herald Tribune,* contacted me for a statement after the broadcast broke.

"Do you feel you pulled a hoax on the Senator?"
he asked.

"I told him that Radio Caroline was a commercial station. So, it either had to be the non-commercial BBC, or a pirate station. He and his press people had plenty of time to consider," I responded.

The story broke so quickly that it precluded becoming an *Enquirer* headliner. Mournfully, I visualized the front page that would never be: ROBERT KENNEDY WALKS THE PLANK, or RFK ENDORSES ILLEGAL STATION NAMED AFTER NIECE.

The *Enquirer* is a weekly. In those days, it took three weeks to get into print. Today, Gene Pope has automated his printing prowess by getting his tabloid out in one week.

But this was probably the first time an *Enquirer* reporter was scooped by his own story. For me, it would never happen again.

Less than a week after the *Herald Tribune* bomb burst, and as the same newspaper ran part II on the Kennedy caper in their Sunday, March 21 editions, Robert Kennedy risked his life to draw public attention from the "pirate" radio fiasco.

For on March 24, '65, Robert F. Kennedy became the first man to reach the peak of the highest unclimbed mountain in North America. Rugged Robert had conquered Mount Kennedy in Canada, and looked out at the world 13,900 feet below.

The climb was alerted to the nation's leading magazines by RFK's press people. And those that had the "pirate" involvement in type, lifted it in anticipation of the Kennedy conquest. Staff writers, photographers and even *paparazzi* converged on the base of the mountain, as did the throngs who believed in Moses and kept their vigil.

When Robert descended, he not only erased an

error, but created an era of hope, pride and rugged determination.

While Robert Kennedy survived and overcame the curse of Caroline, I would continue using the ships for a while longer. Until, that is, the British government torpedoed the floating stations by enacting illegal legislation that ultimately sent them to the ocean floor.

But while they were afloat, the Caroline cover, following the Kennedy episode, became my most effective *Enquirer* camouflage. Especially when I turned the "Candid Camera" on Allen Funt.

"Are you sure this isn't a stunt?" Funt said suspiciously as he tried to read deceit in my eyes, and then in Reggie's.

"If this is a stunt, tell me now. I'm a busy guy and have no time for fooling around, unless of course, if it's for my own show."

The fact that Britain had a highly successful "Candid Camera"-type show running on their own television seemed to dispell doubts that the interview was a hoax, and to confirm that it would indeed run on the Caroline stations. But had the sparsely-domed Funt known that the interview would find its way into the *Enquirer,* his meager crop of scalp hair would have stood on end! He suspected something—and his searching eyes gave me an uneasiness I found difficult to conceal.

Funt was candid when he said that when someone comes near him with a camera, he runs. And it was not because they might take his picture, but out of a gut feeling that he might be belted—with the camera!

Off the camera, Funt said he considered himself a VUP—Very Unpopular Person. Husbands would like to hurt him, wives would like to whip him and others would like to castrate him.

And the reason for all this Funt-directed aggression, he admitted, was because he was the world's number-one snooper, and who likes a snooper?

Funt said that his snoop-show started as "Candid Microphone" sixteen years back. And during this period, he was lucky to have come away with his life. He'd been pushed, shoved, kicked by people who contended that he should not be snooping around—camera or no camera!

He related an incident that occurred at a crowded resort where he caught an amorous couple "being themselves." Noting that their embrace was inoffensive, Funt's cameras ground away, recording a scene Funt thought to be delightfully funny.

But when anxious Allen showed the hot and humorous film to Casanova, the man didn't share his feelings. Instead, he pulled out a long-handled razor and chased him across the grounds. Funt said that he had outrun him easily, but that he was still terribly frightened afterwards.

"So far," he said to us, "my staff has been trying to catch me off guard for "Candid Camera". You sure they didn't put you up to this?"

"No. They didn't put us up to it," I told his secretary over the phone later as I suggested Allen might like to pick up a copy of the January 17, '65 *Enquirer*.

"Why?" she asked.

"Should I be *candid* about it?"

"Oh, I get it," she laughed. "You turned the camera on Allen. Great!"

CHAPTER VII

Zachary Scott, Edward G., Lee Marvin—
Did Being Mean Make Them Happy?

Shortly before a brain tumor in October '65 claimed the life he so enjoyed and held vital, Zachary Scott consented to be interviewed. I scheduled a 12:30 luncheon at Marsh's, which was less than five minutes away from an apartment he maintained that overlooked sprawling Central Park.

Scott, who had made some forty-odd pictures—"I can't keep an accurate count," he said to me—had built his responsible reputation on professionalism. The image of the venomous villain was his trademark, which was supported by a highly articulate, smoothly deep speaking voice that never faltered or failed him.

In the fabulous '40's, the name Zachary Scott was in the same league as Spencer Tracy, John Wayne, John Garfield, among others. Directors found him a devilish delight to work with, though they cast him not as Robert Respectable, and never as Jesus Christ. The closest he might have come to Heaven—or Hell—would be as Judas, but Hollywood never called him for the part.

Instead, he ground out movie memorables such as *The Mask of Dimitrios, Flamingo Road,* and *Mildred Pierce,* among other greats. In 1945, *Mildred Pierce* earned Joan Crawford an Oscar for "Best Actress" and catapulted Scott to even greater cinematic heights.

The name Zachary Scott has always conjured up terrifying thoughts of the loathsome landlord who got his sadistic kicks by serving dispossess notices that would send impoverished, innocent families out into the cold. Or, the brute who tied the movie mistress in distress to a rail as a steaming locomotive converged upon her trembling torso. I had imagined Scott to be a born scoundrel—everything he was on the screen.

Instead, he was suave and highly sophisticated—especially about his image as a screen scum. He had accepted his stereotype, but as I would learn, it wasn't always apparent to him.

"I used to fight the image of the bad guy on the screen," he confessed, sitting in the same seat Chet Huntley had occupied on another interview.

"Then Bette Davis took me aside and gave me a stiff talking-to: 'Don't fight it. Don't be an idiot. The villainous parts are the meatiest and the juiciest. The scripts are better! The lines are better and are more interesting to the public. Who cares about being a romantic character all the time?' Bette lashed into my innocence.

" 'And, who cares about being a leading man? Those are some of the most boring, dullest parts.' She knocked sense into my thick head. I agreed and promised Bette I'd change my outlook.

"How stupid I was before Bette came into my life. I used to *plead* with the studios to give me a leading role in comedy, which is what I had done. But, they would only laugh at me, to my face and behind my back. Then after I had a few wicked roles snuggly tucked under my belt, *they* were doing the pleading—and I was doing all the laughing!" Scott took a drag on a cigarette and changed the topic, temporarily, to Richard Burton.

He said that though Richard Burton received more rave notice from fans and moviegoers, he wouldn't trade places.

"If I was in the position of Burton, I think that would drive me to heavy drinking," he said matter-of-factly, not realizing the ironic truth of his statement. For Burton's drinking would escalate enormously and eventually be one of the key reasons for his final break-up with Elizabeth Taylor.

"Now, don't get me wrong," Scott went on. "I don't hate publicity, and at the same time, I don't dislike it. To be constantly surrounded by vast crowds of people would annoy me very much. In my thirty-one years in the theatre, I was mobbed twice—and on both occasions, it happened in New York.

"At the Sherry Netherland, I was almost killed when a plate glass gave way. That would be some way to go, wouldn't it?" he laughed, exhaling a stream of soft smoke.

"Except for other isolated instances, I can't really say that people have been really hysterical over me. It's pretty difficult for most people to like a louse, which has been my career!"

While Zachary Scott learned to live with his villainous image—until his death—another equally prominent performer couldn't shake the stigma of the terrible tyrannical tintype Hollywood had stamped indelibly, or so he thought, on his career.

One of my agents, a doorman at a swanky Fifth Avenue hotel, tipped me off that Edward G. Robinson had just gone to his room.

After I knocked twice, the door opened and Edward G. asked me to come in.

"What's the rush?" he said, obviously mistaking me for someone else. "I just got back and you want me to leave again!"

"Mr. Robinson, I'm not who you think I am."

"Then," he shouted, "who are you?"

"George Bernard, Trans-Atlantic Features. Didn't the studio set it up?"

"Set what up?"

"The interview?"

"Nobody's told me anything about an interview. And what do you want to know that a press agent can't tell you, anyway?" he became more annoyed at my intrusion.

"I would like to know about your being one of the world's foremost collectors of art," I said, then prayed for a favorable response.

It came. His eyes lighted up. This was Edward G.'s favorite subject and for more than fifteen minutes, I had to listen to a discourse on the merits of the Renaissance versus the Baroque period of painting.

I was growing edgy. This wasn't what the *Enquirer* readers wanted, and I felt that at any second his intended visitor might show up, or a flack from Bavaria Films might call and my number would definitely be up. Edward G. was finishing shooting *Grand Slam* in New York for the independent film company.

"But aren't you embarrassed at the inconsistency of being known as an art lover and an assassin—on the screen?" I had to ask—to shake the interview up.

"You, too," he ranted. "You also see me as a two-bit thug. In spite of all the different roles I've played, you still think of me probably as 'Little Caesar', don't you?"

"Well, yes I do," I had to reply to keep the interview going on the *Enquirer* track.

Robinson had appeared in over one hundred motion pictures in his brilliant forty-three-year screen career, which ended when he died on January 26, 1973.

But it was the role of "Little Caesar" that shot him to stardom in 1930. "And that infamous image has stuck to me like glue," he snapped at me.

The pint-sized Hollywood performer told me that he was no gangster or screen hoodlum, but that he was a fine, accomplished actor who'd been trying to shake the cruel villain label all his life.

He confessed that people, especially those from small cities, actually believed that he'd served time in a federal pen.

"Believe me, I'm clean," he insisted.

"I believe you." I offered comfort.

Edward G. looked angrily at the TV set in the room. He admitted that he hardly ever tuned in his own pictures, especially the gangster ones.

He was unhappy with television, contending that the tube was in major part to blame for perpetuating his "Little Caesar" stereotype.

"Why does TV have to emphasize my gangster pictures? Why can't they play the more rewarding ones?" he asked me.

"Because that's what the public's into," I said. "Just like P.T. Barnum, said: 'Give the public what it wants.'"

"Yeah, but if Barnum had to contend with always being looked at as if he were a common criminal, he'd throw himself to one of the lions in his circus."

Robinson admitted that *All My Sons* and *House of Strangers* were the most gratifying pictures he had starred in. "They helped to reveal the broad range of my acting abilities," he told me. "And in *A Dispatch From Reuters* and *The Prize,* I also portrayed great men of fact and fiction," he exclaimed proudly.

Edward G. agreed that "Little Caesar" was responsible for launching his career, and that the public enjoyed him as the controversial Al Capone-type character who became their image of a Chicago gangster.

Robinson admitted that the slightest reference to crime sent him into hysteria, and that the heartache his son had brought him might have added to his gangster image.

Edward G. Robinson, Jr., then thirty-three, had been prominently splashed across the nation's newspaper pages for his arrests for drunken driving and attempted robbery, which became embarrassing to his dad.

The father told me that it was easy for someone to think, "like father, like son," but the public should remember: "I only made crime movies, and never committed an offense in my entire life."

"In fact, my original intentions were to be a rabbi."

Edward G. added that if he had had a crystal ball in 1930 and he could have seen his monster image building, he would have made a mad rush for the shelters of the temple.

He was sure that the movie associations with Humphrey Bogart and James Cagney had helped cement a criminal image in the mind of millions, "but fortunately, not in the minds of producers."

He had appeared in such top-rated films as *The Ten Commandments* and *Brother Orchid*.

"Everytime I see one of those two-bit, amateur comics mimicking me on TV, I could throw a picture frame at the screen. But I wouldn't want to damage my frames. They mean something to me. The idiot comics who cash in on me as a thug, I couldn't give a darn for."

Edward G. looked carefully at himself in the mirror. "Now, do I look at all like a gangster?" he asked me.

"Today," I said, "you can't tell one from the other. There are gangsters who are cheating the public, and they're in government."

"Don't be philosophical," he said. "Give me an honest answer. Do I look like a gangster?"

I had the interview I needed, so I thought, what did I have to lose by being honest?

"Yes, you do look like 'Little Caesar'," I said.

"But, who is 'Little Caesar?' I'm 'Little Caesar'. I created the role. Look, here. Oh, I'm even sounding like him," Edward G. was growing more flustered.

"I'm only seventy-three now," he told me, looking at himself again in the mirror, telling me that he'd got plenty of good acting years before him. "So, maybe I can bury 'Little Caesar' before he buries me."

Before I thanked him for his time and returned to write the article the *Enquirer* was anxiously waiting to run in their March 5, '67 edition, I felt compelled to tell Edward G. that dispelling the hood image was a waste of time.

He was bucking the inevitable. Not only did TV continue to resurrect his deadly roles, but he had been preserved for all of eternity in that one part that plagued him so much. A museum in Hollywood had preserved Edward G. forever in wax—as "Little Caesar". Better I didn't tell him.

Ironically, Robinson disdained his rough and tough tintype while another box office biggie both liked and likened himself to Edward G. and the actor's cinema-crime cronies.

"I'm a real man. I'm Humphrey Bogart, Jimmy Cagney and Edward G. Robinson all rolled into one," Lee Marvin told me in a corner of New York's famed Rainbow Room following a party for his latest movie, *The Dirty Dozen*. The revelation of his image became the headline of a September 10, '67 *Enquirer* article.

Marvin was boasting that Hollywood was paying him a big bundle for putting his toughness on the screen. And, that Cagney, Bogey and Edward G., in his estimation, were real men, "people the nation should look up to, and respect."

Marvin said that he hated sissies, and that there was a dire need for America to look up to tough people. "Wars," he said, "are not won by the squeamish and the frightened!"

If only the grey-haired Lee knew just how frightened I was during our interview. I figured it was only a matter of moments, not minutes, before my conspicuous note-taking would be detected by the studio press agent. Then I could expect a heavy hand to grab me by the collar of my tuxedo and, in front of everyone, haul me out of the party.

When I called from Trans-Atlantic Features, I was told in the morning that "no press" would be permitted to be at the party. But, if I wished, I could stand in the lobby and take notes while the guests entered the elevator. "That's all," a rude, authoritative female voice instructed.

When I arrived at the lobby, it was just as "Miss Rude" had described it would be, except there were more security guards than I had imagined belonged to any one protective agency. Before the guests could enter the elevator, they had to present their invitation to one guard while another checked it for authenticity, and yet another crossed their names off a master list.

Further, a photographer tipped me off that there was back-up security upstairs, on the sixty-fifth floor, just before the revolving doors to the Rainbow Room and the picture party.

In addition, the public elevators to the floor above and the one below were barred to anyone who didn't have an invitation. And even if you did, the cars were set on automatic control. There was only one stop, the sixty-fifth floor. All the other public cars in the massive building complex were "closed for the evening."

I started hunting for side elevators—those that would take me right into the area and floor of the party, and would bypass the awesome security guards.

Suddenly I spied an open, unattended freight elevator. One summer while I was going to college, I operated a similar type of elevator in Manhattan's famed clothing jungle—the garment center. Once I had run the car recklessly just short of the roof and it took two-and-a-half hours to extricate me and a passenger from the stranded elevator.

As I was closing the door, a voice yelled: "Hey, where ya going with my car?"

I had no idea what the man looked like. It was just a mean-sounding voice. I kept my hand down on the handle and was now passing the eleventh floor. It wouldn't be long before I reached sixty-five. But I resolved to be extremely careful. I had learned something from the jungle car I had operated in 1958, and I didn't want to repeat my mistake. Then it had brought just a tongue-lashing from the manager of the office building. If I damaged the car now, or even got caught in the process, I would certainly be booked on vagrancy, trespassing, theft, and all the other charges in the book.

As I reached the sixty-third floor, I eased up on the hand lever and made a perfect level landing on sixty-five. I heard the elevator motor of the adjacent car and figured someone was pursuing me.

I had little time to survey the area. Only two double doors were between me and the party. I peeped through, and saw a few people chatting with their backs toward me.

A cocktail glass that was resting alongside the elevator car became my prop. Though it smelled of beer, probably used earlier by an attendant, I clenched my hand around it to conceal its empty contents. Then, I walked in backwards as if I had never left, and had been there all along!

It worked. From there I waited for an opportune moment to speak with the hard-fisted, menacing Marvin. But he was greeting another rough character, Jim Brown, who had just retired from professional football as the most terrifying ground-gainer the game had ever known.

After a few moments, Brown moved on and I moved in for the kill.

"Americans need to be bullied," Marvin admitted. "They're too mamby-pamby." Lee said that the Americans could learn a lot from the Israelis, "who," he said, "find that everyday is a challenge to them."

"The Israelis are born men. From the time they are born, they know how to fight and survive—and they fight like no others. They are magnificent!"

Marvin confided in me that he was extremely proud of the Israelis, especially in light of their heroic battlefield accomplishments during the historic June 5, '67 "Six Day War" in which they annihilated the Egyptian army.

"They're something else," he said with pride.

Marvin's pride for the Israelis would have soared even greater had a crystal ball of the future been available. For on July 4, '76, Israeli crack commandos flew some 2000 miles from their homeland to Uganda and gunned down a gang of terrorist hijackers and freed 104 hostages in one of the most daring and spectacularly successful raids recorded in modern times. The heroic siege of Entebbe Airport was a true "mission impossible" that brought the Jewish State the respect and admiration of many heads of state... including the tyrannical Idi Amin, Uganda's President, who cooperated with the terrorists!

Marvin expressed his disgust for war dissenters, urging their being thrown out of the country, or charged with treason. His strong stance on nationalism was understandable. He had dropped out of high school to join the Marines, determined in World War II to wipe out the enemy, single-handed, if need be.

Marine Marvin's sciatic nerve was split, he told me, and he had spent thirteen months in a hospital almost paralyzed. "But I didn't whine or look for a shoulder to cry on. My dad was tough and I learned from him."

In '65, Lee Marvin had won an Oscar for his dual role as gunfighter brothers in *Cat Ballou*—a motion picture with plenty of laughs, but little of the toughness he was boasting of. "It was one of the few films in which I was not all bad. I played it that way."

Marvin said that being mean does mean a lot to him. "I'm as tough on the screen as I am in person," he emphasized. "And, even when I played a good guy in TV's 'M Squad', I was a real mean mother." That last word was omitted when the story ran in the *Enquirer*.

If you've ever seen Marvin get into a fist fight, or fall on the screen, it's really Lee—no double or stunt man. Lee's contract says it.

"Being myself, being the hard man, has made me very wealthy," he went on, noting that every movie he made boosted the asking price for his next film. But Marvin was able to explain his cinema success. "The whole world loves a tough guy," he explained. "Psychologically, I think that most people like to identify themselves with them." That's why, Marvin said, people like to watch him. "I'm everything the average guy would like to be—and isn't."

I saw an angry-looking attendant come through the double doors and surmised that he was the one from whom I had borrowed the freight elevator. He was greeted by the manager of the Rainbow Grill, who reprimanded him for barging into a "private" party—whatever the reason. "You don't come in on a private party," he was screaming.

Even the manager was playing the tough guy. It seemed fashionable. So, as I left, I brushed a guard.

"Why don't you have your uniform cleaned?" I interrogated him. And then I thought, "Why don't I get out of here now and not test my luck

any further?" I quickly took the public elevator
to the street.

Zachary Scott, reputedly one of the richest actors in Hollywood, said, "If I were in Richard Burton's position, I think it would drive me to drink!"

CHAPTER VIII

Unusual Deaths and Near-Deaths!

While working for the *Enquirer* I came to know that the characters running through its pages each issue were limited to a one-week performance. Only, on the most rare of occasions, would they be held over.

The performers came from every walk of life on earth and from beyond this universe. And practically all of them, while they were dead or alive—it really didn't matter—never knew that they would be entertaining audiences on the *Enquirer's* center stage.

Figuratively speaking, Pope was sitting in the audience endlessly searching for exceptional talent. To those who aroused his fancy, he generously allotted premium page position in his next available edition of the *Enquirer.*

The Pope would applaud loudly, almost deafeningly, when the characters boasted of mutilations, especially on themselves. Those who were roasted and toasted—alive—were immediately selected and sent to central casting for make-up and other beautifying, or horrifying, touch-ups.

Others, whose resumes included being boiled or scalded to death, instantly became stars.

In the spring of '65, the following headline ran in the *Enquirer*: FROM HIS CELL, 36-YEAR-OLD PRISONER TELLS: I CUT OFF 4 FINGERS TO COLLECT INSURANCE. For 18 Years, I Tortured Myself To Swindle Companies Out of $13,000.

So much for that performer.

In this chapter three of the most bizarre deaths—and two near-deaths—are brought back by popular demand. I covered their original performance for the *Enquirer*.

In Florence, New Jersey, Miles Lucas died the strangest death on record. I remember the incident so well, for I was asked to photograph the tombstone of Miles Lucas and secure a photo of the deceased from his bereaved family.

Lucas was driving home when he crashed head-on with a truck. The force of the crash sent Lucas's car off the road and into a graveyard.

While the still-moving auto bounced off gravestones in its violent path, Lucas was hurled out the driver's door and died instantly when his skull crunched against a tombstone.

Tragic, but what's so unusual?

The insane irony is contained in the words carved into the tombstone: "Miles N. Lucas. Death Comes Equally To All."

The December 13, '64 *Enquirer* headline read: "MAN THROWN FROM CAR IS KILLED WHEN HEAD HITS TOMBSTONE WITH NAME ON IT."

The man who drove the other vehicle and walked away without a scratch from the collision, told me, prophetically: "They say that everyone's name and number comes up sometime, but I have never in my life seen anything to beat this."

He added that for the first few nights after the tragedy he had had nightmares—and they were all the same variety. He saw Lucas's body flying through the air and his head smashing into the tombstone, just like a guided missile being directed to its target. The man added that he thought the stone, by some unexplainable, mystical force, had been waiting there for Lucas—all his life!

Another eyewitness to the spooky smash-up said that after he observed the same name on the gravestone, he assumed the dead man had been on his way home from visiting his dad's grave. It turned out, however, the man said, to be just an ordinary accident with a "million-to-one coincidence." Eerier than a revelation from Ripley, the tombstone belonged to another Miles Lucas—who was born August 10, 1814 and died April 9, 1900.

A neighbor explained that Miles Lucas "would not" have a tombstone to mark his grave. Miles's survivors, a daughter, two sons and six grandchildren, were all superstitious. They feared that Lucas's sons might die the way their dad had. I guess they had the right to be cautious!

I now had the photos of the crash site and the tombstone Lucas cracked his skull against, but I did not have a head shot of the deceased. And I could not bribe the police photographer for it either. He told me that if the photo got out, the coroner would know that the leak could only have come from one source. And, he was not about to sacrifice a full-time, steady job for a few bucks.

My first efforts with the family failed. They didn't want any part of the press, until I convinced them that the photo was desperately needed to be included as part of a special layout my news agency was preparing on highway safety. Further, I stressed the need for the family's cooperation, which could go a long way in saving lives. "And, if just one life was saved, Miles Lucas's death would not be in vain."

I wasn't sure myself what the connection was between saving lives and the freak photo of a man who crashed into his own gravestone. In any event, they bought it! But after it ran in the *Enquirer*, my phone *did not* stop ringing. I was called every name in the book of rotten names. "How could you? Do you sleep at night? How much did they pay you?" were some of the questions I was speechless to answer.

Didn't they understand I was an *Enquirer* reporter? I had to do my job, and in doing it, I had to be without conscience.

Once a gunslinger thinks of conscience, he's automatically dead. Was I any different?

Did you ever hear of a gun duel ending when one man's bullet entered the other's pistol barrel? Would you believe it really happened in Cleveland during the summer of '65? Shortly after that, my agent there worked very closely with me, piecing together the strange details that would become an *Enquirer* feature for October 17.

Yes, if you've wondered, it was indeed a "million-to-one" freak shot, according to authorities. If it had been evaluated as anything less, Gene Pope would have killed the story.

The freak shot featured a fantastic *Enquirer* layout, which included photos of the marksman, the target, the police sergeant and the hand of an officer showing two similar-calibre bullets that met head-on and then fused together in the barrel of a pistol—also on display.

To relate the confused details of the shoot-out would only put you to sleep. Suffice it to say that this "million-to-one" story stemmed from an argument, and I had to practically pull teeth to extract the statement from the authoritative source who made it.

While these two jerks in Cleveland had demonstrated little regard for life by having almost killed each other with pistols, a ten-year-old who lived near Cape Kennedy's launch pads was musing of missiles and how he, some day, would be a great rocket expert.

He was so interested in rocketry and its benefit to the advance of mankind, that he often tried to hitchhike to the launching areas, but got no closer than nine miles away from the pads.

So, on August 13, he decided to construct and launch a rocket in his own backyard.

And his dream of becoming a great missile scientist might have come true, if only his first experiment in rocketry hadn't failed. For when he built his first rocket and launched it, his dream died with him instantly. The rocket pierced his heart.

The Dade County Sheriff's office cooperated fully with Trans-Atlantic Features in providing me with photos of the dead boy lying face down in his backyard, and of the missile launcher that was made of a U-shaped aluminum tube to launch the cartridge. When he lighted the cartridge stuffed with match heads for fuel, the force of the explosion distorted the tube, which was dramatized by a close-up insert, showing the bent part of the tube. The authorities there also secured a photo of the boy when he was alive and happy, explaining to the parents that a news agency was going to publish the story in the hope, (here we go again), "that the life of an innocent child might be saved". Again, the story was bought.

Though I was paid well for the story, I wondered if the article had any other redeeming value. Boys will be boys, and I seriously doubted whether publishing death shots would deter other youths from engaging in similar potentially dangerous—and deadly—activities.

The story was originally slated for November 7, front or back page, which would have paid more. Pope had tried different payment formulas, and the one that proved most effective was the page-position inducement system. Front page paid tops, which was comparable to the centerfold value. Next came back page. After that, the first five pages of the paper. Then, a full-page story, placed anywhere from pages six through thirty-one paid the same.

When Generoso read my article, he became furious. I had interchanged the terms "missile" and "rocket" and you don't do that when the publisher just happens to be a graduate in engineering from the Massachusetts Institute of Technology. So, I was punished, where it hurts—in the wallet. The story was locked into page twenty-eight, which paid considerably less than the other prize positions of the paper.

I had heard about Pope's penalty policy for seeming inaccuracies, but never thought it would ever be directed against me. Reggie had been fined on January 21, '65 by Ted, under direction from Pope. The incident concerned the story of a woman who abandoned her kid in a cotton field.

On the pay voucher, Ted, an executive editor, wrote: "Please note that on the payment for the above-mentioned story, your fee has been cut by $100 on the orders of the Editor because of an inaccuracy. In your notes you say that the temperature was 'freezing'. The desk checked this and found that, in fact, the temperature at the time was 40-45 degrees. The Editor feels that you should have checked this yourself, and because of this is fining you $100.

"I'd like to say at this time that you've been doing a marvelous job for the paper. Please keep it up—but watch your facts very, very closely, please."

As far as I was concerned, I had watched my facts extremely closely, and had nothing to worry about. I never did agree with Pope's contention that I had incorrectly called a missile a rocket, and vice versa—especially after he "interchanged" their use in a vengeful rewrite of my article.

I did agree, however, with my agent in Philadelphia who suggested that I leave immediately for "the city of brotherly love."

A year before I had become an *Enquirer* reporter, I was an executive at a Philadelphia radio station that was known for breaking major news stories. I was sure, however, that they had no wind of my arrival, or the nature of my visit. I must admit that what awaited me was anything but an expression of "brotherly love," and was instead a memory I'd like to forget.

As I passed Rittenhouse Square Park, I recalled an unforgettable scene when the park had been crowded with devoted fathers taking countless shots of their kids crawling through grass.

About two blocks from the park, my agent met me in a deserted coffee shop. He drew two photos out of a green envelope. One was a headshot of a man. The other made me throw up.

Swiped from the Philadelphia Police Department's secret files, I had in my possession every gore editor's dream.

Little Ronald lived only four months—then he died in excruciating pain. His father had scalded him to death—with tea. The photo confirmed the hospital report. Ronald was burned black from his waist down to the soles of his feet.

The father, whose picture I stared at in amazement, had said that his boy had been scalded "accidentally" when a bottle of tea had been spilled over him.

If it wasn't for a physician at the hospital sensing foul play and notifying the authorities, the father might have walked away with impunity.

Little Ronald died twelve days after being admitted into the emergency ward of Frankford Hospital. He was nine pounds and a bundle of charred flesh.

The father stated to the police that at the time his wife was out, he had accidentally knocked a quart bottle of hot tea over his baby.

After treating the baby with first-aid cream and with butter, he had rushed the infant to the hospital. But the burns were so severe that his son had died. The father was arrested for murder.

The doctor who treated the baby at the hospital testified that it appeared highly unlikely that a bottle of tea could have burned such an extensive area of the child's body. The doctor raised the possibility that the baby had been dipped in scalding water because the burns began just about the waist level and continued down to the soles of the feet.

A detective's report indicated that the hot water in the man's apartment was 154 degrees at the sink and the tub when he went to check it after the baby's death.

The father denied murder, but pleaded guilty to involuntary manslaughter. But before he was sentenced, he told the judge that he "loved" his son.

The story ran on August 14, '66. Just about two years later, Pope ran a related-type piece in the July 21 *Enquirer* edition:

"Doctor's Research Reveals—When A Child Is Murdered, Mom Is Usually the Killer." Part of the piece contained an interview with the learned Dr. Stephen Meyers who stated that children are in more danger from their mothers than from strangers.

But what about their fathers when mom's not home?

On July 31, '66, the gruesome story of a death-determined dad was emblazoned on the *Enquirer's* back page. I wrote the article: "KILLS TWO DAUGHTERS TO PUNISH WIFE FOR LEAVING HIM." How reliable then were the factual findings of Dr. Stephen Meyers?

"Claud Ray, Jr. wanted to punish his wife for leaving him—so he took his two little girls for a last ride, gangland style." Ray picked up his two little girls, seven and nine, one morning, saying he'd drive them to school—but his kids never made it there. In fact, they were never seen alive again—because their 37-year-old unemployed father took them on a detour to death!

The police record indicated that Ray drove his children up along the lonely, deserted seacoast cliffs near Napa, California. And there he committed the most unfatherly show of affection: Ray beat and battered his two girls to death with his fists.

One daughter's crumpled corpse was found a week after the massacre on the jagged rocks below the cliff while the other's corpse was presumed washed out to sea and never found.

There was not even one witness who saw them die or heard their shrieks of agony. Yet the dastardly dad was sentenced to life imprisonment. The jury delivered a decisive guilty verdict as they knew Ray hadn't taken the girls to school as he swore under oath. Reason: he made the mistake of spending their $1 milk money on gas for his car.

The children's mother, Marlene, said that her husband had earlier threatened to kill her and the children for leaving him twelve months before the murders took place. "If I had only taken his threat seriously, my little girls might be alive today."

Marlene admitted that her fifteen-year marriage was living hell. It was filled with fights over money, her other three children and Ray's inability to find steady work. Further, although Ray checked into a mental asylum for a couple of weeks, he was no better straightened out on his release than when he had entered.

The authorities who reconstructed the murder said that Ray had dragged his two little girls out of the car, beaten them to death, "and then hurled their little bodies eighty feet down onto the jagged rocks below the seacoast cliffs." From there, he had hopped into his car and driven through a string of coastal towns, stopping twice. Then around twelve o'clock, he pulled into a

Gualaia, California gas station—which was just a few miles from where his seven-year-old's body was found—and he purchased $1 worth of gas.

At the three-week-long trial, at which Ray maintained his story that he had dropped the girls off at school and had gone out looking for work, the gas station attendant identified the father and placed the time of his stopping there at noon. Ray had paid for the gas with his last dollar—the dollar his wife had given him for the children's milk.

Then at 2:30, to throw everyone off, Ray had stopped at another filling station and called a friend to ask him to pick up the kids. The neighbor told him on the other end of the line that the children had been reported missing from classes since morning. Ray feigned amazement and shock.

Ray was picked up for questioning and since no foul-play evidence had been turned up, including any bodies, he was released. A massive search continued in the area.

But Ray made a fatal error by going to see his wife to taunt her. "He told me to start preparing for the worst. He said he didn't want to be around when the girls were found!" the wife said in the courtroom. When the girl's body was found a week later and an autopsy performed establishing that she had been beaten to death, Ray was taken in again by the police—for good.

I learned, while working for the *Enquirer*, that parents can certainly be problems, deadly ones, to their children. It was a cruel fact. If only we could pick our parents!

CHAPTER IX

Doing The Insane

Arthur William Matthew Carney exuberantly grabbed the "Best Actor" Oscar in April '75 for his penetrating portrayal in *Harry & Tonto.*

Unquestionably, the Academy Award smelled like a bouquet of roses — totally unlike the stenchy stereotype that, until that momentous point in his career, clung like encrusted sewage to his image, but which delighted a generation of tube-watchers in the '60's.

As the witty expert on underground sanitation of Jackie Gleason's "The Honeymooners" which is re-run today in many major markets of the United States, Carney received countless Emmys as the friendly foil to Gleason's hot-tempered characterization of Ralph Cramden.

For one, I couldn't control my laughter. How funny, I thought, to be a human sewer rat!

Whether Pope's people were clairvoyant, I'll never know. But they thought finding the answer was serious business, and less laughable. My partner and I were assigned to find out.

"How insane," I thought to myself.

Getting official clearance from the City of New York for Trans-Atlantic Features came three days later in early February of '65. Even a high-ranking official from the sanitation department was on hand to supervise the entire operation, which began on a West Side street that was blocked off with barricades for this special occasion.

What government agencies will go through for publicity never ceases to amaze me.

Reggie and I hopped into the department's new set of yellow, rubberized outfits. Our boots were practically waist high and the other gear, that might have been used in a New Delhi rain storm, assured us that we were indeed waterproof—except, that is, for the head-piece that exposed our faces.

The manhole was pried open and my partner and I lowered ourselves down a long ladder to where we touched ground some thirty feet below, or so it seemed. Actually it was not ground but gook, of all nauseating varieties.

A department official high above yelled that another manhole was being opened down the block to provide proper ventilation.

I stood six-foot-one. Reggie was about five-foot-nine. The tunnel we were about to enter was somewhere between four-and-a-half to five feet. So, crouch we must, but we didn't want to stray too far from the ladder. Reggie firmly held onto a battery-operated lantern that blasted a blinding beam of light on the pitch black tunnel awaiting us. I adjusted my camera setting, and hoped the available light would be sufficient.

Hunched over, Reggie entered the cavern first. I stooped over and followed the leader, as best I could. After only a few seconds, my back ached from shrill, excruciating pains. I was convinced Ed Norton must have been a sewer supervisor, not an actual worker. For only midgets, I reasoned, were suited for this kind of work— standing up!

The cold winter air from above, mixing with the evaporation of hot steam from the city's offices and apartment houses nearby, fogged up my camera lens. Further, it was extremely difficult to breathe. And what I was inhaling, I felt, was sure to bring on tuberculosis.

I was breathing in the fumes of putrefaction. The handkerchief I had used to dry and clear my camera lens now became my makeshift gas mask.

The pain unabating, I fell to one knee in the

muck and grime of the sewer floor as a half-decomposed rat floated by me. It was too late to capture the evidence on film. But I managed to half-prop myself up. Half was all the ceiling of the tunnel would permit.

Then a flotilla of turds, discarded rubbers (not the kind you wear in the rain), and another dead rat sailed towards me. I quickly got off two shots, not knowing if my clouded lens would pick up anything.

We were at least fifty feet into the tunnel when Reggie screamed to me that he could not go one step further.

Now I was the thankful leader as I maneuvered my hunched frame in the direction of the exit ladder, Reggie following as quickly as was humanly possible in the rear.

For two days after the subterranean ordeal, we couldn't stand up straight, which is a feeling comparable to the bends deep-sea divers develop. But it couldn't be as painful. That I'm sure.

When the voucher arrived on February 11, Reggie fumed over the pay, which hardly paid. The statement read, in part: "Here's our check for $50 . . . A DAY IN NEW YORK'S SEWERS, time, trouble. Thank you."

For what, we wanted to know. Thank you, for what?

Later I learned that Pope had found our story so disgusting he couldn't finish his dinner.

A year-and-a-half later, in July, Pope ran a similar-type story. Dateline: England. "SEWER TURNS INTO GAS CHAMBER AND KILLS TWO WORKMEN. The fumes were so powerful, they turned the manhole into a gas chamber . . . They were killed like rats. The two men were cleaning the 2,500-foot-long sewer of a tanning factory when the tragedy occurred."

So much for sewers and risking human life—for $50.

If that's insane, how would you like to put a lion in your tank and photograph the king of beasts in his own cage? I didn't think you would.

In Willow Grove, New Jersey, which is not too far from Philadelphia, a man kept a roaring lion, as a pet, in his garage.

Needless to say, the animal's owner did not receive many visitors. Simply because they were scared to death of being eaten up alive.

That seems like a reasonable fear, except for the fact that the lion was said to have partially-paralyzed front paws which reduced his mobility to the running pace of a snail, or crippled turtle.

But no one said he couldn't maul a person with his powerful jaws, or leap like a frog.

"Put a tiger in your tank" was popular then. We didn't have a tiger, but we sure had a *live* lion. But that was only "part" of the assignment for the *Enquirer*.

Obviously, we couldn't get the beast into a tank. So we settled for the front seat of our convertible car, thanks to the owner.

But lions—and hawks—have a trait in common. Many are camera-conscious and become jittery. It was apparent even more when the animal leaped over my head and out of the car.

After photographing the male monster gently pawing another lion—a stuffed one—through the opening between the bars of the cage he was now in, I decided to get a few close-ups. But, the bars were in the way and the owner was not about to let his little kitten out again. It had been enough trouble getting him back in the cage.

Assured by the *Enquirer,* and by the owner that Leo the Lion couldn't move, I gingerly entered the lion's den. Quickly, I focussed with my range finder. The glash synchronized as I clicked off two fast shots. I should have learned my hawkisk lesson. For sure enough, the lion took to flight, roaring as he landed within inches of me. I fell backwards and out of the cage.

Ted told Reggie later that he was "upset I cut part of the lion owner's head" in just "one" of the thirty-six pictures I took that day of the man and the monster.

What was insane—the assignment or the *Enquirer,* or me for becoming involved?

When I wasn't crawling through sewers, or into the cage of a lion, I was investigating other insane stories for the *Enquirer.* Like the time my assignment was to look into the presence of human bones that had been discovered in a New York City cemetery by a young *Enquirer* fan who faithfully informed the paper of the occurrence.

Before I left for the cemetery, I made a few phone calls to my agents in the area. Sure enough, there were a series of reports that cemetery officials, under the cover of night, were ordering graves opened. Then, of those deceased who had no living relatives, or friends who would come to the grave, their bones would be discarded into ash cans, and later dumped elsewhere.

It was also said, but never substantiated, that the cemetery was running out of space for new inhabitants. So, they were cleaning the death house—getting rid of the old and making room for the paying new!

I first visited the home of the girl who had called the story to the *Enquirer's* attention, and examined two bones she swore were human. Frankly, I couldn't discern the difference between the metatarsus of a man and that of a dog.

For evidence, however, I kept one. But when I asked her to take me to where she had found the ash can artifacts, she became reluctant to do so, stating that the cemetery made her nervous.

After twenty minutes and a few dollars, I persuaded her to lead me to the exact site where she had first discovered the bones.

No sooner did we arrive than she bolted away and took off as if she had seen the devil. I was now alone in the cemetery. There weren't any bones in the ash can, or in anything else for that matter. How disappointing. A few feet away, however, there was a wooden crate, and now I might be more fortunate.

My rummaging produced a few empty beer cans, some sandwich wrappings and what looked like a bone. I reached all the way in and pulled it out, not really knowing what my hand was clutching.

I actually shrieked as the sensation of feeling flesh became apparent to me, and instinctively threw the bone to the ground. Surely, it might have been from a deceased human, but how could I be sure? Getting it to a medical expert was the logical course of action.

And then, as if out of a book of nightmares, two large-sized mutts appeared and started fighting for the bone. I had not come this far to be robbed of success by two criminal canines. But then another seemed to emerge from a nearby plot. He was attacking me, simply because I was trying to retrieve from his pal pooches what was rightfully mine. But here, possession seemed to be convincingly in the jaws of the dogs. And, you know what they say, "possession is nine-tenths of the law!"

Mustering up some life-saving ingenuity, I turned my camera and strap into a sling and maneuvered it around my head and body like the ball and chain the gladiators used with skin-splitting, bone-breaking perfection in the arenas of ancient Rome.

One dog kept coming at me while the other two continued to fight among themselves. I was frightened that it would break away from the strap and I would be left minus one camera and possibly a life. The sling was also becoming ineffective against the charges of this enraged beast.

Discretion that moment becoming the safer part of valor, I quickly got my ass out of there—with the dog chasing me to the gate and forcing me to jump over. Infuriated, the dog was still barking, growling and gnashing his teeth when I was fifty feet away and rushing to make it an even hundred, and more.

The bone the girl had given me was indeed human, but it was never substantiated if it really did come from the cemetery ash can. Though my information led me to believe the girl's story was accurate, children do have a way of distorting facts. Remember how they sent thousands of innocent New Englanders to their deaths at the stake in the 17th century's horrendous Salem Witch Trials?

Yet again, what were three ferocious dogs doing in a cemetery? Unless, of course, they were to keep trespassers away from evil doings. What do you think? I certainly wasn't going to find out.

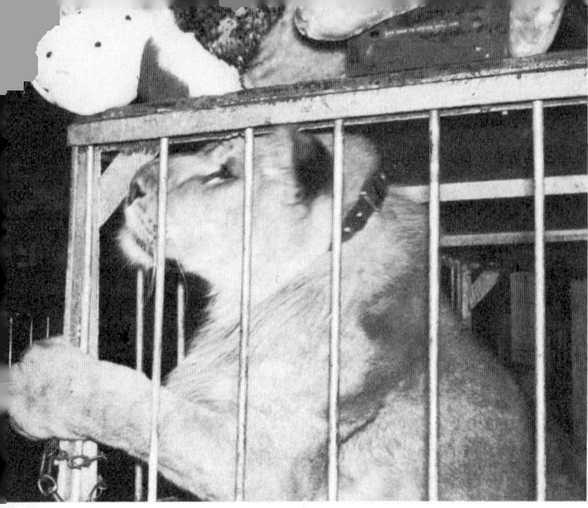

They were "lion" to me when they told me this cat was as tame as the stuffed pussy cat he's playing with at left. (*George Bernard*)

Instead of a tiger, I put a lion in my tank. (*George Bernard*)

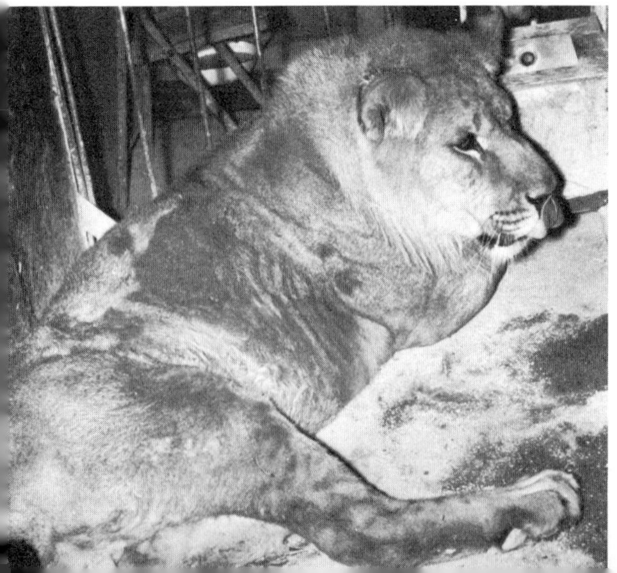

They said the King of Beasts was partially paralyzed, but I felt fully paralyzed when I stepped into his cage to snap a photo. (*George Bernard*)

CHAPTER X

Female Stars Bitch About The Movie Industry— Lee Remick, Lynn Redgrave, Sandy Dennis

"They take our money at the box office, get rich from us, and then they bitch, bitch, bitch about the movie industry. Nothing ever satisfies these ladies of the silver screen!"

Ten years ago, Broadway producer Robert L. Roberts made this statement to me over lunch at Sardi's. Today, he's responsible for two major motion pictures, and he says the situation hasn't changed, except to add: "I *never* hire a tempermental actress, especially one who is sure to bad-mouth the movie industry. Or, even worse, one who would condemn my own films!"

Understandably then, Lee Remick, Lynn Redgrave and Sandy Dennis, three of the screen's leading performers, would never be permitted by Roberts to go before his cameras, and for good reason.

Lovely Lee Remick told me, to my face, that being an actress made her sick. Further, she characterized the movie industry as being infiltrated with immorality, shallowness, phoniness and despair.

Large Lynn Redgrave, at least the way she was made to appear in *Georgie Girl*—the film that catapulted her overnight to stardom, said to me that she was not a "fat slob," and was angry at doing the film.

Screaming Sandy Dennis, sipping a cup of coffee on location shooting, filled my ears with how she hated phony actors, long hours, big shots who boss her around and the people she has to work with.

While Robert L. Roberts has no pity for a performer's personal bitchings, and contends actresses should be grateful to everyone who's helped them, including their fans, Katherine Hepburn thinks differently.

When refusing to sign an autograph for a stage-door Johnny, the disgruntled fan ranted, "We made you what you are today!"

"Like hell you did!" Miss Hepburn retorted.

Like hell Lee Remick would allow her two children to enter show business. In fact, my *Enquirer* story featured the following headline: "I PROTECT MY CHILDREN FROM HOLLYWOOD BY RAISING THEM 3,000 MILES AWAY, Says Lee Remick."

In fact, Lee told me that the only way her three-year-old son and five-year-old daughter would ever get into show business, would be "over my dead body." And the feeling I received was that Lee didn't wish to die. She was vivacious and vibrant, with a charm that radiated excitement. I could hardly take my eyes off her.

Lee admitted that she hardly ever allowed her children to be photographed with her. "I've seen seemingly innocent pictures used by the wrong people to create sensation."

The next words out of her mouth I expected to be a slam against the sensation-packed *National Enquirer.* Instead, she qualified her statement by exposing the culprits who exploited children to be producers, directors and even actors, whom she said were crazy people, "not to be trusted."

She added that these were the exploiters "that I refuse to have my children exposed to. They live in a world streaked with madness."

This explained why she maintained a home in New York for the winter where her children attended school. "I'm protecting my kids from the strange, shallow world of Hollywood by raising them 3,000 miles away."

Lee explained her preparation for the lead in *Days of Wine and Roses*. She had attended several Alcoholics Anonymous meetings in Hollywood and saw what made her sick, reinforcing strong convictions to ban her boy and girl from the screen.

She compared stardom to a drug. "When you remove it, you go into agonizing withdrawal symptoms. It's the same with alcohol," she added.

The Boston-born beauty swore that her kids were going to remain ordinary children who would continue to live in "an ordinary home with an ordinary mother."

I was astounded to learn that Lee's *own* children weren't even aware their mother was a movie star. "And they won't ever find out," she insisted—"until they're old enough to go to the movies!"

While Lee was bent on concealing from little Kate and Matthew the career she had so thoroughly blasted with ringing ridicule, Lynn Redgrave was sticking pins of pain into an imaginary voodoo doll that represented Silvio Narizzano, the director of Columbia Pictures' *Georgie Girl*.

Practically at the gate of tears, Lynn pointed the finger of blame on Narizzano, whose artistic genius, she pointed out, made certain "I'd be a convincing slob." She admitted that padding and ill-fitting clothing helped create the obese image the director "had to have." The make-up and the camera angles selected, along with eighteen pounds "he demanded I gain," made her look the perfect clumsy character.

Lynn was quick to point out that the "extra" weight came off immediately after completing the movie.

She then walked over to the six-foot door mirror and admired herself. Pleased with what she saw, and with on air of confidence about her, Lynn looked out at the city from the hotel window, took a deep breath, and continued.

"It's quite evident I'm not a 'Georgie Girl,' isn't it?" she asked.

"Quite evident!" I honestly agreed and at that precise moment, would have given a King's ransom to hop into the sack with her. But I didn't sense any formal invitation was being offered.

"It's true. I do weigh 142 pounds, but it's really darn well distributed. Don't you think?"

"Extremely well distributed." I was visually raping her.

"And look at these legs," she directed.

In her defense of *Georgie Girl* I was experiencing torturous, sexual sadism. Whether deliberate on her part, or not, I was well aware that British girls were among the most notorious cock-teasers anywhere. I had no way of knowing if Lynn was in league with them, though I had a strange feeling she was not the exception.

"And look at these legs," she directed.

In her defense of *"Georgie Girl"* I was experiencing torturous, sexual sadism. Whether deliberate on her part, or not, I was well aware that British girls were among the most notorious cock-teasers anywhere. I had no way of knowing if Lynn was in league with them, though I had a strange feeling she was not the exception.

The winner of the "Best Actress 1966" award for *Georgie Girl* from the New York Film Critics, she was a member of the most *respected* theatrical family in Britain, if not the world. If I were to try anything, and she screamed for the police, I was sure no one would believe my story. Further, the five-foot-ten-inch attraction was, at the time, starring in the Broadway smash hit "Black Comedy," the lead role she acquired from her convincing portrayal of the "fat slob" in *Georgie Girl*. And, in less than twenty minutes, she would be leaving for the theatre.

I hate quickies. Further, who said I would ever get one? She seemed to like me, but then again she liked many men. "I've got plenty of boy-friends," she confessed, but refused to elaborate on how close, intimately, or otherwise, she was to anyone in particular.

"I certainly hope I don't have to become a cheesecake model to prove I'm attractive," she laughed.

For sure, she wouldn't have done any laughing then if someone predicted it wouldn't be a "cheesecake model" but a prostitute. No, not just any ordinary whore. Only *The Happy Hooker*—Xaviera Hollander! In 1975, the motion picture was released, starring Lynn as the enterprising madame. The book, which originally came out as an original paperback and headed the literary list, became a natural for the screen and several other books to follow.

Ironically, I had been the boyfriend of Xaviera, in real life—for three straight, debilitating weeks. More significantly the Dutch dame, whose real last name is DeVries, pleaded with me—on her hands and knees, and in the sack—to write a book about her life.

"Who's interested in *your* life?" I wanted to know.

"There are stories, true stories," she said, "that would make for a 'best seller'," she begged. "But if you don't write it I still love you."

Indeed, she did, until she left for Puerto Rico and wrote back about a guy she met from New England, whom she also loved. She loved her doorman, the delivery boy, the bartender and everyone who came into her life and left through a revolving door.

The magnetism of the most famous of all

modern-day madams created a mystique that today continues to baffle those who have never personally experienced her multi-faceted charms and taunting, tested techniques.

Hardly considered a beauty, Xaviera could at best be described as mildly attractive, or penetratingly perverse. Intellectually, she was superior to both her perverted peers and jaded johns. She laughed more than she sulked, and she hardly ever sulked at all. And when she made a statement, it had meaning and substance and escaped the trivia status of most conversation.

"You could put a room divider here," she explained, "and move your bar there. Then you could drop the ceiling ..." her mind worked quickly and precisely.

Before Xaviera became a madam ("I'm going to manage other girls and not burn my body out," she would tell me), she really had two basic things going for her. One was her captivating personality. The other was a giant tube of K-Y lubricating jelly, which only the Dutch dame knew how to use with pulsating perfection. Her warm, soft hands and generous amounts of the water soluble cream provided the erotic tremors for the quake.

On one memorable occasion, while our private show was in progress, Xaviera received a call on her blue phone to perform a one-hour number with a husband and wife team. The blue Bell System instrument received higher priced callers than the red phone. Xaviera's fee, including a tip for what she did best, was $300. When she returned, I was fast asleep in her apartment. The nympho shook me vigorously and wanted to continue where we had left off. In fact, I would have obliged, if not for the unmistakable, detectable odor of orgasm and the crust of recently-dried semen still in her hair. Psychologically, it was more than I could sustain. Besides, I was falling for Xaviera and wished to avoid further involvement. So, I decided to spend the rest of what was left of the evening, alone.

Sometime later, when I was an executive at CBS, Xaviera was taping an interview for the company's owned and operated radio stations. When Ms. Hollander spotted me, she threw one arm around me and with the other, squeezed my crotch. How embarrassing! "Do you know her?" the producer of the broadcast jealously queried me.

"Obviously!" I replied, then quickly walked away, hoping the incident would be forgotten, which it was.

Xaviera was a celebrity and I could have flourished in resplendent literary style if only I had trusted her judgment.

But how stupid and shortsighted I was then. I was busy writing a screenplay and didn't attach much merit to her projected project. Robin Moore who authored "The French Connection" wasn't as narrow-minded and readily saw the potential of a harlot's harrowing stories and other confessions. From the book, and even from the movie, he made money, but Xaviera didn't see much, from either the book, or the movie. What did filter back to her went towards paying off greedy, exorbitant attorneys, the I.R.S. and many others to whom she was in debt, Xaviera lamented and swore to me later.

I only slept with Lynn vicariously—through Xaviera. But it was extremely pleasurable. The *Enquirer* was pleased with my story of Lynn, the ugly duckling who became a swan. Accordingly, it ran in a preferential page position of the paper.

Another Redgrave, sister Vanessa, who was getting lots of glamor roles in the movies, especially after *Blow-Up* with David Hemmings in April '67, was not as cordial to this *Enquirer* reporter.

I reached her at the Warner Brothers Seven Arts Hollywood studios where she was in her dressing room preparing for the lead opposite Richard Harris in *Camelot,* an October 1967 release.

"I understand you and your father have had a misunderstanding," I said, hoping to lead her into conversation.

"All daughters have 'misunderstandings', as you call it, with their fathers," she answered evasively.

"But I understand that you *hate* your father." I dropped the bomb which blew up in my face.

"If you think so, then why don't you ask him . . . and why don't you piss against a brick wall?" She punctuated the interview by ending it, then and there.

If I had succeeded with Vanessa, she certainly would have been front-page *Enquirer* timber. Instead, the tree fell on me.

But it was entirely different story with Sandy Dennis on the Warner Brothers set of *Sweet November.*

A call to the studio told my news agency that she would be shooting exteriors in Brooklyn Heights.

Sandy was the winner of that year's Academy Award for "Best Supporting Actress" in *Who's Afraid of Virginia Woolf?* and the *Enquirer* wanted her badly, but only if she would bad-mouth the movie industry. It was always safe to assume that the opposite of what appeared likely would appeal to Gene Pope.

I arrived on the set at 10:30 a.m. I was hoping that this would be one of those days when Sandy would be in a bitchy mood and would pop off about *everything* that bothered her. I hoped she would be irritable and that husband Gerry Mulligan had not satisfied her the evening before. If there's anything that makes an actress edgy, it's sex starvation.

I also prayed that I would not be menaced getting to Miss Dennis! At first I couldn't find her, then I saw her sipping coffee from a refreshment wagon that was pulled up alongside the studio's transfer trucks.

I told her that I was a reporter, but hated going through the studio's press people as "they were impossible to work with. They censor everything I try to write."

Sandy was now in my corner. I could do no wrong. She offered me a doughnut. I accepted.

The crew was setting up transparent orange cellophane sheets over the windows of a quaint brownstone. Sandy stepped to the side to get out of their way.

"I'm sick and tired of being an actress," she confessed. The actors she had to work with, she called "phony". And the grueling, long hours didn't appeal to her either. "And wait until I get inside there," she said pointing to the hallway of the building. "Those lights will be flashing in my face," she moaned. "But the way we're moving, it won't be today. Shit, isn't that a waste of time and money!"

Every other word out of her mouth was either introduced by, or ended with, "shit!" That, of course, had to be edited out of my *Enquirer* interview—Pope didn't go along with vulgarity. He may have liked mutilations, but not obscenity. In a strange way, he was a gentleman!

And sulking Sandy hated all the "big shots" on the set who bossed her around, and moved her here and there "like a piece of freight." But, she confided, even though she hated it all, there was little she could do about it. "Acting is all I know!"

In the film, which I considered to be truly one of the most touching I've ever seen, Sandy plays an amorous kook who has a love for each month of the year—and Anthony Newley is her November love.

Just then an official of the studio called Sandy to meet him by the side of a trailer truck. But before she left me, Sandy whispered gently in my ear to keep cool. "Shit! They don't know what they're really doing. Look, I probably won't be long. Have some more coffee, and wait here."

When I looked back, I couldn't see Sandy anywhere. Anthony Newley was being attended to by a hair stylist and make-up man, which might have accounted for the crowds that started forming. Moments earlier, it was practically desolate on the set.

Two policeman moved a barricade in front of where I was standing.

"Hey, buddy," one cop grunted at me. "Are you authorized to be here?"

"Why, yes," I responded. "I'm a reporter."

"For whom?" he asked.

"Trans-Atlantic Features."

"Sounds like some Mickey Mouse Club." He was getting wise and suspicious.

"Let's see your press card," he asked, practically nose-to-nose with me.

"I don't have it with me," I said.

"Didn't think you would. No card, then off the set, NOW!" he ordered, exercising his authority. His sergeant had probably stepped all over him an hour earlier, or his wife had given him a hard time at breakfast. And, here he was, making my life miserable.

At the time, I didn't have a Working Press Card from the N.Y.P.D. They were extremely difficult to come by, unless, of course, you were a staff reporter for a daily newspaper.

In October '67, just a few months later, I received authorization for a New York City press card. Thus, I had another cover for my stories. The amazing feat was accomplished, once again, through buddy Ben McCall and a contact at the

Halifax Herald newspaper in Nova Scotia, Canada. Those Canadians were fine people and my commitment to them was minimal: I was restricted to celebrities who were in New York and had at one time lived in Nova Scotia. Now, how many are there, really?

One was Godfrey Cambridge, for example. On old Godfrey, who was later to become a good friend, I tested out a $700 spy tape recorder. The case weighed only eleven ounces and was the size of a glass case. The unique feature was found in two delicate microphones that were taped to my chest. "You must have a fantastic memory," Godfrey said. "I don't see you taking down any notes. Are you one of those whiz kids?"

"It's all here," I said, pointing to my chest.

But meanwhile, the offensive officer of the law was chasing me off the set of *Sweet November*. And I had not as yet completed my interview with Sandy Dennis.

After five minutes, I wandered back. I didn't see Sandy, but the cop saw me.

"Hey, if I catch you on the set again, I'll run you in for trespassing, unlawful trespassing."

I wondered what the difference was between lawful and unlawful trespassing. But with no other alternative, I felt compelled to comply with his demand. So I started walking away from the set, but not too far—about fifty feet. Then I ducked behind a tree and watched. The cop was nowhere in sight. I hurried back.

Sure enough, Sandy was looking for me.

"What happened to you?" she asked with sincerity in her marvelous, meaningful voice.

"I went to get a Coke, that's all." I said. For under no circumstances could I confide in her that my reportorial status rested precariously on the most shaky of grounds.

Sandy opened the nozzle of the giant urn that rested on a wooden table a few feet away and allowed a trickling stream of coffee to flow into her cardboard cup. Then she grimaced as if she was drinking a cup of castor oil.

"Shit! It's cold. Oh, well. What do you expect?

"Can you believe all this time we're wasting? Shit, I wish something could be done about it. This damn film keeps me on my feet twelve hours a day, at least."

Sandy admitted that in *Virginia Woolf* she worked fifteen hours every day, just to satisfy director Mike Nichols. She also gave the unequivocal impression of disdain for Nichols, noting how aggravated she became after he accepted the Oscar for her—"as if it was his!"

"It's a real shame I couldn't get to Santa Monica to accept it myself. But I was pooped and had to get up at 5 o'clock the next morning to do a scene."

Sandy Dennis was the recipient of two Tony Awards for her stage performances in *Any Wednesday* and *A Thousand Clowns*.

"There's nothing real in this cotton candy world," she said, as the cop who had left earlier was now staring me in the face.

"What's wrong, officer?" she said.

"You know this guy?" he said rudely.

"Yes, I do," she said emphatically.

"Well, if you say you do . . . "

"Will you *please* leave us alone?" she yelled at him.

Embarrassed, he walked away, muttering to himself as he went.

"Shit, he's got some hell of a nerve. You know, I even hate the cops they assign to the set."

She went on to state that she hated everyone in show business, "except the musicians." Her prejudice was revealed when she introduced hubby Gerry Mulligan to me—a noted jazz musician whom she married in June '65.

"I really don't like anything about being an

actress. Shit, why don't you just call me a kook. I guess I'm not really cut out for pictures—and they're certainly not cut out for me either!"

As I walked off the set, the cop who had been hounding me came over.

"Look, buddy," he began. "I don't know who you are, but if I ever catch you bothering a lady like that again on a set I'm on, I'll run your ass into the precinct—and book you! I don't like a man hiding behind a woman's skirts. I just hope you got your autograph!"

"Shit!" I thought to myself. The four-letter word was becoming contagious.

Now you would think this was a natural for the *Enquirer*. It was, but it didn't get into the paper for quite a while after the interview.

I had made the cardinal error of "shitting where I ate," to pardon the expression. I suggested to the *Enquirer's* editorial chieftain that they consider hiring "a friend," whom we will know as Willie Weasel.

Editors at the *Enquirer* were in short supply. No one lasted for too long and there was a constant turnover.

If Pope wasn't pleased with you, for one reason or the other, chances were that sooner or later—and it was invariably sooner—you were filing for unemployment insurance.

After Pope began serializing assorted sordid books in the *Enquirer*, he would often assign to his editors the task of summarizing other prospects. The editor would be expected to read a designated book, sometimes overnight, and to deliver a "live" verbal report to Pope sometime the next day. Many articles editors were literally living off medical prescriptions and special foods to stem the chronic diarrhea that kept them glued to office toilet seats. In fact, the tension was so great for one editor named Andy that he would shake like a rattle before the Pope. When I visited Andy one day after he had finished playing high-school boy to Pope the principal, he looked like a living corpse. His face was powder-white and his hands were shaking uncontrollably. After Pope required all his editors to have their names listed in the paper each week, Andy resigned. He told me he would die if any of his family or friends ever knew he worked for the *Enquirer*.

Pope turned his staff into jittery jumping beans—and Willie Weasel joined the editorial department. He had worked for a series of gay magazines, and though he swore he was as straight as an arrow, he was probably a little bent around the tip!

Willie was an undetected scofflaw, criminally evading thousands of dollars in violations and other fines, (still unpaid today). He had run away to Europe to work for still another gay-oriented organization in publishing.

After he was canned there, he wrote me. Willie Weasel wanted to return to America, but not without a job. Though Bill wasn't too pleased with his credentials, the guillotine had cut his staff again, and Willie Weasel was given a chance.

Willie's performance was satisfactory, but not by any means great. He did what was required of him, and no more.

And when the blade came down again on editorial, Willie was assigned to this reporter. The Weasel would be processing my stories and that meant checking for spelling errors, reshaping the story's lead paragraph, if need be, or any other changes that were required to enhance the article, without distorting it.

The Weasel would also be processing my Sandy Dennis article.

According to *Webster's Dictionary*, the weasel is defined, in part, as "any of a world wide group of cunning, agile, flesh-eating mammals that feed on mice, rats, birds, eggs, etc." The only thing omitted from the definition is "humans."

Greedy, never thankful for my generosity and assistance in placing him at the *Enquirer,* he resorted to the only tactic he knew—extortion!

"I don't trust your telephones, and I won't meet you in public to discuss it. You'll probably have it bugged, and with plenty of witnesses. I want you to put five $100 bills under a certain tree in Central Park, or you'll never get Sandy Dennis or any of your other twelve articles I'm holding. And if you think I'm shitting, try me."

I could hardly contain myself from bashing his miserable head into the wall.

After I returned from an out-of-town assignment two weeks later, I discovered his threat was not an idle one. Sandy Dennis was still suffocating in Weasel's desk drawer along with the other twelve articles which were growing frightfully older by the day, and all were faced with eventual editorial extermination. Pope was not in the business of printing history happenings. He wanted "fresh" stories for his readers!

I went to Bill with my plight, but he could hardly believe what he was hearing.

Until that point at the paper, every editor had been as honest and forthright as a monastery monk. They never inferred, referred, or even thought about getting kickbacks. Sure, they would joke about my large cash cache, and I would often drown any minor jealousies over a few double scotch set-ups, or a bottle of liquor I'd drop off. Once I even brought by ten six-packs of beer, but no one dared take one sip for fear that Pope would catch them. It would mean instant canning!

Once I satisfied the editorial boys by inviting them all over for a ham-and-cheese on rye lunch. I also featured ten naked strippers who performed with male partners every sex trick in creation. Of course, it was all contained on three twenty-minute stag reels on my eight-mm projector, but the thought was there, and they all appreciated the genuine gesture.

"Things turn out for the best," is just an expression, no more. The only virtue the statement holds is that life does go on and accordingly, things "turn out"—that's all. In my situation at *The Inc.*, however, the turn was in my favor, and I helped steer it in the right direction. For, one evening when the Weasel was walking home from the office, we *coincidentally* came face-to-face. Now I don't really remember what happened too well, but I could swear he was suddenly holding the right side of his face with one hand while the other clenched his testicles. Strange, isn't it! And he was yelling so incoherently. Possibly Bill intervened too. For Sandy Dennis, along with her twelve desk companions who were on the point of expiration in the Weasel's drawer, suddenly came alive.

Before the Weasel was fired for incompetency, he furnished Pope with an inaccurate memo concerning one of my interviews with a marriage counselor. Whether it was out of vindictiveness or a legitimate error on the part of the Weasel may never be truly known. Pope, acutely annoyed, told Nat, another chieftain who replaced Ted, to tell Bill—"Get rid of Bernard!"

"I have my own cross to bear," Nat said to me in the corridor as I asked for an explanation.

But Bill kept me on anyway, risking his own nervous neck—for which I was extremely grateful. *The Inc.* needed good stories and I was batting them out regularly and reliably. I was the Joe DiMaggio of the *Enquirer,* hitting home-runs at a tremendous clip. Frankly though, were my stories worth chancing a high-paying job? I really don't know why Bill went so far out on that limb for me.

Today, when Willie Weasel, who now lives in my neighborhood, sees me at the newsstand, he quickly walks to the other side of the street.

He should only walk off a cliff and do the world a big favor.

Sandy Dennis conferring with husband Gerry Mulligan on the set of "Sweet November." Anthony Newley, her co-star, is in the background getting hair coiffed. (*George Bernard*)

Lee Remick, who hated being an actress, told me she'd rather die than allow her children to appear in a Holly-wood movie.

CHAPTER XI

Freaky-Fetus Finds
And Mistaken Identities

No two *Enquirer* articles, like finger or voice prints, were exactly alike.

On the surface, many of the sensational headlines appeared to ring of repeats or re-runs. But upon further inspection, the differences became apparent.

For example, finding one fetus was unlike finding another. Each, though unborn, had a totally unique past. And while each *Enquirer* story's subject was self-contained and an entity unto itself, each bore a strange relationship to similar stories, and to others seemingly unrelated.

In effect, this is what Chapter XI is all about!

Take the case of Andy Bobinshot who exclaimed: "At first I thought it was a little rubber doll!" But then as he looked closer at the contents of the glass jar he had discovered on his lawn, he realized how mistaken he had been.

For inside the container was the three-month-old fetus of an unborn baby, which was by no means a toy.

The Newark, New Jersey window-washer told me that whoever jammed the fetus into the jar—and discarded it, "rather than give it a decent burial, must have been a fiend!"

How the four-inch, three-quarters-of-a-pound fetus got there became "just another unsolved mystery!" according to the police.

Another eerie *Enquirer* story I reported on that same year, '66, concerned a man's mistaken identity over a living doll—a rubber one! In a strange sense for Fireman Frank Cartica, it was the reverse of Andy Bobinshot's discovery.

As I reported the facts in the *Enquirer*, Cartica put his life on the line to rescue three-month-old Darrow Brown from a blazing Bronx apartment—by bravely and blindly groping his way through suffocatingly thick smoke and roaring flames until he felt a small boy lying on the bed.

Then the six-foot, 225-pound Cartica carried his rescue to the window—where he discovered he was holding a life-sized rubber doll. So he abandoned thoughts of personal safety and dashed back through the inferno where he found the *real* child, unconscious, and carried him through a window to safety.

Using a resuscitator on the way to the hospital, Cartica restored the baby's breathing to normal. Thanks to the fireman's heroic efforts, Darrow Brown recovered completely, and left the hospital in perfect health.

The *Enquirer* displayed an on-the-scene photo of Cartica applying the resuscitator to Darrow Brown. But how did they get the picture that didn't appear anywhere else?

Children do not have an exclusive on chasing the ringing sirens of police cars and fire engines. Several cab drivers in New York City have become extremely adept at the practice, but for different reasons. Many are amateur photographers who supplement their income by selling such photos of homicide happenings, blood-gushing accidents and heroic fire rescues to the New York dailies—and even to the *Enquirer*.

My assignment was to interview Fireman Cartica about his near-blunder and recreate all the death-defying, step-by-step details that a normal person would wish to forget. I had the cabbie's amazing on-location shot, but the *Enquirer* wanted more, including Cartica at the window of the actual burned-out apartment, confronted with the realization that he had made a boo-boo.

Frank's pretty wife and their five boys were seated on the sofa of the Cartica living room as I took a family portrait. Afterwards, the children continued to beam at their dad "who was the greatest in the entire world!"

Mrs. Cartica wanted everyone to know just how brave and special her Frank really was. She also wanted to know where Trans-Atlantic Features would place her hubby's harrowing story.

"In *Life or Look?* she asked, hoping I'd say one or the other.

"All I can tell you at this point," I explained, "is that you will find the article does justice to your brave husband."

I had the intuitive feeling that if his friends at the firehouse saw the *Enquirer* before Frank got a copy, they'd rib him to death. Fearless Frank would then wish he had perished in that fire.

Trans-Atlantic Features received official written permission from the New York City Fire Department to interview Cartica at Ladder Company 48, at his home and at the fire-damaged apartment.

"The boys at the firehouse kidded me for a week or two by singing 'Hello, Dolly!' But I didn't care. I'm just grateful that I recognized the doll in time and that there was a happy ending," Cartica recalled.

Cartica was extremely cooperative. In less than three hours I had taken all the pictures I needed and had jotted down all sorts of quotes from witnesses to the fire. I thanked Frank for his generous time and promised to let him know the moment the story broke, which I did.

"Mrs. Cartica," I said on the phone. "I think everyone at the Cartica household will be pleased with my article. The photos reproduced quite well and the story tells it the way it really happened. The *Enquirer* did a great job with it!"

"The *National Enquirer?*" she said, disbelieving

my revelation. "Oh, no," she cried. "That's terrible. You should have told us. Frank was so hopeful that you would get the story into a better publication. Oh, this is terrible," she went on.

I had fulfilled my commitment to Frank. He was alerted before his fire-fighting friends became aware—by at least three hours.

"Mrs. Cartica, promise me one thing. Go out and buy the paper this afternoon. If you don't like the piece, call me back," I assured her, as if I would have been in a magical position to change the situation.

I never heard from any of the Carticas. But I did forward a copy of the article to the office of the Fire Commissioner, with a recommendation that Frank be put up for several awards, one of which was underwritten by a leading brewery in town.

Enquirer reporters are not totally heartless.

Neither are police officers. They have feelings and know how to express emotion. Examine the Enquirer story of Newark Patrolman Eugene James. For the rest of his life, he will continue to suffer from nightmarish guilt feelings. And all because he wasn't as fortunate as Fireman Cartica. Where Frank saved a life, Eugene took one. Ironically, the official department file on each case included "mistaken identity" where a deceptive toy was involved.

The *Enquirer* headline read: "ANOTHER COP AND I SHOT AND KILLED BOY WHO POINTED TOY GUN AT MY FOREHEAD . . . We Thought His Pistol Was Real."

A box in the upper right hand corner of the page stated: "Patrolman Eugene James, 40, and Angelo Boutsikaris, also 40, saw a man leaving a Newark, N.J. grocery on May 20. The man aimed a gun at James. After shooting the robber, James discovered the gun was a toy and the man a fourteen-year-old boy. Here is James' story—

exclusively for *Enquirer* readers."

Before I turned in my interview with James, I had the officer sign the customary release form as the article was appearing in the first person, in James's own words.

Officer James told me that he was cleared of any blame, but he couldn't put the tragic incident out of his mind.

The law officer added that if the kid hadn't been so huge for his age, the mistaken identity would never have happened. "If a little boy, of say four-foot, came over to you," James justified, "and said 'stick 'em up,' you'd know it was just a joke."

Six months earlier, the *Enquirer* had run an article about a kid who wandered onto the White House lawn with a toy machine gun. When the tyke turned the weapon in the direction of L.B.J., the President's Secret Service treated the matter not as a "joke", but as a dead-serious matter. L.B.J.'s security guards instantly became a human shield, throwing themselves over the President while one of the Secret Service disarmed the kidding kid.

It could have been the "real" thing. Instead, the mess of mistaken identity was averted.

Patrolman Eugene James admitted that his insides had been in knots since the incident had happened and the boy had died.

My stomach wasn't doing too well, either, after I reviewed morgue photos that were slipped to me from the Newark Police Department. Lying on a slab was the well-developed nude body of the fourteen-year-old victim. Like a miniature railroad track, the numerous stitch marks graphically showed where the coroner had made the incisions for the autopsy.

To the lower left of this gruesome, tragic sight, a photo of the sad cop appeared in the *Enquirer,* with this caption: "Still noticeably upset from the tragedy, Patrolman Eugene James sadly holds gun similar to one he used to shoot a teen-age robber to death."

That's what Pope's public wanted in those gore-gushing days, and the illustrious publisher did not hold back.

His fondness for fabulous fetus stories was known around *The Inc*. If a fetus was the fetish of his readers, he complied.

But one story in this category the paper found so utterly fantastic, they discarded it.

Three-year-old Lei Chen Wei actually gave birth to his brother. My agent in Taiwan who, at the time, was the city editor of that country's leading English-speaking newspaper, carefully documented for me the bizarre facts of the birth.

A team of surgeons had removed a fetus from "the neck" of little Lei Chen Wei. The embryo was dead on delivery, but nevertheless, the boy did father his brother.

Two years earlier, in '65, the *Enquirer* ran a similar story. The front page headline glared: "DOCTOR FINDS BABY INSIDE YEAR-OLD BOY."

Again, the dateline was Southeast Asia—Danang, South Vietnam.

While serving with the United States Aid Mission in Vietnam, Dr. Vernon Fitchett conducted one of the rarest surgical operations in medical history.

His patient, Tran Hai, was born with a twin brother—inside his stomach. And for a little over a year, the pug-nosed boy carried his brother inside him. And no one, including the boy's mother, knew the concealed unborn twin was there. That is, until Tran Hai's stomach started to swell up and doctors looked into the matter.

The physicians were startled, but they did the only thing medically possible: they delivered the three pound fetus from the boy.

Dr. Fitchett told the *Enquirer* readers, though at the time he wasn't exactly aware where the story was going, that it was the first time he had delivered, or heard of a fetus being removed from a boy.

Until that time, Dr. Fitchett admitted that all reports of babies delivered from boys in the past had turned out to be hoaxes or just erroneous reports.

The photo that appeared in the article alongside one of Dr. Fitchett with Tran Hai and his mom showed a close-up of the actual fetus to which the boy had given birth. Though decisively dead, the fetus had all the features of a human body—little legs, arms, a head and a torso.

Dr. Fitchett reported that Tran Hai's mother, Pham Minh, was expected to have twins. But for some unknown reason, Tran Hai's twin brother developed inside his stomach, "instead of beside him in the mother's womb."

The boy's mother told the doctor that for a year her son appeared normal, and did all the things healthy children do. He crawled and walked normally and gave no clue that he was carrying a baby.

Then precisely twelve months later, her son began getting pains in his stomach, followed by enlargement of that area.

After taking X-rays, Dr. Fitchett, in a three-hour operation performed the very next day, removed the twin from Tran Hai's stomach. The surgeon estimated that the fetus had developed about four or five months.

Not dismissing the seriousness of the operation, Dr. Fitchett quipped to *Enquirer* readers: "Tran should lead a perfectly normal life from now on—except for knowing, when he grows up, that he was the mother of his brother."

On the Sunday of July 20, '75, after trying for one week to locate Dr. Fitchett in the United

States, I found him at the Naval Hospital in Lemoore, California. Based at the Naval Hospital in Oakland as Chief of Surgery, he was on temporary duty for one week.

"Were you angry, Dr. Fitchett, after you learned of being in the *Enquirer?*" I asked eagerly.

"No, I wasn't at all angry. I must say that I wasn't surprised to wind up in the *Enquirer,*" he said. "Beats me how they come up with those stories. And, they're all true, too," he went on. "A friend in New Jersey wrote me about it, but until this day, I haven't even seen the article. Could you send me a copy?" he asked.

I promised, but the intentions of my inquiry were not solely to get his reactions to becoming a medical page in the history of the *Enquirer.* I wanted to know if he had come across other Tran Hai's in those ten years.

"Mr. Bernard," he began. "There's been about five cases. Three have been in Brazil, Italy and Russia. And the other two I'm checking out, which will become part of a paper I'm presently writing on the subject," he said.

Dr. Fitchett said he was not mistaken about these off-beat fetus occurrences. But he was more amazed at how a former *Enquirer* reporter could track him down "only five minutes after I returned from a month's vacation. Not even my secretary knew where to reach me. How'd you do it?"

I'm sure the good doctor really didn't expect me to reveal the secrets of the tricky trade I had perfected as an enterprising *Enquirer* reporter—of which I was now making good use . . .

CHAPTER XII

Pope's Pets:
Pooches, Pussies And Pigeons!

As the overzealous zoo-keeper, Generoso Pope's wild magazine became the most complete, most diversified and most well-maintained menagerie in the world.

Pope was always so proud of his pets. And when their animal antics and tray of tricks would evoke human sentiment, Gene would instantly release them from the confinement of their cages to his special, sprawling thirty-two-page pet preserve—the *National Enquirer.*

There they'd stay and be able to stray for one week, before being placed by G.P. in *suspended animalation,* until their services were required, once again. But practically all never went beyond the seven-day stand of the issue. Pope didn't believe in over-exposing them when he had an unlimited supply of tasty talent.

Gene's favorites were canines, cats and even pigeons, though he was also intrigued by worms and caterpillars.

And so it was one morning in April '66 that the Enquirer called and asked me to drop by the office and pick up the instructions for my next assignment.

Bill had dropped a car crash in my lap. I still had unpleasantly vivid memories of Miles Lucas flying out of his own car and colliding, head-on, with a gravestone bearing his own name.

But after Bill went over all the story's photo and copy requirements, I looked at him in disbelief. I simply couldn't believe this was what Pope wanted.

There wasn't a blessed soul killed, mutilated,

or even maimed. The assignment, I said to myself, smelled of dog droppings. Nevertheless, I had to investigate a car crashing into a store . . . with a dog behind the wheel.

"It's only a *dog* story. Who'd want to read it but another dog?" I felt compelled to say, and did. "Who cares about pooches? This is the *Enquirer!*" I argued, trying to avoid the assignment.

"Gene Pope cares," he barked, raising the Pope to God! "A good number of our readers are dog lovers—and care! So, if you want to keep Gene happy, you'd better come back with a hefty bone for him, 'Goldmine'. And," he started to growl louder, "I want to see pictures of the dog behind the wheel of the car. And, be sure the dog has a friendly expression on his puss. Our readers don't want to see a dog-faced dog!"

When I arrived in Vermont, I located the officer at the crash location who was an eyewitness to the incident. The policeman said it was "the craziest thing" he had ever seen. After all, what else could he say without appearing retarded?

He did say that two days before Christmas, a woman had parked her car outside the local post office. So as to avoid stalling in the biting cold ski area, she left the engine running—and also left her two mischievous pooches inside the car. Porky, a mixed terrier, was in the front seat while Gibby, a cross-breed Maltese-cocker, was in the back.

Investigators at the scene of the accident theorized that Porky must have knocked the automatic transmission into "drive"—and the car took off!

The woman heard her car motor roar and rushed out of the post office. But it was too late. All she could do was watch helplessly as the auto took off and traveled about three hundred feet.

There was panic as pedestrians ran for their lives and those in cars jammed on their brakes.

The uncontrollable car banged brutally into and knocked down an iron railing, snapping off the intake pipe of a bank's oil supply.

Gaining more speed—to about thirty-five mph—the car shot across the street and crashed clear through the wall of an appliance shop coming to a final halt in the store's kitchen—leaving a $3000 trail of damage behind.

But the dogs suffered not a scratch. They were only howling wildly when their owner reached them, and started barking herself at the animals.

The woman promised she would turn the engine off whenever she had occasion to leave the dogs in the car.

Now is there any real moral to this mad assignment? If that woman ever takes her pooches to the post office and it gets cold again, as it always does in Vermont, rather than risk a fine by taking her prohibited pets into a government building, she will undoubtedly, if she hasn't already, keep the engine running.

Then, could the message of this magazine story be that every car owner make sure that his, or her, dog learn how to drive—just in case the car starts running away while master is not there? Or is the lesson learned that there is none?

While Gibby and Porky received a terrible tongue-lashing, they had miraculously cheated death. Closer to my New York home, however, thirty minutes drive from the city, in Paterson, New Jersey, their barking brothers were not as fortunate.

The *Enquirer* headline read: "CITY EXECUTES 20 HEALTHY DOGS EACH WEEK—BECAUSE OF AN OLD LAW...It Says Pooches Can't Be Adopted—They Must Be Destroyed."

I was thoroughly appalled by Paterson's "Death Row" for dogs, which was never empty. For, each week, an average of twenty-five condemned canines made the short trip to the execution chamber. There they were gassed methodically in the same style that California had been notorious for disposing of condemned human criminals: a gas pellet was dropped into the water solution to make death come mercifully faster. That was the way, if you will recall, the late Susan Hayward went in the movie, *I Want To Live*.

The dogs that were destroyed also wanted to live. But they were the innocent victims of an old local law that dated back forty years and was based on an earlier ordinance passed in the 1870's.

My super-stringer, Bernard Silverstein, who covered the City Hall beat for the *Paterson News*, took time off his lunch hour to pass me through security at the Paterson pounds. Bernie was one of the most competent newsmen I had ever met. Aside from a nose for news, there wasn't anyone in Passaic County he didn't know, which made my job easier. A good agent in an unfamiliar area can be an excellent seeing-eye dog.

I thought it strange that the municipal pound-master could auction off even a stray pig, if he ever found one. But there was no legal way of disposing of a stray dog—only death!

And though many of Paterson's people in '65 would have liked to purchase the doomed dogs, the law specifically said *no*. Only the rightful registered owner could reclaim his pooch. And if he didn't before seven days, the animal was destroyed.

Gene Pope's heart was in the right spot—for Spotty, Spanky, King and all the other poor pooches who would soon be silenced. No more whimpering, whining or tail-wagging.

The article ran on page three of the *Enquirer*, which was great page position. The photos included: "LAST DAY—A few hours after Danny tried to adopt him, this innocent pup was put to death in the pound's gas chamber."

Another was captioned: "TURNED DOWN—Twelve-year-old Danny Lawrence, shown playing with doomed dogs, offered to provide a home for one of the friendly puppies—but it's impossible because of an old ordinance."

And the third photo showed the actual doomed dogs in the death chamber, moments before their lives were snuffed out.

It was all I could stand. Bernie took the photo as I turned my back on the pooches, but not their plight.

Pope and I could do no more. After the article appeared, letters of support literally flowed into the *Enquirer's* mailroom. But if change was to come, it had to be from others. Pope could only highlight the dogs' destruction and continue to push for reform. He was not a judge, nor a legislator, senator, congressman or assemblyman. He was just one dog-gone dedicated publisher. Sure, his primary motive was to sell papers, but he didn't have to extend himself that far. Anyway, what publisher in America isn't devoted to raising circulation!

Ten years, one month and a day later, out of profound curiosity, I decided to see if things had changed in Paterson.

Brilliant Bernie was still on the City Hall beat for the *Paterson News*. He gave me the gruesome report. The method of exterminating the dogs had changed, but the law was the same.

"More than ten years ago they were using gas pellets—and sometimes a truck to pump gas into the dog's execution chamber," he said.

"Then, when 'no-lead' came out, the executioners were discovering that the dogs were lingering on—some twenty minutes—before taking the last count.

"So," he grimly added, "the city began paying a veterinarian a thousand dollars a year to do the job more effectively, and with relatively no discomfort to the dogs. The vet injected sodium pentothal into the dogs, and that was that.

"It was better than the gas pellets and the truck that pumped the stuff into the chamber," he noted. "More humane!"

"But I'm afraid that the 19th-century ordinance will never change for Paterson," he fretted. "I believe it's that way now throughout the state. But the city of Paterson will not assume any responsibility for reprieving a dog's death sentence—unless, of course, as before, the owner reclaims the animal within seven days. If the city were to release dogs to anyone who wanted them, Paterson might become the target of litigation—especially after the animal took a chunk out of someone. No, sir. It might seem cruel, but Paterson considers it practical."

Bernie contended that New Jersey was not alone in its stringent policy of destroying stray dogs in the absence of the rightful owner.

While dogs were tragically being put to death, a Captain Haggerty was busy being their psychiatrist, and training both the normal and emotionally troubled pooches for a productive life. Haggerty, during my *Enquirer* interview a decade ago had his head cleanly shaven like Yul Brynner, and owned one storefront operation in the Bronx. Today, his bow-wow business has expanded to Manhattan.

In another location, careless cats were also being put to death. I shuddered with disgust after I read an *Enquirer* account of how a self-proclaimed mercy-killer of pretty pussies would spend all her waking moments catching stray cats.

She moved through the streets as cunningly as a cat and, before the animal was aware of what was happening, he was in her sack. Then, the woman placed the cat in an air-tight miniature chamber and watched through a transparent glass as the poor creature died agonizingly from suffocation.

The wicked witch justified her deadly deeds by proclaiming she eased the widespread, needless suffering of stray cats who might have starved, developed diseases or might otherwise have had to endure a miserable life on earth.

While this fiend who dealt in the supposition of "might" was rivalling Paterson in executions—their number and efficiency of operation, a mouse was biting a cat and escaping without even a scratch. Not the greatest story in the world. But Pope ran it as a part-pager anyway.

Pope's pigeons were not fairing well either. Either they were being shot at, or not fed properly. Examine *The Inc.'s* headline from February 7, '65: "COOKS HER BOYFRIEND, FEEDS HIM TO PIGEONS!"

Six months earlier, the *Enquirer* had presented: "HIS GUN'S FOR HIRE—TO KILL PIGEONS!" Dateline: London. Pope thrilled at foreign pieces as they were sure to create the impression with the reader that the *Enquirer* had reporters everywhere.

But why Pope's peculiar aversion to these delightful feathered friends who soiled the nation's park benches with their frequent droppings? One editor laughed and said that Pope's nest-like hair once became the successful aerial target of a pigeon, and he never forgot the incident.

But this particular full-time pigeon exterminator, at the time the interview ran, admitted he'd blown to bits 400,000 of the dark-skinned doves. He was a true professional assassin of pigeons who would stalk the streets every night, rifle in hand, eagerly searching for his next victim.

Peter Noteboom in Orange City, Iowa was also hunting for pigeons—enough of them to bring in vast sums of money that were hardly chicken feed. But unlike the British bird-blaster, Noteboom didn't kill any. "I never shot a pigeon in my life," he revealed. Proud Pete just made them available to others, so that they could do the killing.

For fourteen years, Noteboom had been collecting pigeons and selling them—primarily to sportsmen who wanted to shoot at them, mostly with double-barrel shotguns.

Since he started in the pigeon business, Noteboom said he was personally responsible for the death of—by shooting—one million birds in various marksmanship competitions. About another million more fortunate pigeons missed the hunter's bullets and flew to safety.

"I feel awfully terrible at the thought of pigeons getting killed," he said, feeling that if he didn't supply them to such shooting events, most of them would be murdered as pests anyway.

"At least," he said. "They have a flying chance!"

I wondered how he would have reacted to my suggestion that I take a shotgun and offer him a running chance down the road.

Now, you would think that the story was all wrapped up. Wrong. The *Enquirer* wanted more. One, a photo of Noteboom. Two, a shot of Peter's pigeons. Mission was accomplished on both fronts.

But the *Enquirer* wanted to know exactly how much the shitty pigeons dropped in his bank books.

"Trans-Atlantic Features cannot run the article, Mr. Noteboom," I said apologetically.

"Why, Mr. Bernard? A deal is a deal. I gave you the pictures and the facts. In return, you promised to get me some foreign pick-up in the press. Now, are you going back on your word?"

"No, I'm not," I said. "But you are not telling

me what you make, and I can't run the story unless I show readers that you're a success at what you do."

"Well, if it's not going in tne U.S., well, all right. I'll tell you. I buy pigeons for 20 cents each and sell them for 50 cents."

"How many pigeons do you sell a year?" I asked, the answer being crucial to the assignment.

Noteboom paused, thought a moment. "On the average, about 150,000 birds a year and since I started in the business, my profit has been averaging *over* $30,000 each year. There's hardly any competition for me and my basic expenses are a telephone, four trucks and three hired drivers. And, of course, air-transport costs." Noteboom paused again, laughed and added, "Hey, here's something for your article . . . I'm the 'Pigeon King' of America."

"No, Mr. Noteboom," I thought to myself, "You're 'Mr. Dead Duck of America' and I've set you up, and shot you down."

Simple multiplication told me that Noteboom at that fourteen-year point, had earned over $400,000. And in the coming years, he would pass the half-million mark.

The *Enquirer* headlined my article: "SELLS TWO MILLION PIGEONS—EARNS 400G PROFIT."

"Wait until the I.R.S. gets his ass." Bill couldn't stop laughing. "I'll bet you my last dollar the guy's never reported his real earnings."

Until that point, Bill was probably right. After all, how can you keep track of pigeons—unless, of course, by their droppings?

While enterprising Peter Noteboom was busy carting pigeons to their deaths—to an upcoming World Championship Live Pigeon Shooting Match in Mexico City, an industrious woman in Florida was selling live red worms by the cupful as bait for the sharp tip of a fisherman's hook.

Widowed three times, and left alone to support her three sons, courageous Jeanne Martin, 35, converted the backyard of her Miami home into a worm farm.

The owner of a nearby grocery suggested to Jeanne that she give worms a go. In a short time, after purchasing 10,000 giant African red worm breeders, known as night crawlers, and putting up a business sign in her backyard, she had a thriving business.

The breeding worms were put in pens. Jeanne provided fertilizer and good earth. After three weeks, the eggs hatched.

Fishermen flocked to her backyard to buy all they could get at 60 cents per cup with fifty worms in each container. Jeanne was selling fifty cups a day and was expanding her business. She took out a loan of $500 and purchased 250,000 more breeders.

But the elements conspired against her. Two weeks later Hurricane Cleo hit Miami and drove the worms out of their pens to die.

"The worms were scattered everywhere," she recalled. "In the kitchen, bathroom, even in our beds." The Martins salvaged as many of the critters as they could find alive, but most of the crop was lost.

Just then, another storm developed. Mrs. Martin's crop started blooming again as the Dade County Planning and Zoning Board informed her that she would have to close up shop. In other words, she was told to go fish for income someplace else.

Mrs. Martin told me that the Board was acting on the complaints of neighbors who called her "Worm Woman" and said the neighborhood was zoned for homes, not businesses.

Jeanne fought back, and hard. In the end she won the right to continue selling her worms.

After I left Jeanne, who was a delight as a mother and as a person, I went back to my hotel room by the ocean. As I typed the article in my room, I started scratching. First my back, and then my leg. Sure enough, three red worms were sharing my room.

Did you ever think that worms don't like to be devoured from the end of a hook by foolish, ferocious fish? Well, sometimes they live to ravage resort towns and eat everything in their paths. They are also disciplined and march, like soldiers, together in large numbers.

Thousands of crawling, wriggling, green and black-striped caterpillars—called army worms—swept over beach fronts, lawns and patios during one memorable Memorial Day weekend in '65 at Virginia Beach.

I was assigned to the story by the *Enquirer*.

The resort community was finally getting back on its feet when I interviewed some of the townspeople.

The actual first invasion force was observed by a fourteen-year-old girl who was cutting her family's lawn when she saw dozens of the caterpillars crawling all over the grass. She described them as each about 1½ inches long. They had come out of a nearby cornfield in search of food after devouring everything edible in their breeding ground.

"They crawled all over my feet," recalled the girl. "I just jumped away and ran into the house."

Her mother quickly used a forceful water hose to knock the army worms off the walls. She made sure to seal all the windows from the caterpillars that had hatched from moth eggs by the hot Virginia weather.

In the service, I had been stationed at Fort Eustis, just forty minutes by car from Virginia Beach. When I would spend my weekends at the beach, it would often become hot enough to fry an ostrich egg on the sand, no less hatch an army of raging, rugged worms.

Townspeople even admitted to being bitten by the wormy soldiers as they advanced. One such casualty was Nancy Gray who was bitten while standing on her lawn.

One resident tried both a dusting compound and then a chemical solution, "but the worms seemed to thrive on it," she said, and they kept on coming.

When nightfall came, the invasion was in full force. Crops and trees were all destroyed. The police and firemen were helpless to bring in aid from city, state and federal government agencies.

One homeowner said he even used a blowtorch on the caterpillars after all the insecticides had failed. But that, like all the other defensive measures, failed.

It wasn't until the holiday ended that an effective plan was put into operation. The town council commissioned pest-control companies to destroy the invaders.

All the residents quarantined themselves in their homes and made sure to carefully lock all windows. Then the companies sent planes into the air, loaded with killer pesticides. And for more than twelve hours, the planes' engines were heard as the crafts sprayed the area with a thorough chemical dosage.

Finally, as if out of a science-fiction movie, the caterpillars began to shrivel up and die. The spray had worked.

Then, the strangest thing happened. The army worms disintegrated to dust and blew away in the wind. The people of Virginia Beach came out of their homes and many cried with joy, while others said silent prayers of gratitude for their deliverance.

The town council estimated that $7,000 worth of damage was caused by the 10,000 destructive caterpillars.

But the town took a pound of prevention. Regular spraying of the area was ordered for each year, to insure that Virginia Beach would never again be invaded by the same army of destructive worms.

So much for Pope's pets.

Peter Noteboom on his Orange City, Iowa pigeon ranch. He sold the birds as living targets for "sportsmen."

A load of pigeons on their way to Havana to become sitting ducks for gun enthusiasts, (below). (*Peter Noteboom*)

Captain Haggerty, analyst and trainer to canines, shown with photo of U Thant, whose dog he trained.
(George Bernard)

Giving counsel to a client over the phone for a canine-in-distress. *(George Bernard)*

CHAPTER XIII

Pope's Confessional For The Stars Made Public!

Getting stories from the stars for the pages of the *National Enquirer* was like enticing them into the black booth of a confessional.

But instead of the ordinary priest or rabbi playing the attentive, consoling lay psychiatrist — who listened to their gripes, feats, admissions of guilt and sin — the Pope, through his reporters, would be their true confessor.

And while the performers would offer penance, tape recorders and shorthand notes would record their inner-most secrets — for the *National Enquirer* .

During February '66, Jerry Van Dyke told the *Inc.'s* readers: "I WANT TO MAKE EVERYONE FORGET I HAVE A BROTHER."

Brother Dick Van Dyke was in his fifth successful TV season while Jerry's NBC series, "My Mother, the Car" had lost its novelty appeal and was now flopping in the ratings.

Diagnosing Jerry's undue hostility towards Dick as unresolved sibling rivalry, I played shrink and became a good listener.

"Dick, Dick, Dick, That's all I ever hear," Jerry groaned.

Jealous Jerry confessed he wanted absolutely no sympathy from Dick—"just to be bigger and better than he ever was, or will! I get violently sick when people refer to me as 'Dick's little brother' or 'That's Dick Van Dyke's brother. What's his name?' "

The blond-haired, handsome Jerry revealed that he often hated his brother for being too sympathetic and understanding towards his professional problems. But jolted Jerry just wanted the public to wake up and realize he was a special, talented somebody!

To beat his brother in the business as a comic, Jerry admitted he had become a thief in the process.

"I've stolen his routines and hoped they would go over big for me." He began reeling off one confession after another. He even admitted stealing Dick's facial expressions and gags.

Jerry, three years younger than Dick, said he had watched his brother work since they were teenagers. And he even tried impersonating him, but no matter what he did, it didn't work right.

Foreseeing the imminent ax of the network's executioner falling on his show, Jerry prayed for a big break to come along, as if by a miracle. Then he grew hostile adding: "Yes, I need something real big, because I want to make everyone forget I have a brother at all!"

It was obvious that Jerry was always overshadowed by his brother—"ever since I can remember." He confirmed my suspicions, without any hesitation, adding that he was always "the kid," even though at the time he was thirty-four years old and Dick was thirty-seven.

Jerry revealed that Dick had surpassed him in everything—except in athletics and strumming the banjo. But that wasn't what built show-business names into big stars, he reasoned.

He was correct, but wrong for not having changed his last name. Other brothers were succeeding in show business, and the public wasn't even aware of their blood ties. For instance, take James Arness of the long-running "Gunsmoke" TV series and Peter Graves of "Mission Impossible."

As Jerry jumped out of the confessional, Fred MacMurray entered. *Enquirer* headline: "I HAVE 300 PAID HOLIDAYS A YEAR."

"I got it made," fabulous Fred began. "I have $1 million in the bank and I don't have to take orders from anyone." He added that if he didn't feel like working, he didn't have to. And most of the time, he didn't feel like working.

"I have 65 working days and 300 paid holidays a year," he laughed, "and get to pick the days I work on my TV show, 'My Three Sons.' " Slightly tanned and extremely rested-looking, he appeared to have just come out of his swimming pool in Brentwood, California.

"What was Fred's problem?" I asked myself. "Was he turning into a bum?"

He said if he wanted to be a "bum" he could, an extremely wealthy one. But he was not.

"Bums don't work at all," he said, admitting he just works enough for his friends to think of him as a part-time loafer. Fred considered being half a loafer as better than none at all.

In '66, Fred, who confessed to living for leisure, was in his sixth blazing-hot rating year on "My Three Sons." He didn't know at the time of our interview that it would continue as a super-hit for more than a decade.

Fred couldn't see people breaking their necks at the studio five days a week when he could make a fortune working only one. Millionaire MacMurray admitted growing interests in lemon and orange groves, oil wells plus a hotel in Acapulco. Today, he has added to that investment list a sprawling 2,300-acre ranch in northern California with more than 350 head of prize cattle.

Fred was absolutely certain that he put in less time on the job than any other leading actor or actress doing a weekly TV series. And, as he left me, he patted himself on the back with a sense of accomplishment and pride.

If Fred "millionnaire" MacMurray labored the least, my next confessor strived the strongest.

Barbara Stanwyck, 58, star of TV's "Big Valley," said: "I WORK 16 HOURS A DAY, SEVEN DAYS A WEEK—AND I LOVE IT."

Strange, isn't it: Jerry Van Dyke didn't work enough. Fred MacMurray loathed labor while silver-haired, brassy Barbara couldn't get enough of the commodity.

"I'm a lusty broad," she admitted, a statement too suggestive for the *Enquirer,* so it was cut from my article.

In the palm of my hand, I held a miniature index card on Barbara Stanwyck—born Ruby Stevens in Brooklyn, July 16, 1907. As the youngest of five children, she broke into show business at the age of fifteen with the role of a chorus girl.

From there came seventy-five movies and four Academy Award nominations. Her name became a household word throughout the world.

Barbara admitted that the thought of not working frightened her to death. There was a time, she recalled, when things weren't going well for her. "I hadn't made a movie in some time, and there were no signs that anyone was going to give me a job."

She couldn't settle down. She'd pick up a book, any book, and throw it down after reading about a dozen pages. Then she tried going for long walks to divert her mind from the boredom and anxiety of not working. The walk turned into a run—"though I had nowhere to go."

Then Barbara tried organizing a small-scale acting school, "but everything I told the few actors and actresses who attended sounded stale and old-fashioned."

"The Big Valley" came along and Barbara immediately signed the contract. "I bless the day I got the role of Victoria Barkley in the series," she said, for she became a working actress again.

The 110-pound star, who said she felt like

twenty, was as trim as ever. In fact, Barbara possessed all the virtuous enthusiasm and nervous energy of a young starlet—a third of her well-preserved age. Remember, she was fifty-eight then.

I listened with compassion. She said that many on the set disliked her and this upset her considerably. "Some of them call me a slave-driver, and I can't say I blame them either. I work sixteen hours a day, seven days a week—and I love it." That became the *Enquirer* headline, exactly the way she said it.

Her hectic schedule, if she didn't watch it, I felt would surely bring on a heart attack. Barbara admitted she got up at 4:30 a.m. and worked right through until 8:30 p.m.—without a day off. The series was shot Monday through Friday, "and I come in on Saturday and Sunday to go over next week's script."

As for the good old days in Frank Capra's *Ladies of Leisure,* the 1930 hit that made her a star and *Sorry, Wrong Number* from which she became known as the neurotic heroine, Barbara said there was no time in her crowded day to dream about them. "I'm too busy for that!"

Barbara mentioned that columnists and others in TV were beginning to call her the female Lorne Greene. "He's great in his 'Bonanza,' role—but I know I'm better in mine. If he's the 'Big Daddy' of TV westerns, then I'm going to be the 'Big Grandmother'," she vowed.

A decade later, both "The Big Valley" and "Bonanza" were still on the tube — in re-run throughout the country. Undoubtedly, the popular series were dubbed in countless foreign languages.

Her professionalism and dedication to the television industry did not go unrecognized. Barbara Stanwyck received the coveted Emmy for "The Big Valley," becoming, unquestionably, the 'Big Grandmother' of the westerns, as she had so determined.

Only recently, Richard Long, Barbara's TV son, passed away. Ironically, Lorne Greene's big boy, Dan Blocker, who portrayed Hoss Cartwright, also died.

In "living" death, however, one of the most sensuous, seductive-looking actresses became one of television's hottest revivals.

Carolyn Jones took her seat in the confessional. The *Enquirer* typographer began assembling the December 19, '65 headline, "Carolyn Jones, 'Morticia' in TV's 'Addams Family', Says: IT TOOK A DEATH-LIKE ROLE TO BREATHE LIFE INTO MY DYING CAREER."

The headline was Pope-perfect. He loved it! The combination of a personality profile—and the perverse—was right in thunderous tune with the image of the *Enquirer* during the mad, monstrous sixties.

While Barbara Stanwyck jumped for living joy when television beckoned, contemplative Carolyn, then thirty-three, almost let it slip by.

Before the spooky spoof came along, nobody could even remember who she was. Her credits on the screen included: *The Bachelor Party, A Hole in the Head,* and *How the West Was Won* —"but all anyone remembered was my chewed hairdo," she said.

The big break came when cartoonist Charles Addams selected Carolyn to portray the character "Morticia" in a new TV series.

After having read the first few scripts of the series, Carolyn was still undecided. She couldn't make up her mind. But being desperate for work, the role made her mind up. "And, it's been the biggest and most successful decision I've ever made."

How fitting, I thought, Morticia in a confessional: her white, death-like facial make-up, luscious blood-red lips and long, jet-black hair that captivated fun-loving "sick" audiences.

To most, there's nothing humorous about death. And the "Addams Family" walked a very thin censor's line.

"I even watch the scripts to insure that they don't injure anyone," Carolyn confessed. She added that extra precaution is taken not to ridicule the dead, but on at least one occasion, she said, "we goofed!"

As if to plead for a remission of sin for desecrating the dead, Carolyn confessed an impropriety: "In one episode, Gomez, my husband, played by John Astin, needed signatures to enable him to run for mayor. So, Uncle Fester, played by Jackie Coogan, got names by copying all the names off headstones in the cemetery.

"But it took a death-like role like this to breathe life into my career," she admitted. "You might say I've been dead lucky."

Indeed she has been lucky. The dollars from her re-run residuals continue to arrive.

Rod Steiger wasn't confessing anything. He was boasting. "I'M A GREAT ACTOR" ran the March 24, '68 *Enquirer* headline.

Energetically egotistical, Steiger opined that he was one of the true remaining "great" actors—"the rest are either dead or at the end of their careers."

The movie greats Steiger was alluding to included Spencer Tracy, Paul Muni and Frederic March.

"I count myself in that group," he said. "There aren't many of us."

Born Rodney Steven Steiger on April 14, 1925, he is considered by his peers to be one of America's greatest performers—on both the stage and the screen.

Steiger said that actors like John Wayne, Paul Newman and Charlton Heston—"the big box-office successes"—aren't necessarily great. He labeled them "formula men," adding, "Once you've seen one of their films, you've seen them all."

I couldn't argue with Steiger's sound praise of his illustrious, many-faceted career. Could one man play so many characters, so convincingly?

In *The Pawnbroker* he had played the lead. He was a politician in *Dr. Zhivago,* and a gangster in Al Capone. Steiger portrayed Napoleon in *Waterloo,* and in *The Mark,* he'd been a psychiatrist. A general in *The Girl and the General* and a prosecuting attorney in *The Court Martial of Billy Mitchell* were but a handful of a larger fistful of those unforgettable, diversified roles he'd played over the years.

Rod has gone on record stating: "I think of acting as an immediate reward and an immediate death. The greater the moment on stage, the longer the mourning."

For his best efforts in United Artists' *In the Heat of the Night,* Steiger won the "Best Actor" Oscar.

Next on line was a bearded, boasting hippie-type. The *Enquirer's* photo editor was already scouring the city and calling American International Pictures for stills from *The Wild Angels.* The typographer and the layout men were standing by, waiting.

The August 28, '66 *Enquirer* headline would read: "Henry Fonda's Son, Peter, Boasts: I'M A HELL RAISER ... I'M THE NEW JAMES DEAN."

Young, twenty-seven-year-old Fonda was my age. Actually, he was three months older and lived in the same neighborhood. During the confession session, he preferred to stand, and I joined him.

Fonda's new movie, *The Wild Angels* was one of the most controversial, brutal films to come out

171

in the sixties. As the leader of an outlaw motorcycle gang, he portrayed a lifestyle that was not
uncommon to him away from the screen.

"I'm too cool and too hip for this world," he
confessed. "I don't follow any rules. I don't think
about tomorrow. I do whatever I want to do. I'm a
hell-raiser—I'm the new James Dean. To hell
with conformity!"

Fonda recalled all his harrowing motorcycle
runs in the picture that, he said, gave the producers ulcers. Then he compared his living to
that of the late James Dean. "He used to live fast
and furious and never worry about the conse-
quences. And I believe there's a need for a suc-
cessor to James Dean . . . and I'm it."

Peter said that Dean was a symbol of the
tough, free rebel, a label that Fonda felt the
world needed.

I wasn't quite certain what he meant. What
was "needed?" But I didn't wish to interrupt
Fonda's concentration.

Proud Peter filled me in on some of his LSD
trips. "Man," he said to me, "I've been through
the best and I've seen the worst—the very worst.
And I know for sure where I am on this planet."

Physically, he looked stable, but I wondered
what damage had been done to his brain.

Fonda's fondness for drugs was delicately
snipped out of my article. Pope never condoned
statements, or stories, about drug addiction. He
wasn't on Fonda's trip for drugs, alcohol or other
artificial stimulants or depressants.

The Wild Angels set the stage for *Easy Rider*,
which made Fonda. And again, the film allowed
him to be himself on the screen. From then on, he
was no longer known as "Henry Fonda's son,
Peter."

Peter Fonda, in "Pope's confessional", tells me, "I'm a hell-raiser. I'm the new James Dean. To hell with conformity!"

CHAPTER XIV

My Man Chu In China

By the early spring of '66, with Reggie firmly entrenched in the music business, I had established for Trans-Atlantic Features a vast, highly efficient network of news spies throughout the country. Most were on the full-time staffs of the leading dailies in the country: the *Boston Globe, Detroit Free Press, Miami Herald, Cleveland Plain Dealer, San Francisco Examiner*, and others. I even had spies planted in the *Enquirer* organization. This enabled me, on occasion, to deliver a completed feature article to *The Inc.* —even before they had officially given me the assignment!

I had men—and women—in Greece, Italy, Germany, France, Holland, Norway, Sweden, Denmark, Israel, the United Arab Republic, and the Soviet Union.

In Moscow, agent Alexei turned in a comprehensive report on Leonev Shchotnikov, a Russian judge who, while heavily into vodka, ran down four people. The first three died when the intoxicated magistrate accidentally lost control of the wheel. The fourth, an eyewitness who had jumped to safety, planned to identify the judge for the hit-and-run crime—unless blackmail money was paid. The judge reasoned that the extortionist was better off dead than alive. So he arranged to have him meet his end on a deserted street. And when the man appeared, he was met—head on—by Shchotnikov's car. To make absolutely sure the man was dead, your honor honored his body by rolling the car wheels over it eleven times before speeding off. Finally, the judge became jittery and confessed, passing an automatic death sentence on himself. Three months later, he was executed before a firing squad.

My man Manuel Perdova (an alias), in Argentina, was an excellent informant. He heroically managed to break through an iron veil of official police secrecy to report the facts of "an internal police affair" that became a "world exclusive" for the *National Enquirer.* The May 8, '66 headline read: "WOMAN DETECTIVE MURDERS POLICEMAN ... When He Tries To Call Off Their Romance."

Periodista Perdova even managed to smuggle out of Argentina the grim photo of the detective lying dead at a railroad station after his pretty police pal had pumped three bullets into him.

Detectives Francisco Gamalero and Pauline Sanders had been tough on criminals—but soft on each other. And for about three years, the two super-sleuths had worked as a team—to cover up their own secret love affair, because Gamalero had a wife!

While their police work was smooth, their romance wasn't. And Gamalero signed his own death warrant when he finally decided to end their overtime affair.

But it wasn't that easy. Pauline flew into a murderous rage after he broke the news to her on a Buenos Aires commuter train. And as he stepped off the train at a suburban station, she whipped out her service revolver and pumped three slugs of hot lead into his back. He died instantly. And she was apprehended thirty minutes later.

That story has special application today to the wives—and husbands—of police officers. If you weren't aware, many police departments are new co-ed. Men and women walk the same beat and are assigned to each other for patrol car duty.

While I had competent correspondents in such

out-of-the-way places as Greenland and South Africa, I was missing a man in China—and needed one who could organize and dispatch reporters throughout Southeast Asia.

Then a contact at one of New York's Chinatown newspapers gave me the name of George P. C. Chu, the crack city editor of Taiwan's leading English-speaking daily, the *China Post.*

I drafted a five-page letter to Chu in care of his newspaper. Then I waited for a reply.

After eight days, Chu cabled me at Trans-Atlantic Features, hereafter referred to as T.A.F.

"Dear Mr. Bernard: Received your detailed proposal. Please send T.A.F. press credential. Have several unusual current stories. Will send photo and story descriptions by letter. Pleasure to be your agent in China. Sincerely. George P. C. Chu."

From that moment on, my man Chu in China did the job. Story leads started flowing in from Japan, South Vietnam, and all other parts of that distant side of the world. Chu even developed a first-person interview with a defector from the infamous "Red Guard," the young militants who had been terrorizing mainland China.

My man Chu helped turn editions of *The Inc.* into "the *National Enquirer* of China," so it seemed. Seeing ethnic names like Liu Tang-kun, Li Ming-sheng and Wen Mei-fang became as common as finding soy sauce in a Chinese restaurant, and the stories were as appetizing as lobster Cantonese.

On August 21, '66, the *Enquirer* devoted the entire back page to this story: "MAN LIVES AS A NUN IN CONVENT FOR 17 YEARS."

It was the most thought-provoking, brain-boggling revelation the paper had ever printed. But it only ran after Chu had documented the evidence to the full satisfaction of everyone on the *Enquirer's* editorial staff.

It was amazing, but thoroughly true. For seventeen years, Chen Jui had impersonated a nun in a Buddhist convent. And not one of the sisters, who had chanted prayers with him and worked alongside him in the rice fields, ever knew that Chen was a man. The only individual aware was the abbess who had accepted him as a novitiate in 1949.

Then after seventeen years, the abbess decided to disclose the identity of the forty-two-year-old male nun. Fortunately, one of Chu's own agents, working exclusively for T.A.F., came up with the lead. It was a stroke of good Chinese fortune that the strange story had not appeared in their local press. I feared Reuters or other news agencies would pick up the story and teletype it all over the world.

Chu had immediately wired me the facts and within ten minutes, the *Enquirer* gave me the go-ahead.

In turn, I wired Chu: "Congratulations on story scoop of male nun. Must have quotes from Chen and Su Ta-cheng, abbess at the ancient Fengshan Temple in Chi Hu. Photos urgently needed of Chen before he entered convent and as male nun in religious clothes. Also, must have photo of abbess and dormitory where Chen lived. Take extra care. No leaks. Wire progress. Sincerely. George Bernard, Trans-Atlantic Features."

Using a T.A.F. press credential, Chu was permitted to enter the nunnery and interview both Chen and the abbess.

"It wasn't too easy at first getting the abbess to talk," Chu later told me. "She greeted me warily, but then I used my powers of persuasion," he added.

The abbess told Chu that she had finally decided to disclose the secret on the birthday of Buddha, "because Buddha had freed Chen of his mental anguish after his wife had deserted him. Buddha gave Chen the power to forget his worldly cares and I wanted to make this merciful act known."

Chu recalled that when he asked to see Chen, the abbess was at first against it. "But then I charmed her into it. She motioned for me to follow her.

"Chen appeared shy. His head was shaved. And the long robe he wore made him pass easily as a nun. If the abbess had not revealed Chen's secret he could have gone on indefinitely. Even possibly for another seventeen years," said Chu.

Chen told Chu that when he was twenty-four, he married a beautiful girl from his village. After only a year, she ran away. Chen searched the countryside for his wife until the strain and anguish brought on a nervous breakdown, and he entered the hospital.

After two months, Chen was released from the hospital. His concerned relatives suggested finding another wife, but the embittered Chen said: "I could never trust another woman. But my family was persistent. So I went to work in a monastery not far from my home to get away from them."

Chu reported that Chen became distraught when his relatives invaded the monastery and pleaded with him to remarry.

"Then it occurred to me that I could escape them by going to a nunnery where male worshippers could not enter."

Chu said that Chen was twenty-five when he had first approached the abbess at the Fengshan Temple and begged to be admitted.

The abbess told him that her first reaction was to turn Chen down, but his persistent nature and deep religious convictions impressed her.

"It didn't seem too difficult to charm her," Chu admitted. "I had the same good fortune as Chen in getting admittance to the nunnery, except I didn't stay for seventeen years," he laughed.

"Since there were no religious or man-made laws preventing a man from entering a convent, I decided to take him in." The wise abbess also reasoned that Chen would not interfere with the females there. Her thinking was that since the nuns had taken their religious vows that denounced worldly pleasures, a man's presence would not concern them. Further, she added, "what was the matter anyway with a man and a woman worshipping Buddha together?"

But so as not to frighten the nuns, she used discretion and did not inform them of Chen's male identity. Further in Chen's favor: the abbess herself had experienced a broken marriage thirty years earlier and was sympathetic to the plight of the unhappy male applicant.

For thirteen years Chen was isolated from the other nuns by separate sleeping quarters. "During those years I watched Chen very closely," the abbess told Chu. "Then four years ago, I gave him permission to mix freely with the nuns. He was a man of the strongest moral codes and an extremely devout Buddhist. I never regretted admitting Chen to our convent," she said.

The article seemed so incredible to Pope that the doubtful publisher ordered further substantiation. My man Chu was wired to furnish a copy of Chen's I.D. card which the abbess stated was issued after his true identity had been disclosed.

Within one week I had it in my hands and personally dropped it on the editor's desk. But the verification didn't stop there. Pope had Chen's face compared by an expert with the facial features of the disguised male nun. After this checked out, a Chinese journalist was brought in to study the I.D.—to ascertain if that indeed was

Chen. Finally, the story ran.

In a lengthy letter from Chu, he filled me in on upcoming stories. "A man was sentenced to death on February 7," he wrote.

The man whose life was in deadly jeopardy was Liu Tang-kun and his life literally hung by a hair—a pubic hair!

Liu, a doctor, had been arrested and brought to trial for raping and then murdering a nurse. The authorities, Chu reported, used brutal methods to extract the confession. But the tell-tale evidence was found in the victim's vagina. Lab experts had matched a single pubic hair found there to that of Liu.

"Efforts to get on-the-spot morgue shots of the dead nurse have been made . . . the picture of the nurse before her death, and a reprint of Liu are only pictures I have thus far. Also I am trying to get exact ages of both nurse and doctor."

But before Chu could continue on the assignment, Bill killed the article. He was afraid that pubic pieces would offend the Pope and he didn't want to show poor judgment before his boss. So I received reimbursement for my expenses, which the paper recorded as an "undeveloped fee."

A story that Chu had assigned to a colleague in Japan involved a medical inhumanity to a child. Chu wrote in the same letter: "Regarding Dr. Iwahashi, the butcher, and Toshihiro Furkawa, the unfortunate boy, Erai Yatsu (a pseudonym for our Japanese reporter) thinks it is impossible to get pictures of the boy. He has the doctor's picture, parents of the boy and place where brutal operation took place."

I wired Chu: "Nothing is impossible. If he can't secure photo, I'm taking him off case immediately. No more assignments. Get back to me soonest . . ."

Within ten days, I had the completed story.

The preferential back page of the August 28,

'66 *Enquirer* read: "DOCTOR CASTRATES A ROWDY 10-YEAR-OLD TO QUIET HIM DOWN."

And it was all true. When the child didn't respond to tranquilizers or other medical treatment, the doctor castrated the youth. The barbaric surgery was performed without the permission or knowledge of Toshihiro's parents—and was illegal!

But the fifty-six-year-old physician was not penalized for his butchery—because he was the only doctor in the small town of Kobayashi, Japan, and his services were vitally needed.

Reporter Yatsu spoke with the boy's parents, who revealed that the child's life had been filled with tragedy. During Toshihiro's infancy, he developed polio. At the age of six, the polio spread to his brain and the child was forced to drop out of school.

At the age of seven, the disturbed boy had set fire to his home. At eight, he had attacked a little girl. At nine, his devilish deeds of mischief included: turning in false fire and police alarms, breaking windows with rocks and trying to split a child's head open. He had even managed to push a parked car over a ledge into a river.

His hostile, **aggressive** behaviour continued. Toshihiro broke windows, kicked doors, attacked elderly patients and even tried to pull up nurses' skirts.

The doctor told my agent that he tried every medical procedure in the book to quiet the rowdy kid, but nothing worked.

"So the only way to quiet him down was to castrate him," the doctor told the reporter.

On August 22, '65, Dr. Iwahashi performed the operation—and Toshihiro Furukawa was robbed of sex for life.

Until the operation, the youth had been so violent that the doctor had advised the parents not to visit their son. But three months later, they decided to pay their boy a visit. And when the mother asked about her son, the nurse told her: "Your boy is well, except we had to castrate him. He was so violent."

Rushing into the room, the terrified mother confirmed the nurses's report. She bundled her son up and took him home. Then she called the police.

The doctor didn't deny conducting the castration, but another eminent physician disagreed with the doctor's methods. Dr. En-Yu Shioiri, Chief of the Neurosis Section at Tokyo's Keio Hospital said that sometimes castration worked, and other times it did not. Further, "The patient's behavior patterns might not necessarily be changed until ten years later, if at all."

Under Japanese law, castration is illegal without exception. The Eugenic Protection Law states that a physician may sterilize, not castrate a mental patient—but only if it is deemed necessary for the public safety. To sterilize, the government's Prefectual Eugenic Protection Committee, which administers the law. must give approval. Because the lad was only ten years old at the time of the castration, the permission of the parents was absolutely necessary. But the good doctor never did any of these things, or consulted anyone.

The authorities said that jailing him would cause a "medical panic" in the community. But the doctor, who continued to practice medicine, offered to patch it all up. No, once the testicles were snipped off, that was that. And if indeed, Dr. Iwahashi did attempt a testicle transplant — for the patient he castrated — it would not only have been an *Enquirer* first, but a medical one.

But what's a pair of human balls worth anyway? Dr. Iwahashi estimated the value at $60, which he sent to the bereaved parents, "so as to forget the whole thing," said the mother.

They sent it right back, however, and I'm sure, to boot, they would have liked the money to accompany a swift kick in the doctor's balls.

Harry Golden wrote a memorable book, *Only in America*. But no part of the world could rightfully match Southeast Asia for its unbridled brutality towards fellow human beings. Sometimes, however, the brutality was self-imposed.

The Japanese castration was popular with the *Enquirer* readers. But when my man Chu came up with a child-castration story in his own backyard, Taiwan, I had my doubts if it wasn't too soon for another.

Did you ever hear of a child who, by getting even with his parents for a broken promise, cut his balls off in the process? Chu heard and so did the *Enquirer*. Even quicker than the O.K. on the Japanese castration, I was wiring Chu his instructions.

Hsu Tsing-tsai was three years older than Toshihiro when the tragedy occurred. And it happened because his parents didn't take him to the zoo as they had promised. To compound the matter, the boy's mother was out for the night and the father away somewhere—and the youth had not eaten breakfast, lunch or dinner. He was, however, eating himself up with brooding about his loneliness.

Chu recalled: "The boy felt vindictive, spiteful. He convinced himself that his parents didn't care about him so he decided that they never should have any grandchildren—if he could help it! So he took a kitchen knife out to the backyard and castrated himself. If the boy's father hadn't come in the door a few moments later and rushed him to the hospital, the youngster would have bled to death."

The doctors at Shanhsia's hospital in Taiwan told Chu: "The boy kept repeating later that his

existence meant nothing at all to his parents.
'They don't care about me, so why should I care
about them,'" the boy told the physicians.

Dr. Lin Hung-wei told correspondent Chu how
the boy performed the surgery on himself: "As
the boy recalled, he first grabbed hold of a very
sharp kitchen knife. The kind that you could slice
meat with. Then he strode up onto a little knoll
behind the house and stripped off his trousers.

"Then, he sliced open his scrotum and cut off
both his testicles—and threw them away. Blood
began to gush from the wound and he fainted.
The next thing he remembered was waking up in
the hospital. But that was many hours after he
was out of the emergency room. It took several
doctors to stop the bleeding and close the wound.
I was one of them."

Reluctantly, the lad went home a week later.
But he was never the same boy.

Bill wanted to know which testicle fell to the
ground first and where he threw them away.
"The left one," I answered quickly. "And he
threw them at a hungry giant moth that happened to be flying by." Bill laughed. "O.K.
'Goldmine'. You . . . and your man Chu did a great
job. It's all set for the August 16, edition! 'BOY,
13, CASTRATES SELF—BECAUSE PARENTS
NEGLECTED HIM.' "

Moral: when you tell your son he's going to the
zoo, be sure you keep your word.

Chu was simply amazing. While city editor of a
leading Taiwan daily, he still managed to supervise all of T.A.F.'s Southeast Asian affairs.

I considered Chu to be not just another
"China-watcher," but the Walt Rostow of the
Orient when it came to developments in Asia.

As a native of Shanghai, Chu had left his home
and studies to join the Free Chinese Army as a
P.F.C. in March 1949 while only seventeen. In
less than two bitter months of fighting, the city

fell to the Communists. For his patriotism, he was promoted to the rank of Second Lieutenant. G.P.C. Chu recalls: "I led the evacuation across the straits to Taiwan. The promotion was only on paper, as my platoon was composed only of myself!"

Along with other casual personnel, including batallion and regiment commanders who were without troops, Chu was assigned to a reclamation farm in Yi-Lan County in eastern Taiwan. There, early in 1950, he performed research in hog-raising and vegetable-planting. But that was not going to be his career. Instead, he completed his secondary education and entered the Political Warfare College, a training ground for the responsible post he would assume at both the *China Post,* and as an agent for TAF.

Did you ever hear of newly-weds getting a divorce, so that they could work together? Again, Chu did. It made an excellent human-interest, off-beat article. Living together for the lovebirds wasn't a problem, but working together was.

After getting maritally hitched and obtaining teaching jobs at the same school in Paiho, Taiwan, they learned of an antiquated regulation that specifically prohibited any school in that country from employing a husband and wife at the same time.

The school officials, after discovering the infraction, said that one of them would have to transfer to an out-of-town teaching job. Wei Yung-sung, twenty-seven, and his pretty wife, Pai-hua, twenty-one were perplexed. They couldn't quit as they were legally obligated for two years at any school where the authorities wished to assign them. Having attended a tuition-free teachers' college, both were bound to that obligation.

A transfer was out of the question, because the

only post offered was in a town very far away. The couple couldn't live without each other, so Chu reported.

Living apart meant extra expenses, which they could not afford. Besides, Wei was going to night school and didn't wish to leave his studies there.

"There was only one way out," Wei told Chu. "We had to get a divorce. We love each other. But we'll have to stay single for two years—officially, anyway."

Wei and his bride did just that. They got divorced so that they could work together in the same school. Officials of the school were so impressed with their love for each other and dedication to teaching, they turned their backs on the fact that they were unlawfully living together.

While two people couldn't see enough of each other, a nineteen-year-old bride was becoming bored with her generous thirty-five-year-old hubby. Chu-tung Wang discovered his dream girl in a whore house of Taiwan. And since Mei-yu Huang was a slave, he shelled out his life's savings to purchase her freedom. Then he married her and offered the girl of sin a life of respectability.

But the clean life bored the young bride and as soon as the honeymoon was over, she demanded a divorce from her engineer husband.

"And when he refused," Chu reported, "she repaid all his kindness—by lacing his food with rat poison and watching him die in agony."

The girl made this statement to the police: "He was honest and sincere and all that. But he was so dull and uninteresting, I couldn't stand living with him—which really was worse than living back in the brothel.

But was it better than dying? Mei-yu was sentenced to die for her crime before a firing squad.

Oddly enough, she had almost engineered the

perfect crime. She put a box of strong rat poison in her purse and after going to a movie with her husband, Mei-yu suggested having a bite at a local snack bar. But before Wang began eating, she sent him to the counter for a slice of pineapple. And while he was away, less than a minute, she laced his beef noodles with arsenic. When he returned he ate every last drop, poison and all. When he got home, he complained of pains and doubled up with stomach cramps.

Ignoring his wife's advice that "it's nothing to worry about," Wang went to the clinic, his evil bride following and hoping he wouldn't make it. Though he managed to stagger into the hospital on his own steam, he really didn't make it. While doctors were treating him for food poisoning, he died one of the most violent of all deaths—screaming and writhing in agony—while his wife looked on silently.

The police were summoned. After conducting an investigation, they saw no foul play. After all, Wang did not die from food eaten at home. Further, the waitress at the restaurant testified she served Wang and his reformed whore.

Wang was buried, but though the case was formally closed, it was not closed permanently. Kai-ting Liu, one of Wang's closest friends, went to the police and raised doubts and suspicions about the sudden death.

The police exhumed Wang's body from his grave and performed a thorough autopsy. The lab tests were conclusive. Wang's stomach was lined with arsenic.

Mei-yu was picked up immediately and brought into the police station for questioning, and under fierce interrogation, she broke down and confessed her dastardly act.

Chu photographed Wang in his coffin. In addition, he furnished pictures of the victim while alive and a jeering candid of his ex-slave who was "bored to death" of her husband. The *Enquirer* article even featured a picture of the actual sales girl who sold the rat poison to Mei-yu.

Two other Chu contributions are worthy of comment. "GIRL, 5, KILLS PLAYMATE, 4, THEN VICTIM'S PARENTS ADOPT HER." Also, "CHATTER OF MONKEYS HELPS SAVE MAN FROM BEING RIPPED TO PIECES BY A 500-LB. SAVAGE BEAR."

Though I'm running out of chapter space, suffice it to say that headlines tell a lot. And your vivid imaginations from the all-encompassing *Enquirer* headlines, some of which are masterpieces, could probably come close to reconstructing the actual, stranger than fiction, events.

Ever grateful to my man Chu, I felt obligated to repay his good work. The *Enquirer* had prospered, while Chu and his team were paid royally for their highly professional services. T.A.F. flourished as well.

Finally, the opportunity arose.

After seven years as city editor, he was accepted for a fellowship at Southern Illinois University. But Chu's passport was soon to expire. And it wasn't too easy in those days to get out of the country, even for a city editor.

On March 22, '68, I wrote to James Wei, Director, Government Information Office, Taipei, Taiwan, Republic of China. I requested permission for T.A.F. correspondent Chu to cover the International Sinologist's Conference that was currently being held in the U.S.

It worked. Chu received full cooperation from his government in "securing closer media ties with the United States." Today, with America's "friendlier" stance towards mainland China, my letter would have probably been filed in the "circular files"—the waste paper basket!

Two years later, Chu received an M.S. in Journalism from S.I.U., followed by a Doctorate.

In America to stay now, with his three children and pretty wife, Dr. Chu is an Assistant Professor in the University of Detroit's Political Science department. His writings have appeared in the *Sunday Times of London,* the *Washington Post* and the *Detroit News,* among other papers.

And from Birmingham, Michigan where Chu makes his home, he is the enterprising managing editor of a Jack Anderson-styled, hard-hitting *Enquirer*-fashioned news service "To More Than 2,000 Daily & Sunday Newspapers."

Other subscribers include TV stations in America and feature syndicates in Australia and Manila. He is presently in the negotiation stage with tabloids in Tokyo and London.

In a typical, recent issue crammed with "exclusive news and views from all over the world," Chu's CONTINENTAL NEWS FEATURES reported some of these scoops: "Mao on Sex" . . . "Arafat Sets Up Office in Prague" . . . "New Fad of CIA Bashing Hurts M15" . . . "Egypt's Garlic Saves Czech Cuisine" . . . "Peking Selling Tibet Treasures for Nuclear Arms."

At the accelerated rate Chu's going, it won't be long before one reads: "My man Bernard in New York." All the best to Chu!

My man Chu from China posing with his wife and their little Chus. He was responsible for coordinating many fantastic and fascinating stories that appeared in the *Enquirer*.

CHAPTER XV

Galella, Camera & Co.—Tallulah, Twiggy, Burl, George Segal and Angie Dickinson

During the mid-sixties, America's best-known "paparazzo" photographer was a virtual unknown.

Ron Galella, a second-generation Italian-American, was five "darkroom" years away from a highly-publicized confrontation with the widow of John F. Kennedy. Their heated "day in court" would begin February 16, '72 and continue over seven weeks.

When it was all over, Jacqueline Kennedy Onassis had delivered a decisive blow to Galella's freedom of the press. Jackie's court-sanctioned "free-floating" anti-magnetic field had limited Galella's Nikon from approaching her within fifty yards. On appeal, the restriction was reduced to twenty-five feet. But Ron's real victory came in the overwhelming recognition of his work—from the press, his peers and the public at large.

And so it was at one of those typical celebrity parties in Manhattan that I first came in contact with Galella. Betty Lee Hunt, the noted theatrical press agent, was introducing the sprightly, debonair Bobby Short to New York. Angela Lansbury in a mini-dress barely at the crotch level was joined by sexy Rexy Reed and other personalities in toasting and well-wishing.

Even Tallulah Bankhead made one of her rare appearances. The "Darling" dame wore a sash across her chest that said "BETTE DAVIS." Initially, she fooled me. The resemblance was uncanny!

My good buddy, Ben McCall, still not aware of my *Enquirer* connection, was a close friend of Betty-Lee Hunt. So, when we arrived, our names were on the invitation list. I was the only journalist at the party, and Ben the only photographer. That is, until ten blinding flashes went off near the door, where Ron Galella made his entrance.

In a matter of moments, the paparazzo had used his flash like a smoke screen and was shooting the stars in the center of the restaurant. Betty Lee looked astonished, but said nothing. She was the toughest publicist in the business for adhering to an invitation list. "If you're not on my list," she would say, "you ain't getting into my party!" Apparently, she knew Galella's ability to place pictures of her clients in national magazines, so she made the exception.

Ben was about to take a full-time job with the Metropolitan Museum of Art in their photo department and his understanding wife Mable wanted him home evenings. So, I was on the lookout for another photographer who knew what was happening—when and where. After Galella and I exchanged business cards, Ron left for another "beautiful-people" bash. I remained.

At the time, I had no way of knowing that my business card would lead to another successful, anything but boring, business arrangement. Remember, I had first met Reggie that way—at a party.

I couldn't remember when the *Enquirer* had last printed an expose on Tallulah, except for some possible column tidbits. Every chance I had, I would go through back issues of *The Inc.* to determine which celebrities hadn't been heard from for a long while.

"You look great, Tallulah," I complimented her. She gave me an endearing hug, pulled back and in her characteristic charm said to me: "Darling, you're so kind."

She asked me how I enjoyed the party and I said it was a reporter's dream.

"Well, Mr. George Bernard Shaw," she began, holding my shoulder with one hand while the other draped around a liquor glass. "I'll give you a story. I may look divine, but darling, I'm not going to be around too much longer."

I fortunately had clicked on my spy tape recorder. The two miniature mikes were taped to my chest and I made sure to be practically on top of Miss Revelation. Though there was a heavy chatter, I was confident my $700 recording gems that were being used by Soviet spies as well as the U.S. intelligence, would do the job.

"You see, I'm dying of emphysema. And there's nothing that you, or my doctors, or anyone in this world can do about it. Now that we understand that, what are you drinking?" she said, downing her drink and swiggling an ice cube in her mouth.

"I don't think I'm drinking tonight," I said.

"Oh, what a party-pooper you are," she laughed.

Tallulah coughed violently, her throat becoming even more raspy and husky. "I'm not long for this world. You do believe me?" she questioned. I nodded.

"Good," she went on. "Look, I have no real regrets. Sure, I would have liked my last Broadway show to go, but it didn't. And I've made *some* good movies and did whatever I wanted to in my private life, which really wasn't private."

Just then Betty Lee took Tallulah by the arm and led her away to another part of the party. B.L.H. not only put the affair together, maintained security, but she was New York's answer to Elsa Maxwell. It was her job to mix people together and make sure they were having one delightful evening, for which she was getting paid.

I said my goodbyes to all and hopped a cab to

my office where I transcribed my interview and wrote the article. And the next morning the *Enquirer* was jubilant. That is, until they decided to request my tape for their attorneys.

With a glum look on his tired face, Bill broke the news: It was "too hot to print," he said regretfully. "Your tape checks out, and all that. The writing is fine and we'd love to run it on the front page. Nobody's denying that she said it. Her voice is unmistakable. But she might have been drunk when the remarks were made and believed, actually felt, that she was dying of emphysema. Her doctors might have thought differently. No, 'Goldmine', we can't take a chance with this one."

I was more than just mildly disappointed, though I understood his point. But how it must have burned the *Enquirer's* attorneys when Tallulah's prediction became deadly accurate. For, on December 12, '68, a year and some months later, she died of double pneumonia and emphysema.

Burly Burl Ives was opening on Broadway in "Dr. Cook's Garden." Earlier in the morning Bill's instructions were: "We understand that he eats like a hog and loves anything he can stuff into his mouth. See if you can get him to admit that he's a fat slob. That's the only angle we want developed into a story."

Ron Galella, with whom I was now working, picked me up in his beat-up green Rambler. The paint on the hood had been scorched off by a hot summer's sun. And the fenders were banged up from quickly getting into and out of small parking spaces between assignments. (At that time, Ron was living in the Bronx. A few years later, his fame would create more assignments than he could handle. He would be trading in one orange Firebird for another and living in resplendent style.)

We moved swiftly through the stage door past the guard. Ron knew the backstage layout of the theatre and we had no difficulty finding Burl's private dressing room, which was anything but private. Photographers from the Associated Press, United Press International and local newspapers were relentlessly firing their flashes.

Galella wanted an "exclusive" photo session and desired different shots than those that would appear in the later editions of the newspapers. That moment Burl was gleefully posing for the press, not aware his show would receive unanimously unfavorable reviews within a few hours, and be forced to post a closing notice.

Before we knew it, Burl had slipped out of his costume. Now in his street clothes, he was walking out with the press.

"See you later at my party," he told two visitors in the doorway to the corridor.

"Mr. Ives, you were fantastic!" I said, not having seen the show. Galella was speechless.

"I'm glad you enjoyed it," he said happily.

"I'm a reporter, and this is my photographer, Ron Galella. Could we chat with you and take some pictures, say, at the party?"

"Now, how did you know about that? It's supposed to be a secret. Oh, I get it. You heard me say it."

"If we didn't have sharp ears, we wouldn't do our job well," I said.

"True. True. Well, O.K. Sure, we're having my favorite food, Chinese. Now I have to make one stop, but just go by to my place. I'll see you there later. You have the address?"

My mouth was watering, not so much for the Oriental delicacies expected on the Ives menu, but for the set-up. What could be more perfect for a hatchet job than the comfort of a man's own place? I was sure Burl would be so at-home, he would open up his stomach to me.

If I secured the interview, Galella's photos would be purchased by the *Enquirer* to accompany the article. And now we were working together, undercover, for the rewards. On other than celebrity stories, I would work alone—as writer and as photographer. But when it came to stalking the stars, I couldn't be concerned about a camera's F stop or if the flash battery was properly charged. I needed all my wits just to get the interview. Preying on personalities was a difficult game.

When Galella and I arrived at Burl's dainty duplex on West End Avenue, we were looked at suspiciously by a woman who came to the door. She was Burl's trusty press agent who doubted the authenticity of our invitation. Still, though, she permitted us to join the party, and wait for the arriving big one.

Ron and I had not eaten dinner, and we were ready to tear into the hot buffet table of hot-and-sour pork, fried rice, spare ribs and the succulent giant-sized fried shrimp. But the press agent kept staring. Then a grey-haired man and what looked to be his wife, or mistress, started eating and Ron was off and running. Ravenous Ron soon became satiated, as content as a cow left to graze endlessly on generous green grass.

The food was superb. I came nowhere to matching Ron's voracious appetite, but I wondered where was bouncy Burl? Then, as if he had heard my prayers, Ives arrived at his own party. I wondered if he had knocked off some stage-door cutie on the way.

A servant brought out a new spread of food, which consisted basically of what was displayed earlier. Ron eyed the table of savory offerings, belched, and let discretion conquer dreams of assaulting the succulent spread of Chinese goodies.

Before he even greeted his guests, big Burl

headed for the chow. Instantly, Ron's camera went into unobtrusive action. And finally, the moment was right. Burl had moved over to our corner of the room.

"How do you like the food?" he asked, adding: "You know, we made it ourselves." He put down his plate. This was Burl's sixth, and all looked alike, except the first two plates were stuffed three inches high and brimmed with the works.

His stomach protruding conspicuously over his bobbing abdomen, Burl swung his arm over my shoulder. "Now, aren't you glad you came?" he said.

"The food was great!" I said. "Did you have any?" knowing full well that he, moments earlier, had languished in it.

Galella took that picture.

A photograph of me with a star as big as Burl would never run in the *Enquirer*. An undercover reporter would have to be insane to expose his face. But the picture did graphically serve as conclusive evidence that the interview transpired, if the situation ever called for substantiation.

"I had six plates of the stuff," Burl laughed.

"But, aren't you afraid of what people will say?" I asked.

"What the hell do I care what people will say. I'm the boss here, and I'll eat to my stomach's content," he went on, patting his belly.

"But you wouldn't want to be known as a hog?" I queried, adding, "it's not healthy."

"I am a hog," he admitted. "And I'll never die from too much food. From something else, someday possibly. But not from food," he resolved.

Burl's suspicious press agent was giving me dagger eyes. And when Burl finally excused himself to go to the little boy's room, she rose from her chair and marched over.

Miss Inquisitive, who said she tried to read our

lips, demanded to know every word that had transpired between us. I thought it was none of her business. And I would have told her so. But I didn't want to draw any undue attention to my reasons for being there.

"We were just discussing Burl's culinary preferences," I said with a straight face, but a crooked tongue. The inquisition of Ives didn't stop there.

For three days following my interview, I took her call at T.A.F. And, each time she called—and it totalled seven—the message was practically the same. "Mr. Ives is a very special, proud man. He is a respected performer. And I'm sure you would not do anything to dispel that image. Now, if you were to print anything unkind, I would have to refer the matter to our attorneys. Do I make myself understood?"

Though I had a full contact sheet of photos of Burl Ives gobbling down chunks of chow, I advised the *Enquirer* of my misgivings and requested the article be silently put to death.

"Goldmine," Bill said to me. "You've got all the substantiation, but if you'll rest a little easier, we won't run it." And they didn't.

During the summer of '67, Galella and I approached George Segal at Alexander's department store in Manhattan. The handsome actor was appearing in conjunction with Twentieth Century Fox's *The St. Valentine's Day Massacre*, in which Segal played the part of Peter Gusenberg, gangster Bugs Moran's right-hand man. George's personal appearance was being staged in the store's radio-record section by the studio's beautiful press agent, Marilyn Stewart.

The angle of the story was that he appeared in so many films as different characters, that he could never readily be remembered for just one of his fine portrayals. The *Enquirer* wanted me to find out why a man of his tremendous talent had

198

never become a super-star.

In those days, who knew of George Segal? But I think that morning in July at Alexander's, I developed an insight into why Segal lacked the vision to become an immortal in the industry to which he dedicated his life.

Like a chimp, Segal jumped up on the counter, crossed his legs like "Sitting Bull" and snapped at me like a turtle—throughout the interview.

Then he began to make a series of silly faces at me, and wouldn't stop until a fan tapped him on the shoulder for his autograph. Which he gave willingly. A young man standing next to me was so bored of Segal that he actually fell asleep waiting for a friend to get Segal's signature on a piece of scrap paper.

When you really think about George's strange apprenticeship, there's nothing wrong with having worked as janitor, ticket-taker, soft-drink salesman, usher and understudy before making the big leagues—according to the International Motion Picture Almanac. But, George, enough is enough. You're out of your adolescence.

Ron and I had more than enough rejections from press agents on the phone who demanded to know where T.A.F.'s stories were to appear, before allowing us interviews with their clients. So when A.S.C.A.P. scheduled a gala Lincoln Center black-tie affair in October '67, Ron and I decided our personalities would be our invitation.

Our approach and entry was simple. It was like loading a machine gun with an ammo clip and then blasting away. Except, with our plan, no one would get hurt and no one would be aware. So, Galella turned on his flash and I strung a camera around my neck, and we blinded our way into the party. When a flash is going off, who ever looks at who's doing the flashing?

With Galella's trusty gun continuing to blaze, we managed to quickly find an unoccupied, isolated table in the corner of the ballroom. We waited for about five minutes before getting up and surveying the situation. If no one had challenged us by then, it was a fairly safe assumption that we were now part of the party.

There was the irresistible Angie Dickinson. How fortunate Burt Bacharach, I thought. How many men envied the popular musical composer, not for his music but for the gorgeous gal from Kulm, North Dakota he took out of social circulation to be his bride?

I knew the five-foot-five, 114-pound dazzler was in town, but wished I had reviewed more carefully the Dickinson file folder at *Enquirer* research. However, I did recall her fondness for writers. And after all, I was a journalist . . . even if only for the *Enquirer*.

And so when benevolent Burt got up from the table to refill the glasses at the bar I slipped into his seat. Sometimes an undercover reporter has to wait all night for his entry, which, if taken prematurely, can mean disaster.

In a few moments' time, Angie was tightly clutching my hand, as if she had known me, "a writer," all her life. Her face was alive with excitement. Whatever I said evoked the right response as she gripped my hand harder, with feeling, and then let her own hand slip to my knee.

She had become Dickinson, I remembered, while attending Glendale College. Her first husband was college football star Gene Dickinson and she was born Angeline Brown on September 30, '32. She got her first big break after being a starlet when producer Howard Hawkes discovered her while talent-scouting for a new face, and she subsequently starred in *Rio Bravo, Point Blank* and *Pretty Maids All in a Row.* A one-time mayor of Universal City, she confesses to being a hopeless baseball addict.

There was nothing modest, however, about

Angie Dickinson. She told me she was a great actress, which she was, but wanted more work. "It was fine being the wife of America's greatest contemporary composer," she said, "but my career is equally as important. If one falters, it affects the other."

While she spoke of herself, she was intrigued by talking to a writer, right in the flesh. Angie wanted to know what novels I had written and what type of surroundings were most conducive to turning out my best work.

Her hand then left my knee and clutched my hand again. I was transfixed by the face of a true goddess, and I was helpless to do anything about it.

Suddenly, Galella's strobe wasn't blasting white light anymore. And, for good reason. He had vanished from the area. And it only took me a few seconds to realize something was wrong. It was the feeling of calm before the storm. And it came close to raining down on the back of my head.

For, standing over this reporter, and looking down on me with raging vengeance in his jealous eyes, was hubby Burt. Angie was simply speechless as she withdrew her hand. Immediately, Burt put the two drinks on the table. Then I noticed him clenching a fist. But before he could direct it towards me, I plunged my hand into his and shook it vigorously, properly introducing myself.

"Your lovely wife has been telling me all about your perfect marriage, Mr. Bacharach," I said. "I'm a reporter."

Composer Burt bought the story, but the hand-holding session registered an F Flat, and "F" was for trying to *fool* him.

The next morning, the *Enquirer* gave me an "E" for effort, and an "F" for *failing* to pick up on Angie's special "friendship" with the late J.F.K.

"You had her in the palm of your hand"—which I certainly did—"and you let her slip away," Bill moaned.

Today Angie is "Police Woman" on the top-rated NBC-TV program. What I wouldn't give to put her in hand-cuffs . . .

"How about a scoop on an actual banana-puffing party?" I asked Bill. "You bring that story around here," he said, "and Pope will strangle you with the peels. You're not serious, are you?" He really wanted to test my sanity.

"Just a thought," I said, matter-of-factly.

Of course, Pope wouldn't go for it. Getting high on banana fumes, to Pope, was no different than marijuana, which he despised.

In the absence of petrol, bananas were even said to fuel the trucks of guerrillas in '43 wartime Manila. The energy was supposed to be in the dried skins. But I didn't get the knockout feeling the press agent for the banana-sniffing machine wanted me to experience—and believe.

The girls demonstrating how it worked were clad only in the scantiest bikinis. Ron even tried to pick up one of them, but she flatly refused his proposition. After all, he wasn't the household word he is today. He was just a hard-working, diligent free-lance photographer who had little time to wine, dine and romance a girl. "My work comes first," he would often say. "Women, though they are important for my survival, are secondary. A woman can pick up and leave you after she says she loves you. But a man's work, his accomplishments, will never abandon him. They remain forever and beyond."

Ron sold a photo of the banana bash to a leading German magazine, and I happened to be in that frame. Translated to English, the caption erroneously assumed: " . . . drug addicts at a typical New York City party."

I was pretty angry at Ron for not controlling

the editorial content of the caption. I would later learn, however, that once a photographer sells his pictures, especially overseas, he has lost control of what is said editorially about them.

My anger really didn't have a chance to reach dangerous proportions. Twiggy, right atop the *Enquirer's* "most wanted" list, was coming into New York.

Bill's instructions were to evoke controversy. "Don't come back and tell me she said, 'I'm so frail, I haven't had my period since I missed fish and chips two months ago.' I want a real blockbuster, 'Goldmine.' We're counting on you," he said.

For three days straight, Ron and I kept close surveillance of a photographic studio in Manhattan's East 60's. Finally, our break came when a secretary to Bert Stern, the renowned commercial photographer, admitted that Twiggy was scheduled to be at the studio the next morning, around 9:00, "or even earlier," she said. "But may I ask who you are?" she asked. She never got a straight answer.

Twiggy, the seventeen-year-old British-born Leslie Hornby, was the fashion rage of the world. Her manager-boyfriend, Justin de Villeneuve, was overly protective, especially when the press tried to get too close to his live puppet. Justin wanted the media at a distance, about that of a cannon's shot.

It was midnight before we finished checking out other celebrities at the Plaza, Waldorf and other hotels and night-spots. As Ron was notorious for oversleeping, it was decided he would stay over at my place, but not in my apartment. I've always been a light sleeper, even in the Army. And Galella, among other things, was a snorer.

So, I gave the former Air Force aerial photographer summer-camp bedding I had kept as a souvenir from the service. And instead of shooting the stars, he slept like a bear under them—on the roof of my fourteen-story apartment building.

When I nudged him at 7:00 a.m., he was still snoring loudly. Even the pigeons who normally would congregate about the running water hose were too frightened to land.

After shaving, showering and grabbing a quick breakfast, we double-parked in front of the studio, and waited. At precisely 9:00 a.m., a beige Rolls Royce pulled in front of our car and two people hopped out.

"Wake up, Ron. It's them," I yelled.

Ron jumped out of the car as I emerged coming up directly in front of Justin who was lugging a heavy black bag up the stairs. Twiggy, the most beautiful of all branches, was already on the top landing.

"Twiggy, Twiggy," I shouted, which couldn't help catch their attention.

"Yes, what is it?" Justin muttered.

Ron kept shooting, but didn't say a word. There goes my interview, I thought. Then the thought occurred to me. Why not? It was so perfect.

"I'm the former head of Radio Caroline for this country," trying to affect a semblance of a British accent. I figured they would be more cooperative to a countryman. And, I was right.

"And," I continued, "I'm doing an article on both of you for Trans-Atlantic Features that will appear in Europe."

"On both of us?" he queried.

"Yes, you're the man who made the woman," I said. "What do you mean 'made'?" he laughed. "Sure, come on in, but we can't give you too much time.

"But no flashes, please. It hurts our eyes," he instructed.

After warming them up with small talk, I got into the interview, and the lead evolved unintentionally when I asked Twiggy what she liked best about America.

Sensing that I was not really an American, but somehow British, she exploded: "If it wasn't for the quick money, I never would have set foot out of England. In America, I've been pawed, squeezed, ridiculed, berated and constantly laughed at."

Both Twiggy and her twenty-seven-year-old protector concurred that autograph-seekers bugged them enormously. And music was the only good thing about being in the states, Twiggy confessed as she pumped a quarter into the juke box standing in the corner of the studio. "But I can't say the same for the people who dance to it," she added.

Twiggy admitted that she was abused on the dance floor of the "Electric Circus" discotheque the night before. "A strange-looking girl grabbed my arm to see if it was real . . . and a man tried to pull my leg off as a souvenir of the evening. Then," she went on, " a bearded creep made an effort to verify whether there was any chest cleavage under my shirt."

The hottest number in modeling, who was the subject of two ABC Specials, countless other TV commentaries and print pieces, went on and on. She even said that there were those who hate the success of others, "especially of me, I'm the rage of the sixties. And I'm also in a personal rage," barked the brittle British branch of beauty.

The October 29, '67 *Enquirer* front page said: "EXCLUSIVE INTERVIEW REVEALS: TWIGGY HATES AMERICANS ... BUT LOVES THEIR MONEY." Galella, who was fortunate to get off a few frames of the couple ascending the stairs, made that edition with a giant photo of the British beau and his talkative Twig.

If the branch was ever burned for her frankness, and set afire for refusing future interviews,

I was responsible. As with everything else in life, they survived the interview in the *Enquirer,* and left for home shortly after.

It's pretty hard to stay in a country, especially America, after you've admitted loathing their people, but loving their dollars. Is it any wonder stars won't open up to reporters without their press agents sitting alongside?

Tallulah Bankhead, sporting a banner that read "Bette Davis", told me "Darling, I'm not going to be around too much longer. . . ." (*Ron Galella*)

Big Burl swung his arm over my shoulder, his stomach protruding over his belt like bobbing blubber. "Now, aren't you glad you came?" he asked. (*Ron Galella*)

I interviewed George Segal at a department store while an under-enthused shopper fell asleep. (*Ron Galella*)

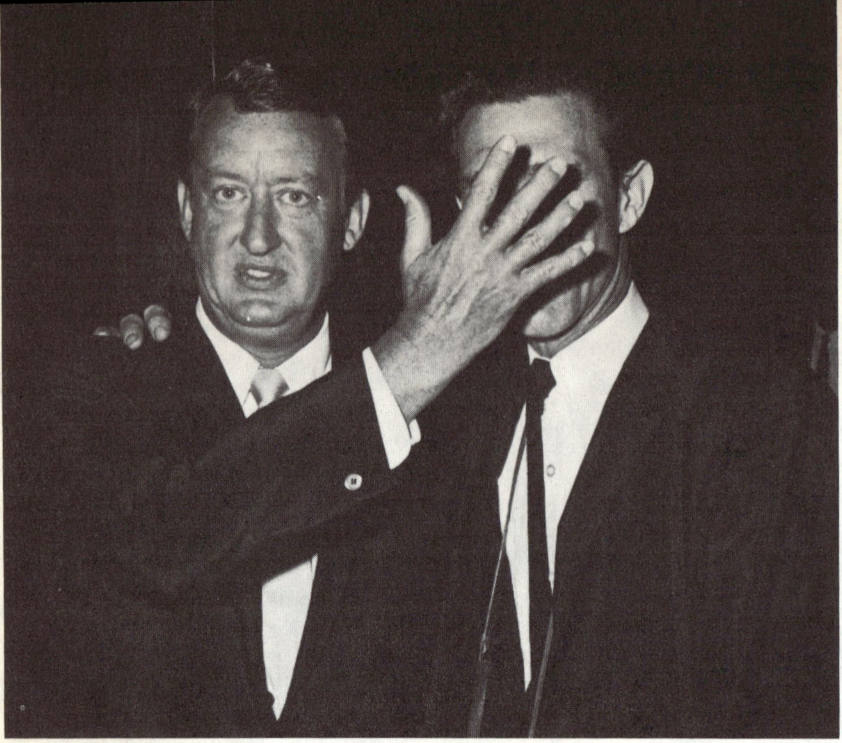

Comic Tom Postom holds his hand over my buddy Ben McCall's puss (above). Ben saved my life, on an earlier occasion, from the ferocious clutches of Robert Mitchum. (*Ron Galella*)

Angie Dickinson was more intrigued with my being a "writer" than with her own career—until, that is, her husband brusquely interrupted our chat. (*Ron Galella*)

A banana-smoking soiree in Greenwich Village. You were supposed to get high—you didn't. A German magazine altered the caption and indicated that the party was for drug addicts! (*Ron Galella*)

I caught the trim Twiggy and her all-business boyfriend
for an interview that became a blockbuster! (*Ron Galella*)

CHAPTER XVI

Judy Garland And The Kennedy Clan

Perturbed, our energy drained from driving endlessly in circles for a parking spot in the car-congested Broadway theatre district, Ron pulled his jalopy into one of the high-priced garages off Sixth Avenue in the Fifties. I was convinced that the bill for a few hours would be greater than what this beat-up hot box on wheels could bring at any used car lot.

Street parking was so tight we couldn't even slip into a spot by giving the parked cars in front—and back—a simple nudge, which is a common practice in New York. It was so bad that a law-abiding pooch couldn't even use the street to properly do his duty.

This night, however, we couldn't afford to be late. Judy Garland was opening a four-week run at the Palace, which had to be one of the most significant events of the '67 season.

Earlier that day, Bill had briefed me. The only angle that would be acceptable to Pope was Judy's connection with J.F.K. "If you don't get a Kennedy story from her, don't bother at all. Nothing else will do," he said firmly.

I understood why: the *Enquirer* had covered Judy's seesaw career meticulously in its other unpredictable aspects.

May 3, '64: "Liza Minnelli's Angry Cry: MY MOM, JUDY GARLAND, IS PERSECUTED . . . She's Been Hurt Too Many Times And She's Suffered So Much."

July 3, '66: "I'VE HAD 4 HUSBANDS & 3 NERVOUS BREAKDOWNS SAYS JUDY GARLAND. IT'S MORE THAN ANYONE SHOULD HAVE TO TAKE."

July 31, '67 would not only have to be the night that Judy soared at the Palace, but that undercover men Bernard and Galella succeeded.

Bill Doll was the press agent for "Judy Garland, at Home at the Palace." Doll knew Galella well, especially after Ron's photos of the publicist's accounts had wound up in several prominent national publications. In those days, Doll's office was the biggest in the business. He had also been instrumental in building Mike Todd's giant image. And so it was understandable that he'd be commissioned to arrange Judy's press for the Palace.

Over the phone, Doll gave Galella permission to shoot the stars in the theatre lobby, which in those days, and even now, is all most press agents will permit. Funny, publicists want "press" for their clients, but they seem to act contrary to good business practices and often either exclude the news media, or invite those who won't even write a kind word or print a solitary mention.

When we got to the theatre lobby, Ron popped off some fifty candids of gown-garbed celebrities and their escorts in black-tie attire as they entered the electrified-with-excitement theatre from limousines and taxis.

To maintain proper crowd control, the local police precinct rushed over foot-patrol officers and additional barricades were quickly set up. There were the customary bright lights, a plethora of press photographers. And of course, there were the throngs of ogling onlookers who pushed and pelted each other to gain a moment's glimpse of the arriving celebrities.

About five minutes before curtain time, Galella and I moved in swiftly with a wave of ticket patrons. Then we waited in the rear of the theatre until most of the crowd had taken their seats. For how else would we know what seating was available? Suddenly, a few feet from where we were standing, Judy emerged and made her grand entrance down the aisle to the stage. The applause was deafening, and she hadn't even delivered a half note.

We grabbed two back seats on the aisle. Galella began to adjust his telescopic lens as I began to write down opening night observations. The click of Ron's Nikon was muffled by the roar of the audience as he started shooting the glistening Garland using the illumination of the theatre spotlight. Today, shooting inside a theatre during a performance without written authorization is a crime in New York State. Then it was different, though not encouraged.

Spying an unoccupied seat up front, closer to the stage, I left Galella. We arranged to rendezvous in half an hour in the rear, after he varied his shots by taking pictures from the balcony.

To get a better insight into Garland's magnetism, Ron and I decided to be backstage spectators. So we left the theatre during intermission. We moved quickly and confidently through the stage door entrance and were not even questioned. It's like anything else. If you move with authority, others assume you belong. Conversely, when you're frightened and show it, you're stopped.

But the only thing that Judy had going for her that evening was charisma. Certainly, it wasn't her voice. In fact, it broke occasionally, contrary to reports and reviews in the local press. But her frenetic fans were amply satisfied. And they applauded, and continued applauding, even when she stood momentarily in silence, not uttering a word, or singing a nostalgic note.

Before Judy finished her act, trouble developed. She was singing into a dead mike. The technician had apparently thought the show was over, which it soon was for him. His lack of professionalism and Judy's rage would bring down his final curtain. For the anger burned in Judy's penetrating eyes as she glanced in the direction of the technician who finally got the sound system working again. When Judy performed, you never knew when she was finished. Thundering applause and screams of "more, more" would bring her back for several "extra" numbers. The technician should have known better.

I knew it would be extremely difficult to interview Garland in her dressing room. It was too small and too many visitors would be sure to distract her. Further, she probably wanted to get her breath after singing herself to the point of exhaustion. So, while Judy was singing what she swore to the audience was her "last" number—Ron and I made our exit. Galella had secured a marvelous set of candids, but if I didn't get my interview at El Morocco, there would be no story to accompany Ron's shots. And the *Enquirer*, on this assignment, would not be buying the photos without the interview. Ron was free to go anywhere with his superb shots, and often did. But my only market was the *Enquirer*– and *The Inc.* required undying allegiance and exclusivity. I was not permitted to write for any other publication.

We split the outrageous parking bill and raced over to the "El-Mo." Ron swung two cameras around his neck and a battery pack to power the flash unit hung over one shoulder.

Many elegantly dressed guests were arriving. Bill Doll was stationed at the door while his staff was carefully checking the guests' names off a typewritten list. On the Second Avenue side of the night spot two notorious gate crashers were desperately trying to pry the side door open. A lanky, curly-haired gay guy and his naive mother had slipped by the press agent and his staff during the distraction of four fans trying to push their way into the party.

The next few seconds would be the most critical. Ron and I had come so far, and we didn't know how Doll would react to press inside a private party.

But just to soften and hopefully camouflage our impact, I briskly walked over to Doll, whom I had never met formally, and congratulated the press agent on a fine show, as if he had anything to do with the choreography or staging.

Beaming with pretentious pride, Doll thanked me. Yet he still didn't know who I was. Then I pulled him to the side and shouted to Ron:

"Photographer. Take Mr. Doll's picture," which Ron did, as I passed by the press agent, smiling all the way as I entered, backwards, past the desk and into the party.

Ron, using his native ingenuity, came through the door a few minutes later, shooting Doll and guests as he went. Again, it was like a blazing automatic weapon going off—and it worked. Today, this technique of entry is used to perfection by a lot of party crashers who make a regular diet of celeb events, and who haven't spent a cent for a cup of coffee, or a hot meal, in all their degenerative years. In fact, many of these crashers are on the welfare rolls with phoney press cards and cameras without film. They ruin it for the legitimate guys, like Ron and myself.

Angela Lansbury arrived as two photographers followed the fringes of her sleek, chic gown, their strobes blazing. Angela was everywhere, and so was Earl Wilson. Earl was, and always will be, a gentleman. The congenial columnist never knew my name, my occupation, yet he always extended his hand in friendship, which might explain why he's so loved.

Vaudeville veteran John Bubbles and Judy's daughter Lorna Luft made their entry. John and Lorna had turned in spectacular performances in "Judy Garland, at Home at the Palace."

It was growing late. I seriously wondered whether Judy would come to her own victory party. She was known to be irresponsible, but the thought of disappointing her friends and followers seemed unlikely.

I could hear loud cheering. Judy was walking down the aisle of El-Mo. She had a better chance of surviving outside as she was mobbed, and hugged, and kissed by everyone inside.

It was a good fifteen minutes before a seat directly opposite Miss Garland became vacant. Thank God! This was as good a time as any to give it a go. So, I grabbed Judy's hand and kissed her on the lips, certain I would get away with it.

"Fantastic! Superb!" I shouted.

"But who's this guy? Where do I know him from?" she was probably thinking to herself, as I slipped into the seat. We were alone at the table and I hoped it would remain that way.

"I'm a journalist, and I made this special trip to see you. You are unbelievable," I said. "But may I ask you something? Is it really true that you were friends with J.F.K.?"

"Yes, we were good friends. But, look. I don't wish to do any interviews," she insisted.

"But this isn't an interview, Miss Garland. I'd just like to quickly clear up a few points. You really weren't that tight with the Kennedys?"

"Not *that* tight," she became enraged, but not at me—at the fictitious report I had manufactured right out of the blue. I always had been good as an ad libber. I was sure she would now be on the defensive.

Guests were now passing our table, stopping momentarily, staring at the ninety-five pound, forty-five-year-old entertainer before moving on. Garland was now in a tantrum and could not be tranquilized by anyone, until she had set the record straight, which she did for me.

"When Jack died, part of me died with him. For

he was more than just the President of the United States. He was my best friend. He was my confidant . . . my platonic friend. And most important, he was like a psychiatrist to me," she admitted, which became the lead paragraph of my "exclusive" interview.

Frances Gumm, known to the world as Judy Garland, continued praising J.F.K. as being the type of man others should emulate. Courageous, intelligent, perceptive and intellectual were the adjectives she selected to describe John F. Kennedy, "a man's man," she noted, whom she knew "eight or nine years" before he entered the White House.

In 1960, Judy campaigned vigorously for John Kennedy overseas to land servicemen's votes in what turned out to be an extremely close election.

On August 13, '75, at a gala party honoring the forty-four-year-old, one hundred two-story Empire State Building, in which an actor in costume portrayed King Kong and a model simulated Fay Wray, Lorna Luft told me it was doubtful she would campaign for Teddy Kennedy as President, if the Massachusetts Senator jumped into the race. "My mom did it for John, now you're asking me about Ted. I'm not into politics," she said, skirting the question, and changing the direction of the interview to prolific praise of Jacqueline Onassis: "She's a great, courageous woman and I love her as much as my mother did."

Half-sister Liza Minnelli was also noncommital. At a chic, midnight, black-tie bash given by designer Halston at his virginal white-interior duplex off Park Avenue in the East Sixties on September 15, '75, Liza said it was not uncommon for Lorna to change her mind. "Lorna can tell you one thing today and do a complete about-face tomorrow. But as for me," she said, smiling in adoration at husband Jack Haley, Jr., the

Twentieth-Century-Fox movie mogul, "I'd sit down and have a long talk with Ted, then I'd be able to tell you if I would support him."

But at El Morocco that night in July, '67, Judy confessed that her relationship with J.F.K. had always been "platonic", and "never" sexual. She viewed John F. as a man of great insight—"far ahead of his years," pointing out that if John had not been Chief Executive, he could have become a prominent lawyer, a fabulous financier or, and probably best, a psychiatrist.

Of all the men in her life, Jack was the "only" man Judy could confide in. And when a marriage problem developed, J.F.K. was there to offer his advice—even though she knew the answer to resolving her dilemma. "But I had to hear it from Jack's own mouth to accept it," she revealed. And even when she had problems with her short-lived TV show, President Kennedy was there to lend a compassionate ear. Problems of morality and conscience were also dropped on Jack's tired shoulders. "All I would have to do was pick up the phone in L.A., or wherever I would be at the time, and call the President—person-to-person," she pointed out proudly, consistently getting through to him—at all hours of the day and night. The President, she revealed, *never* avoided her calls by leaving word he was not in, if he was.

Jack's approach to resolving her dilemmas always took the intelligent and "successful" approach, she recalled. And he never minded how often Judy would call, she said. "Jack never regarded me as an interruption," she insisted. "I became a welcome opportunity for him to unwind and relax. This is what the President told me, and I believed him."

Judy noted that while J.F.K. was alive, she was as much a "problem child" to him then as now. Sipping a drink and holding back a flood of tears, she continued: "Now I am forced to make my own decisions—even if they are snap ones, at times. But it's better than none at all—even if you're wrong. I fired the sound man an hour ago, just before I finished my act. In the past, I'd probably have said nothing to him. I would just have suffered in silence. This time I took action. The President, I'm certain, if he was alive, would have been proud of me."

A tear trickled down her cheek as she described having lunch with the Kennedy clan at the White House. "I'm still very close with Jackie. I have a picture of John and Jackie and yours truly," she went on with a catch in her voice. Then a strange-looking man in full dress, glarey-eyed and hostile-looking, probably from one too many, took up residence at our table. Judy had to get up and let the man get in the middle seat, which he requested.

Galella who was photographing our interview, looked up attentively at the mere mention of Jackie's name. In five years, he would be focusing on the former First Lady, not solely through the lens of his trusty camera—but face-to-face in a courtroom. The *New York Times* would call the confrontation, "the best Off-Broadway show in town," the quote Galella would use in his top-selling book, JACQUELINE ('74 release), which immortalized their unusual "love-hate" relationship. Galella would be out some $42,000 in court costs while Jackie's own attorneys would be forced to sue the widow of John F. Kennedy and husband Aristotle for approximately ten times the total expenses incurred by resilient Ron—$400,000, (they settled for $225,000)—just to be paid for "services rendered" and "other related" costs of the courtroom confrontation. It was even reported that Ari came close to divorcing his "extravagant wife" over the Galella money matter.

Against the business acumen of father Joseph

Kennedy, Judy saw herself as a waste. While he was working financial miracles, her fiscal policies were fiascos. "I've always been in hock, or at the pawn shops," she said to me. The money that came fast and furiously for Judy, left even quicker. She admitted that if Ted and Robert were her brothers, growing up might have been more bearable.

During our protracted chat, I had not taken one written note. It was all in my head. Sometimes tape recorders and note pads frighten off a personality. And I was sure that if I had dared, I would have drawn undue attention. After all, this was a "special" party for Judy Garland, not for a camouflaged reporter of the *National Enquirer*. And to complicate matters even further, the people who were sitting alongside our table out of listening range, were trying to distract my distraught subject with hand and finger gestures. That night everyone wanted Judy's time. But if I continued the interview any further, I would have had a difficult time recalling it verbatim.

So I thanked the glittering gem for all her time and dashed for the men's room, and into an open toilet stall. Then I pulled out some paper and started writing down everything she said.

My miniature tape recorder was in repair at the factory in Stamford, Connecticut so I was back to pad and pen. After a few minutes, someone with a brusque voice kicked the side of the stall.

"Hey, buddy," he said rudely. "What are you doing in there—writing your life story?"

He was close. Not mine, but Garland's. To keep him from suddenly barging in on me, I had to use some sound effects. This consisted of pulling off a few yards of noisy toilet paper. And I was sure it sounded just like I was in the final stages of doing what, to most people, came naturally.

When I finished, the guy almost knocked me over getting into the stall, which I kicked, too, and in a disguised voice said: "Hey, buddy. You gonna be in there all day?"

Later, I told Ron about the toilet tale. He found the washroom incident so comical that the *paparazzo* photographer almost ran the car into a parked police emergency truck.

Pope was so elated with the scoop, I was told he did another of his famous dances. "Judy Garland Reveals: I WAS JFK'S PROBLEM CHILD." The headline was mounted along with my other front page breaks on the *Enquirer's* front wall in the editorial office. Ron's photos appeared with the provocative piece, his pictures more lifelike than the El-Mo party, if that was possible. Galella, a photographic wiz, was a graduate of L.A.'s Art Center College and a former *Life* magazine staffer, where he skillfully learned the art of darkroom printing. No wonder his photos seemed to jump out of the page. In May '76, Galella's second book, *Off Guard,* would produce the single greatest photographic achievement in the *paparazzo's* life.

No one knew it then but this was Judy Garland's "last" interview before the grave. Judy, who had started on the stage at age two and one-half, was dead at forty-seven.

Now you would think that any story pertaining to the Kennedy clan automatically made the *Enquirer*. Earlier, on May 24, I had conducted an "exclusive" interview with Senator Edward M. Kennedy, one of Judy's favorites. But the scoop session didn't appear in print immediately.

Teddy had escorted his mother, Rose Kennedy, to an elegant reception for the Duke and Duchess of Windsor at the Bergdorf Goodman department store across from the Plaza Hotel.

I was there with a young lady who drew more attention than the royal couple—from Senator

Ted. Out of the corner of his roving eye, Kennedy kept an obvious focus on my date. Karen Lee was more stunning, more spectacular-looking than the sophisticated models of London and Monte Carlo who often displayed the chic Bergdorf Goodman fashions.

I quickly sensed that alluring Karen was both a delightful decoy and a tantalizing temptress to snare the Massachusetts Senator—for the *National Enquirer*. I had not known in advance that the Kennedys would be attending the New York event.

After briefing Karen of my aspirations, we strode chatting in the direct path of the Senator. And as I looked up, he was still standing there, his gaze transfixed on my lovely date.

"Senator Kennedy. My name is George Bernard, and this is Karen Lee."

"A pleasure to meet you, Karen, and you, George," he said, never taking his eyes off her.

"We're invited to a movie party for your dear friend, Alan King," I said, offering another lure.

"Yes, Alan is a dear friend. But when and where is the party?"

"Michael's Pub. Can you come over and join all of us?" I asked.

"I first must take my mother home. But, after that, I'll join you. And, thank you very much. You will be there, too, Karen?" he inquired.

"Yes, I will," she said seductively.

Half an hour later, despite a dreadful driving rain, the Senator strode briskly through the club doorway and chatted excitedly with the comedian and Mrs. King.

How frustrating. Here I invited my prey to the lion's den and a comedian plays a joke on me by snaring him for himself. Finally, however, I was able to buttonhole the boyish-looking lawmaker in a dark corner of the dining area off the bar.

Kennedy was reluctant to speak at first. "I just said good-bye to Alan, and to remain here talking to you might offend him," he said apologetically. I thought I was the guy who invited him in the first place. The nerve. And of all times for Karen to be freshening up in the powder room. But I pressed a rum-and-coke into Edward's eager hand, and he stayed for another half hour. Actually, rum-and-coke was his favorite drink. So, while I fired away with questions, Ted polished off four stiff ones—more rum than coke.

But the Senator didn't forget. "Where's Karen?" he asked. I looked around. "Why, here she comes now," I said with glee in my voice. Her appearance at that moment surely influenced the politician to remain a while.

Initially, we spoke about his back. Although it was injured in twenty-six places from an earlier plane crash, the Senator looked to be in good health.

"Don't be deceived by appearances," he said. "I'm feeling better and getting around more, but the pains persist. And at the reception for the Duke and Duchess there was so much pushing and shoving, I have a few aches to bring home tonight."

"Speaking of royalty," I said, "there are many in America who feel the Kennedys are trying to establish a presidential dynasty. What are your feelings about this contention?"

"Bobby pokes fun at that illusion every chance he gets. He doesn't agree with it at all. He also denies the rumor that everytime there's a new cabinet position, he has another kid," Ted said, neatly side-stepping the question with a joke.

Ted's piercing eyes got under Karen's skin and she stepped back a few feet as Ron Galella took a photo of the interview. Was this the same man that Judy Garland would wish as a brother?

Kennedy denied that he or brother Bobby were

interested in the '68 Presidential nomination. "It would be a disaster for Bobby to try and knock L.B.J. out of the political box. He wouldn't have a chance. L.B.J. is too strong," said Ted.

Edward admitted that he was torn between devotion to his brother, Robert, and support of the President. "Yes," he said, "it does place me in a disturbing position. I do not take sides, however." Instead, Ted said he buries himself in other projects that divert his mind from the problem. Ted listed these therapeutic preoccupations as immigration reform, refugee matters, the poll tax. But the Senator was remiss in failing to state another involvement—girl-watching, or was it "chasing"? I wasn't sure.

How could Ted have known that his dilemma would be resolved by time and a dreadful destiny? Bobby was L.B.J.'s most severe critic on the President's handling of Vietnam and was making his aggressive bid for the top job in the land when an assassin's fatal bullet buried his dream forever. And how could Bobby have known or Teddy predicted that L.B.J. would not run for re-election?

But fearing that perhaps he was saying too much, Ted Kennedy quickly finished his rum-and-coke, said a hurried goodbye, especially to Karen, and walked back into the rain.

There is a story, however, late vintage, of Ted and a former politician, also good-looking, named John, and their special "friendship" with a modern-day Japanese "Dragon Lady" who is presently a known New York model. The story describes how this Asiatic beauty successfully played these two political birds against the middle. Both Ted and John (the latter's bid for a Presidential nomination flopped miserably), would visit this young lady at her East Side apartment—without either knowing of the other's existence. On one almost embarrassing occasion, each sent a poinsettia plant to this cunning cutie—from the same florist in her neighborhood.

But does a man's fidelity really matter? Elliott Roosevelt, years after F.D.R.'s death, wrote of his father's "extra-marital" affair. And Jack Kennedy, while married and in the White House, was said to have indulged. Yet, both proved to be superior Presidents of the United States—in spite of it.

The *Enquirer* didn't run my '67 Kennedy interview. Said Bill: "You really came up with some interesting stuff. But political stories, even the best, aren't what our readers want to read. Here's a check for $50 anyway."

Oh, how right he was! In the April 21, '75 *Newsweek,* two staff writers noted: "Interestingly, the *Enquirer's* recent interview with Richard Nixon in exile did not sell well—'politics and religion are dead,' says Pope."

Judy Garland was attentive to my queries about the depth of her relationship with J.F.K. (*Ron Galella*)

At the Empire State Building, I interviewed a gorilla called Ping Pong—who was aping his ancestor, King Kong— while Galella readied for photos. Model Ashley Todd pretended to be damsel-in-distress Fay Wray.

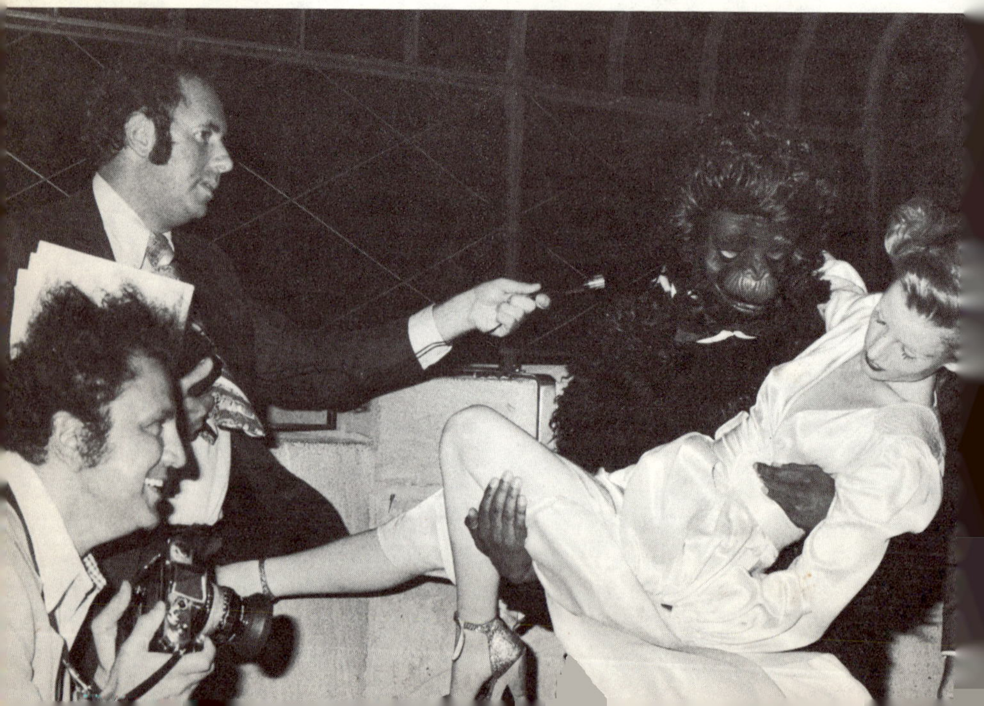

Senator Edward Kennedy told me about a rift with brother Bobby as he downed a few at Michael's Pub. (*Ron
Galella*)

And here's Karen Lee, the eyeful that
Teddy couldn't take his eyes off!

CHAPTER XVII

UFO Goof-O

"DO WE FACE INVASION BY SUPERMEN?"
"DOES THE AIR FORCE TELL US ALL THEY KNOW?"
"ARE THE UFO'S HERE?"
Provocative headlines, aren't they? In the *Enquirer's* June 26, '66 issue, this same article raised the fear of a future flying-saucer war.

On July 23, '67, the *Enquirer's* cover story revealed: "SOLID SAUCER EVIDENCE SHOWS ... SAUCER LANDS IN VIRGINIA ... Police Examine Part of Evidence Left By Saucer ... Leaves Road Aflame ... "

March 31, '68: "RUSSIANS SAY THAT FLYING SAUCERS EXIST ... Top Russian Scientists and Military Leaders Now Believe Flying Saucers May Be Visitors From Other Planets and are Spying on the Earth. Leading Soviet experts say that Unidentified Flying Objects seem to be directed by highly intelligent minds that could be conducting surveillance of the earth in a military fashion."

August 12, '75: "Terrified Pilot Says: Three UFO's Took Control of My Plane ... Baffled Air Traffic Controllers Track Them on Radar Screens."

Unidentified Flying Objects and their haunting hum of dire portent aroused the imaginations of Middle America, as Pope learned quickly. Perhaps Pope's penchant for this perplexing phenomena was rooted in the widespread hysteria of '38's "fictionalized" account by Orson Welles of a Martian invasion. For although listeners were advised before each segment of the drama that they were listening to only a dramatization—not the real thing—the network was jammed with calls of inquiry, threats and general hysteria. In fact, many residents of New Jersey where the Martians were supposedly landing, actually began to evacuate the state.

To escape the perils of boredom, people become masochistic. They crave and cling to fears, especially of the unknown. Yet these same fears offer hope. So contends Jack J. Leedy, a prominent New York City psychiatrist who feels that life on other planets, free of wars and pestilence, is the hopeful dream Americans want to read and fantasize.

With this premise in mind, I approached Truman Capote on October 25, '67. The occasion was an opulent dinner-dance party at the Americana Hotel honoring the premiere of the movie "Camelot." Richard Harris, who portrayed King Arthur in the film was there, and so were Pat Kennedy, model Penelope Tree and Faye Dunaway.

Truman was twitching his left ear and peering affectionately at me through his stylish sun glasses. I flattered him for fifteen minutes by discussing his best-seller *In Cold Blood*. Then, gradually, I shifted the issue from death on earth to life on other planets.

The *Enquirer* had tipped me off that he was deeply interested in UFO sightings and might be writing a book on the subject, which if true, would have made a blockbuster article.

But as soon as I mentioned the word "UFO" he turned into a raving, rancorous, rambunctious individual. I was sure that this Martian-mannered man was going to blast me in the face with a spray of hot coffee or slap me with his flying fingers that looked like little tentacles.

"That's what you were after all the time—wasn't it?" he screamed. The perceptive peanut continued his tirade: "You didn't want to hear about my book at all, did you? Well, you aren't the first who's bothered me about the subject. And, you want to know something, I'm *not* going to tell you either. Now, please, please leave this table, immediately!"

Even Ron was frightened. I certainly had outstayed my welcome. Further, the press agent for the party was approaching and it was time to depart—"immediately"—as troubled Truman had so entreated.

Galella, who was enamored with Britt Eklund, did not wish to leave the festivities. So I waited in the lobby for him, far away from the maddening Capote. But how embarrasing! That's what an *Enquirer* reporter must expose himself to, day in and day out. And anyone who says otherwise is a liar.

Could Capote have come to earth in a capsule from outer space? Though he was listed as being born in New Orleans in September '24, I considered the possibility that the five-foot-three falsetto-voiced darling of the "jet set" was really a rockets' expert in a daffy disguise from another world. Why would he get so upset at the mere mention of a UFO? Unless, of course, he didn't wish to draw attention to the forbidden subject, or himself in that celestial connection.

Bill contended that people of prominence, as Capote in publishing and U Thant in the pursuit of world peace, might be privy through their powerful posts of influence—to classified UFO information.

I was instructed to get to U Thant. Then, I was to persuade the U.N. official to elaborate on the following angle, providing, of course, he accepted this premise: ONLY THE FEAR OF ATTACK FROM OUTER SPACE WILL SAVE THE WORLD.

Bill wanted U Thant to say that the U.N. was ineffective in keeping the three great powers,

Russia, China and the U.S., from averting eventual war. And that only through the real threat of invasion from the skies would the world bury their differences and unite as one to fight their attackers. Bill had read, he thought it had been in the *New York Post,* that U Thant believed in the presence of UFO's, which I was supposed to confirm and develop. But coming up with an angle is one thing. Getting U Thant to agree to such a contrived interview was another, and a difficult assignment.

After getting absolutely nowhere through U Thant's secretary—"He's all tied up for a month and a half, sorry," she said—I decided to make my own appointment unscheduled and unannounced.

It was a few minutes past 6:00 p.m. I quickly flashed my New York City press card and passed the guard at the U.N. gate. Fortunately, the guard failed to look at my special admittance pass, which I didn't have. I entered the building and made my way to a black-tie reception the Secretary General was holding for several foreign ambassadors.

From behind a pillar I observed U Thant talking with the Ambassador from Albania. I also noted several plain-clothesmen who all had the same "detectable" look about them. Who did they think they were fooling? Probably, they would have been more effective in uniform, for they didn't fool me—and I felt I wasn't putting anything over on them either.

When the Albanian Ambassador turned his head to greet another dignitary, I moved in quickly. The U.N. undercover boys were now on my tail, but stopped short when I extended my hand in friendship to U Thant. From all appearances, we could have been best friends or working together for world peace.

"You're looking extremely well," I said to U

Thant.

"Yes, thank you," he looked puzzled, still smiling. "But where do I know you from? Your face looks familiar, and I must apologize for not remembering," he said humbly.

"I'm a foreign correspondent," I said, showing the U.N. leader my press credential. "I'd like to know your thoughts on UFO's. Do you think that an attack from outer space would help unite the world?" I asked, as the Albanian Ambassador now returned his attention to the Secretary General.

U Thant was not smiling anymore. "This is no place to ask me a thing like this," he said, becoming flustered.

"Can I make an appointment with you at your office for tomorrow to discuss the matter?" I said, trying to salvage the situation.

"No, no," he cried. "Whatever my views are shouldn't reflect any position of the United Nations. Please, this is no place to discuss the matter."

Reading wrong-doing, two of the U.N.'s guards began to move in on me. I shook U Thant's hand vigorously, thanking him for his time, which he didn't give me.

No one put a hand on me as I went through the front exit. But as I looked back, there were five of the super sleuths standing and staring at me, probably in disbelief. They had never met the likes of George Bernard.

I was baffled by the reluctance of people to discuss flying saucers, men from distant planets and weird worlds beyond our own solar system. But Bill didn't take me off the inter-planetary beat.

A man from Syracuse, New York was one of a thousand-and-one calls that would flood the *Enquirer* switchboard each month. At least, that's what their blond-haired, blue-eyed operator told me.

Oscar James told Bill he had actually seen five green-and-orange colored creatures emerge from a saucer-shaped space craft that landed—in his own backyard. They were three feet tall and had four arms with seven fingers on each hand.

I actually got to speak to James, or whatever his real name was, when he called the paper back at a prescribed time.

"Yes, Mr. Bernard. They came and left. But I get the feeling they'll be back soon," he said excitedly. "One of the creatures even waved to me. But I want you to come up here and do a story on my experience," he said.

I looked in the Syracuse phone directory. There was no Oscar James listed. And people in the vicinity of where he had said the James family had a seven-room private house, never heard of the man or experienced seeing either the questionable space ship land or take off.

So, I recorded the story as another UFO—Unidentified Freaky Oddball.

I was particularly intrigued reading the *Enquirer's* May 24, '70, page nine headline: "U. of California Professor Builds Flying Saucers That Really Fly ... And Claims Every Family Will Own One in the Future."

The story began: "Paul Moller believes in flying saucers. He should—he's building his third one." The article by Yvonne Dunleavy went on to report that Professor Moller contended that his saucer would solve the traffic problem in America. It could be parked in the garage and could take off and land in a driveway or the parking lot of an office.

Anyone could learn to fly the saucer and it would cost less to operate than a six-cylinder car. Further, the purchase price would be around $4,000. It could fly a mile high and at a speed of 165 mph. In '67 he gave the invention its first test flight.

After putting down the article I wondered if
any of the reported UFO sightings could at all be
attributed to Moller's machine.

In '67, there seemed to be an inordinate
number of UFO sightings. The three most prominent, those that received the greatest press attention, were: January, Mt. Clemens, Michigan;
June, Alberton, South Australia; October,
Trinidad Island.

Then in '74, Generoso Pope included these unexplained sightings in a giant-sized advertisement that appeared in the *New York Times*.

The illustrious publisher reached further for
media acceptance by running the same advertisement in the trade magazines, *Advertising
Age, S.A.M.* and *Advertising News of New York*.

The ad featured photos of twelve unexplained
sightings, beginning with what appeared to
be a flying saucer approaching a farm in
McMinnville, Oregon, on May 11, '50. The headline read: "WE'RE OFFERING OUR READERS
$50,000 TO PROVE THESE AREN'T FRIS-
BEES."

The advertisement asked the reader if he or
she would be willing to grab a movie camera and
walk up to some gleaming, humming object that
just landed in their backyard.

For $50,000?

"Well, here at the *National Enquirer* we've established a continuing offer—$50,000 to the first
person who can prove to the satisfaction of our
panel of experts that a UFO comes from outer
space and is not a natural phenomenon."

The ad stated that the *Enquirer* also offered
smaller rewards for "less-than-total" proof. For
example, the enticing copy stated, "On October
18, '73, an Army helicopter was flying south of
Cleveland at 1500 feet when suddenly a sixty-foot
cigar-shaped metallic-gray UFO hovered over

the chopper. The four-man Army crew put their craft into a dive but, instead of descending, they soared (were pulled?) up 3800 feet in seconds—it would normally take over a minute to make that climb. The UFO disappeared.

"After study, the U.S. Army agreed to let the *Enquirer* make a $5000 award to the crew. Frankly," the ad continued, reaching the point of delivering a sales message, "we find these stories fascinating—and hard to ignore. So do our readers. And it's this sort of unique, exciting editorial that gets the main credit for our whopping 31.1% jump in circulation over the past year."

Using the alias of Bill Carlin, I phoned Bert Halperin, Director of Advertising for the *Enquirer* at their sales office on East 42nd Street in New York.

"No, Mr. Carlin. No one has yet claimed the $50,000. But, Mr. Pope is hoping," he said to me on July 28, '75.

I'm sure Mr. Pope is praying that someone does relieve him of the award money. For what's a mere $50,000 for a story worth $5 million anyway?

Remember the popular quiz shows of TV's early years? The sponsors were crossing their fingers, and saying their prayers that the cocky contestants would break their banks, a sure-paying method to increase viewing audience and boost the ratings. On other occasions, the advertisers were reported to have even "prompted" the contestants to insure their success.

So don't think that Pope wouldn't like to give that dough away. And, who knows, someday soon, maybe a week, month or year from now, a little old lady in Boulder, Colorado or a high school dropout in Peoria, Illinois may claim the fifty big ones. And then the *Enquirer*, and the world, will know substantially more about the worlds beyond our own . . . hopefully.

His tresses thinning, tiny Truman Capote peered at me affectionately through dark shades. Then I asked him about UFO's—and the little man reacted like someone not from this world. (*Ron Galella*)

CHAPTER XVIII

The Shrinks

What do you really know about psychiatrists, psychologists and all the other therapists, otherwise known as "shrinks?"

For instance, were you aware that in January '68, the month a comprehensive article appeared in the *Enquirer* on the subject, *The Inc.'s* readers learned that psychiatrists' suicide rate was four times that of the average person? Oddly enough, psychiatrists, whose responsibility it is to prevent suicide among others couldn't do it for themselves. They were committing suicide at a far greater pace than any other group in America.

The astounding article revealed that their suicide rate was seventy per 100,000 and experts believed that was a conservative figure. Further, a third of those suicide cases were doctors under forty years of age.

On July 23, '67, the *Enquirer* printed this headline: "PSYCHIATRIST JUDGED INSANE AFTER 50G'S IN STOLEN GOODS ARE FOUND IN HIS HOME." The article concerned a resident psychiatrist at Yale-New Haven Hospital who, until his apprehension by authorities, had the police totally baffled for two years. This kleptomaniac would steal almost everything that wasn't nailed down—tables, chairs, desks, typewriters, cameras, nuts and bolts.

If you still haven't formed a definitive opinion, consider an *Enquirer* interview I conducted in the spring of '68: "TOO MANY PSYCHIATRISTS ARE MONEY-HUNGRY DOCTORS WHO VERY OFTEN DO MORE HARM THAN GOOD—These charges come not from disgruntled patients, but from a prominent psychiatrist."

Were you aware that many psychiatrists prefer administering electric shocks instead of employing chemotherapy? Reason: the former is considerably more profitable, financially, than the latter. And analysts often transfer their own negative habits to their patients: smoking cigarettes and cigars, taking calls during sessions with patients, and remaining on the phone for long periods of time. A considerable number of psychiatrists will not transfer their patients to another doctor who might otherwise provide better treatment. Reason: as before, greed. Concern for the pocket before the patient!

This particular psychiatrist, a crusader for reform in the medical profession, never dreamed that a simple lunch we had together could have brought on acute indigestion three weeks later. For when the article broke in the paper, the shrink's wife, fearing possible repercussion from the American Psychiatric Association, collapsed in her kitchen. The maid had picked up that particular *Enquirer* from the local newsstand, not knowing her employer was plastered within. And when she laid it down on the kitchen table to conduct her household chores, the doctor's wife started reading it. In a few moments, the maid heard a loud thud. It took fifteen minutes to revive the poor woman who was still sobbing and ranting when the psychiatrist came home for dinner. And the reception he received left him black and blue for weeks. It was such a good story, and the doctor was so intelligent, I had to give it to *The Inc*. I simply had to.

It is said that many therapists enter their profession because of a psychological flaw that prevents them from being normal. Thus, they spend a miserable existence trying to find themselves through their patients.

During one routine interview with a female

analyst discussing the motivations of crime, I
observed her preference for young girls. In her
late fifties, she smoked a cigar, had a razor-cut
hairdo. Only photos of young, innocent-looking
girls were displayed on her desk, table and three
walls of that room and while I was leaving, I
couldn't help but observe a nude girl standing
behind a partially-opened door that could have
been a bedroom. The shrink also observed the
door ajar, but said and did nothing, not wishing
to draw further attention to the embarrassing
tell-tale.

While waiting for the elevator, I wasn't quite
sure if I had been witness to an illusion or to the
very private life of a sick shrink. Then again;
what was so sick about having a naked girl in
waiting?

Then the sound of the elevator's motor was
punctuated by the shrill sounds of screaming
from the psychiatrist's pad. I was certainly curious, but definitely not a voyeur. And anyway, I
had to get back and transcribe the interview. I
imagined the therapist to be torturing her victim's flesh with the smoldering tip of a bull whip.
But indeed if that was happening, it was their
affair. Different strokes for different folks, but I
really never knew for sure who was doing the
stroking. I assumed the young girl to be the
strokee, but who could be sure?

On another occasion, a hulking, black-bearded
psychiatrist propositioned me to go to bed with
him. And only after I threatened to walk out of
his office and leave the interview behind, did he
apologize for his perversions in public.

And while we're on sissy-shrinks, another psychiatrist related to me the case history of a
homosexual patient who wasn't responding to
treatment. So the concerned analyst referred the
young man to a colleague, whom he had the
greatest respect for and felt would be successful

at implementing an effective therapeutic program. Then, about a month later, the patient called his former therapist to report how pleased he was with his new psychiatrist—whom he was now sleeping with!

We are also aware of some salty malpractice suits registered against psychiatrists by their female patients. Recently, a young woman won a sizeable six-figure settlement against a New York City psychiatrist, in which she alleged the analyst induced her to join him in sexual intercourse—a form of therapy she considered later to be coercive and improper. The judge concurred, initially awarding the plaintive $350,000, which on appeal was reduced to $150,000—and finally $25,000. The noted psychiatrist, whose analytical comments appeared often in the *Enquirer,* and regularly in such magazines as *Cosmopolitan,* among others, is still practicing his profession, sex excluded. "Her case was all based on lies," the shrink told me over the phone on July 29, '75. "And I'm going to fight it to the bitter end," he added. I wish him luck!

Or how about the case of a Park Avenue plastic surgeon who, because of marital difficulties, sent his wife to see a psychiatrist. After six months, the shrink presented the surgeon with an enormous bill, and the wife furnished her husband with divorce papers—she was marrying the marriage counselor. I know the bizarre facts of this all too well. For while I was an *Enquirer* reporter, I sent a girl friend for a consultation with the doctor about her crooked nose. After she woke up in the recovery room, saw the doctor's big blue eyes and remembered his great green money clip, it wasn't long before the two went before the justice of the peace.

It was this same surgeon who would prepare a series of sketches, before and after, of how Lady Bird Johnson would look if she had her entire face reconstructed. The *Enquirer* angle was: LADY BIRD JOHNSON, WHO WANTS TO BEAUTIFY AMERICA, IS UGLY ... But Here's How She Would Look After Surgery." The doctor got cold feet and demanded I return his property, which I did.

With all their flagrant frailties, promiscuities and perversions, Pope was still proud of his stable of shrinks. While he would punish them publicly by publishing their incongruities, he would invariably allow these analysts to play God to his readers. At other times, if the shrinks weren't cast as Messiahs, they were billed as prophets of great psychiatric advances.

And so on August 4, '67, I was assigned to interview a shrink who claimed a cure for the mentally sick—poetry. Dr. Jack J. Leedy maintained an office on East 86th Street and after ten minutes I wasn't sure whether I was in a Turkish bath or the boiler room of the building. A lone fan in the corner tried to do the job the air-conditioning system couldn't accomplish. There was none.

Leedy, who belonged to the American Medical Association, the American Psychiatric Association and had more medical affiliations than I believed existed, told me that "forty-five to fifty" percent of his private patients had been discharged after his treatment of poetry.

The people that Leedy claimed to be helping through "poetry" included hundreds of drug addicts, alcoholics, homosexuals, transvestites and many others.

As Leedy told of his success with "poetry therapy," I turned from skeptic to believer. For as Leedy explained, "P.T." was devised to mirror a patient's own state of mind. The patient was then able to recognize his problems and become inspired to overcome and conquer them.

The associate attending psychiatrist at Brooklyn's Cumberland Medical Center had been encouraging his patients for more than eight years to read, memorize and listen to poems as part of their therapy.

My second visit, included in the same article with Leedy, was at Project Teen Aid, a community action program in Brooklyn for pregnant, unwed teenage girls. Leedy was a special consultant to the program.

Elnora Dumas, a director of the program, told me that the unwed mother, who was forced to drop out of school, best expressed herself through poetry. "Thus," she said, "we're able to get to the core of the problem—why she'd get pregnant." Leedy said he believed poetry to be far more than just a form of entertainment: "I believe it is meant to inspire and elevate the human spirit as well. In doing so, it can salvage human lives that might be wasted in misery."

I was so pleased with the article and my photographs, I insisted the *Enquirer* run my byline, George Bernard—which they did.

I was gratified again when Leedy turned out two books on his therapeutic tool: *Poetry Therapy* and *Poetry the Healer*. Further elation came to me after Leedy reported that because of my convincing November 26, '67 *Enquirer* story, a veteran's hospital in Arizona was devoting a special wing of their medical complex to the treatment of war-disturbed American G.I.'s returning from Vietnam—with "poetry therapy."

Leedy and his work, virtually unknown to the media before my *Enquirer* break, was now receiving extensive editorial consideration in *Life* magazine, the *New York Times,* the *New York Daily News,* the *Wall Street Journal,* and other leading newspapers and magazines.

Another psychiatrist I would interview for T.A.F. was an inventor, of sorts. Dr. Robert Ravich insisted on knowing where my article would appear. In that sense, he was no different than Leedy, who for a week would call and question: " *Life, Look,* the *New York Times?*" "You never know, Jack," I would say. In the end, from one *Enquirer* scoop, he made them all—and more. So I really did not mislead dear Jack. But even after the story appeared in the *Enquirer,* Leedy would accept the initial disappointment philosophically, like the poet that he is: "Well, it is a newspaper ... better than the 'Gezundheit Gazette.'"

But Leedy was short-sighted. The *Enquirer* was more than a newspaper. It was an institution that was gradually getting away from stories of the sinister and the sensational. Gradually, *The Inc.* was gaining respectability, on its way to becoming a "family" consumer paper. According to figures released by the Audit Bureau of Circulations as of June 30, '67, the *Enquirer* was reaching an average weekly circulation of 935,456. Eight years and one month later in April '75, Jackie at the funeral of Ari, as featured in the *Enquirer,* would boost that one edition to an audience of 4.8 million.

Again, as with all the others, I had to use my powers of persuasion to get the interview with Dr. Ravich. The September 3, '67 *Enquirer* back-page headline would read: PSYCHIATRIST'S TOY TRAINS PUT ROCKY MARRIAGES BACK ON TRACK."

Can you believe that playing with model electric trains was serious business for the good doctor? For a fee of $30 each session, now considerably higher, Dr. Ravich would sit couples on either side of a table. Then they each would send their own little toy engine from one end of the track to the other. A wife who wouldn't give her husband the right of way might be revealing her stubbornness. Or a husband who dropped a little gate that forced his wife's engine to take an alternate

route, might be indicating his hostility towards
her.

The Manhattan psychiatrist told me that "life
is a game and all games have rules. By applying
the rules to the world of electric trains, I found I
could trace the reasons behind marital upsets."
Ravich revealed that just from playing with his
toy trains, he was able to discover whether a wife
who claimed that she wanted her husband to
succeed was secretly yearning for him to fall on
his face—or if a husband was too domineering—
or if each harbored destructive hostilities towards the other.

I even permitted my picture to appear in the
Enquirer article playing Ravich's game. The
caption read: "TRAIN TEST: In photo top of
page, wife (played by professional model) pre-
pares to send her little toy engine along the
tracks during psychiatrist's test, while husband,
posed by *Enquirer* reporter George Bernard,
starts his train." The day the story broke, I called
Ravich to get his reactions. He had already seen
the article: "Mr. Bernard, your story is 100% accurate, and the photos tell the story. But, why
the *Enquirer?*" He hung the phone up, and probably rode one of his trains into a wall.

My *Enquirer* "exclusive" was picked up by the
prestigious German magazine, *Stern*. It also was
lifted by *Look* and other publications. So, why so
angry, Dr. Ravich? Didn't you know that a story,
like anything else has to start somewhere? And,
in one way or the other, everyone copies and tries
to emulate the *Enquirer*.

Then the *Enquirer* wanted to know why American women spend billions of dollars a year on
beauty aids. Dr. Joseph Haber, Chief of Child
Psychiatry at Coney Island Hospital in Brooklyn, became my candidate. It would have been
better to find an analyst more closely involved
with the beauty aid industry. The fact that Dr.

Haber's specialty was children's abnormal behavior, didn't concern the *Enquirer*. As Bill would say: "If the man's a psychiatrist, he is a superman, as far as Pope is concerned. Use him!"

Said Haber, in part, on the American woman: "She's a jealous, neurotic female who changes her husband or boyfriend as often as she changes her wig or hairdo . . . She cannot stand stability. She is always craving a change. That's why the beauty parlors succeed—they offer constant change with new hairstyle after new hairstyle."

Shrinks are entertainers, at least the ones I came in contact with for the *Enquirer*. And after they saw themselves in the *Enquirer* and were still jolly, I had them in the palm of my hand for untold future stories. Yet, I never paid an analyst for his time. As extreme egoists, seeing their name in print was consideration enough for their scholarly time and effort.

"Spell my name correctly and mention my latest book," they would ask of me in return.

Did you even wonder why cancer of the cervix and the rectum go undetected—until it's too late to do anything about it? The *Enquirer* did more than wonder. They assigned me to find out. Pope was convinced that the blame rested with general practitioners, the family doctors, who for one reason or another, were negligent. So, the instructions were to pit doctor against doctor, and not give the GP's a chance to defend themselves from the scathing shrinks.

Before I could come up with three psychiatrists willing to be interviewed on the controversial issue, I had been rejected by nineteen. "I'll not stick my neck out, even though I believe what you're saying is true," said one. "That's hogwash," offered another.

The *Enquirer* story had a lengthy headline, possibly the longest in the paper's history: "Many doctors fail to detect cancer because they are too timid to examine nude patients. Statistics show that one woman in every 20 in the U.S. eventually will develop breast cancer—yet a panel of leading psychiatrists said many family doctors are too bashful to find out whether patients have early symptoms."

The "panel" was in the imagination of the *Enquirer* rewrite man. For there never was any panel, just three out of twenty-two who were willing to agree with the Pope premise. If I wanted to prove that "Honest Abe Lincoln Really Had the Look of A Criminal, Says a Panel of Three Leading Psychiatrists," all I would have to do is go down the line. After speaking to maybe seventy-five shrinks, I'd have my panel.

Since I've already intrigued you with the subject, let me not leave you hanging with the desire to know more. About doctors' negligence, Dr. Margaretta Bowers told me that "many are afraid". Dr. Giovanni Sacco said that "many are bashful," while Gothard C. Booth's indictment of general practitioners was that "sometimes they are too squeamish." And it was even said by the threesome that GP's are afraid to look at a nude woman during a routine examination because they associate an undraped female with the cadaver they cut up in med school. Many are squeamish about touching sexual areas because of childhood teachings and taboos. They fear they just might get sexually excited if they were to examine a nude woman and are terrified that a patient might scream or accuse them of taking liberties.

Don't laugh. There is a high degree of validity to what the shrinks say.

Psychiatrists would also be called on to play fortune-tellers. In the absence of "the real thing," a shrink would become a salient substitute, and possibly more effective. You could get an analyst to say almost anything about everything. A shrink could be operated like a marionette with little, if any, difficulty.

When the sudden end of the May-December marriage of Frank Sinatra and Mia Farrow occurred, the *Enquirer* wanted to know why.

Most assuredly, it would have been sure suicide to approach Frank directly on why he conquered in love and failed in marriage. And, it was a sure bet that Mia Farrow wasn't going to say a word on the subject.

The morning the *Enquirer* tried to reach me, I had overslept. My alarm failed to go off, and my phone receiver was accidentally kicked off the hook the night before. When I checked in with Jerry at the paper, he was furious.

"Where the fuck you been, Goldmine?" he screamed. "We've been trying to reach you all morning, and I had to give a plum away to someone else."

I knew he had probably called the verifying operator, so I couldn't say that I was busy taking a story down over the phone. So I told him the accidental truth and pleaded to get the story that had already been assigned.

"Well, all right. But the other guy's got at least three hours on you. The first one to bring in a 'signed' complete story from a psychiatrist-marriage counselor on why Sinatra and Farrow busted up, gets $1,000 from Pope . . . no page position, just cash. Be gone with you now. And, one other thing . . . "

"Yes?" I said.

"Good luck. You'll need it."

How about, "Frank Sinatra never really had time to study the inner needs and moods of his woman—he was too busy having fun with his friends"? Or, how about, "Mia was probably not a real love object to him. She was something he needed to build his ego"? Boy, this was easy, I thought, and in less than twenty minutes, I had completed the piece.

"Hello, Sam. George Bernard . . . Yes, Sam. I'm fine. Listen," I said excitedly over the phone. "I can get you a great plug for A.F.T.L.I.," I went on, which means Association For Feeling The Truth and Living It, Dr. Sam Greenberg's self-help group that he founded and would die for.

"Don't move from your office, I'm hopping a cab to Brooklyn right this minute. I want you to read something."

In a half-hour I was dashing out of a Checker cab and through Sam's front door.

"Sign here!" I said. The cab driver was keeping the engine and meter running.

Sam read my article quickly, came to the part about A.F.T.L.I.—liked what he saw, and signed.

And thirty-five minutes later, I was dropping the story onto Jerry's desk—less than two hours after I had first received the assignment.

Isn't it insanity to believe that shrinks should have the answers to the problems of "others"— even those they've never met face-to-face? I knew that eventually their speculations would backfire.

On March 3, '68, my *Enquirer* interview with psychiatrist Joseph Haber revealed: "WHY JACKIE WILL NEVER MARRY AGAIN." Not too long after the article appeared, in October '68, on the private Greek island of Skorpios, Jacqueline Kennedy became the wife of Aristotle Socrates Onassis.

In the March 31, '68 *Enquirer,* I interviewed a psychologist and a psychiatrist. The centerfold spread stated: "WHY BOBBY KENNEDY WEARS HIS HAIR LONG." Leedy speculated that Bobby still wanted to hold onto his youth. Further, that Bobby felt that the country belonged to the young, and if he was to become a presidential candidate, he wanted that audience to feel he was a part of them. Leedy even added that Bobby's long hair was a possible rebellion against the memory of his late brother, J.F.K., the authority figure.

Leedy was pleased with the article, especially when the *Enquirer* didn't fail to mention that he was director of the Manhattan "Poetry Therapy Center."

Psychologist Harold Greenwald, a noted author, suggested that Bobby might have equated long hair with being a "swinger." He could consider himself an honorary member of the jet set. But Greenwald was quick to point out that Robert's rebellious look could also turn off would-be supporters. The noted psychologist pointed out that long hair could alienate those who are bald or balding. "It's psychologically as bad as flaunting money before a poor man," he said.

Just as Lon Chaney turned into the wolf man before your movie-going eyes, Bobby's long hair was shown as it progressed from a crew-cut in '60 to hippie-length proportions in '67. But did you ever consider that maybe the pictures selected were taken at various stages between haircuts?

After that, I participated in a giant article on why Dr. Spock openly defied the U.S. government. Again, I called upon my stable of shrinks, and they didn't let me down. For the December 10, '67 *Enquirer,* I interviewed Leedy to find out why Lynda Bird Johnson had made a mad dash to the altar. No sense thinking too long about why. Just use your imagination and you'll probably come up with the actual psychiatric speculation as it appeared.

Then on July 21, '68, the *Enquirer* ran this bit of hypocrisy: "4-Month *Enquirer* Study Reveals —ALMOST EVERYONE IN AMERICA IS UN- HAPPY, FOR THE FIRST TIME IN OUR HISTORY."

If you really think about it, what are they say-

ng? Granted, times always tend to appear worse
than they actually are, and every generation of
American feels he's living through a depression.
But "everyone" at one point in the day is "unhappy." Also, at one time during the day,
"everyone" wipes his ass with toilet paper, or a
reasonable facsimile. So, why not that headline
as an attention-grabber?

There's a saying: "Don't carry good things too
far—you'll ruin them!" And that's exactly what
Pope did with the shrinks, other doctors,
educators and scientists he had featured. He felt
compelled, as if by the will of God, to tell the
nation's business-brains and intellectuals who
read the *New York Times* that even the shrinks
read and love his paper. So why not collect a
couple dozen analysts and take out full-page ads
somewhere classy like in the *Times* and the *Wall
Street Journal?* That's exactly what Pope did on
April 18, '74.

"WHAT LEADING SCIENTISTS, DOCTORS,
PSYCHIATRISTS AND EDUCATORS LIKE
ABOUT THE NATIONAL ENQUIRER." Below
the startling headline ran twenty-six testimonials that were culled from the '73 *Enquirer*. And
beneath them was a sales reminder that the *Enquirer* is "NOW AMERICA'S #2 NEWSWEEKLY
FOR THE ENTIRE FAMILY. CIRCULATION
3.9 MILLION. WE HAVE GOOD NEWS FOR
YOU."

But, two months later, on June 13, the *National
Enquirer* purchased identical ads in the *Times* and
Journal, but this time the news they were giving
was bad. Under the heading, "AN APOLOGY,"
the ad stated:

"The *National Enquirer* wishes to advise the
readers of this newspaper that the use of the
names, attributed quotes and, in some cases,
photographs of a group of leading scientists, doctors, psychiatrists and educators in a full-page

advertisement which appeared in the *New York Times* on April 18, 1974 was without their prior knowledge or consent.

"This statement is being published at the request of Dr. Rene Jules Dubos, Dr. E. J. Lieberman, Dr. Natalie Shainess and Dr. Edmund Sonnenblick, who have notified the *National Enquirer* that if they had been consulted in advance, they would never have consented to such use, both on ethical and other grounds."

The Inc. quoted Dr. Dubos in the original ad as saying he was "delighted to see the *Enquirer's* circulation recently top three million. It just shows that the American people really appreciate a good product." Now here's the kicker: Dr. Dubos, a Pulitzer Prize-winning author and professor emeritus at Rockefeller University was not even aware of the ad, until it was brought to his attention. Further, the eminent scholar had *never* had a copy of the *Enquirer* in his hands. And his only connection with *The Inc.* came during a telephone interview with an *Enquirer* free lancer, in which the doctor stated firmly that he never made the remarks attributed to him in the ad.

Dr. Lieberman, a Washington psychiatrist who was also shown in the ad reading a copy of the *National Enquirer*, revealed that he was interviewed by a husband and wife team from *The Inc.* who requested he pose for the shot, saying: "Our readers like to see people that we interview reading the *Enquirer*."

Needless to say, Drs. Lieberman, Sonnenblick, Shainess and Dubos were furious. It seemed inconsistent with Pope's policies that the proud publisher would have proceeded to feature these testimonials if he knew the circumstances by which they were allegedly and questionably obtained.

Regardless of what you may say about Gene

Pope, the man is not a phoney. And while he does peddle strange-styled stories, he, personally, attempts to convey truth. Good for you, Gene!

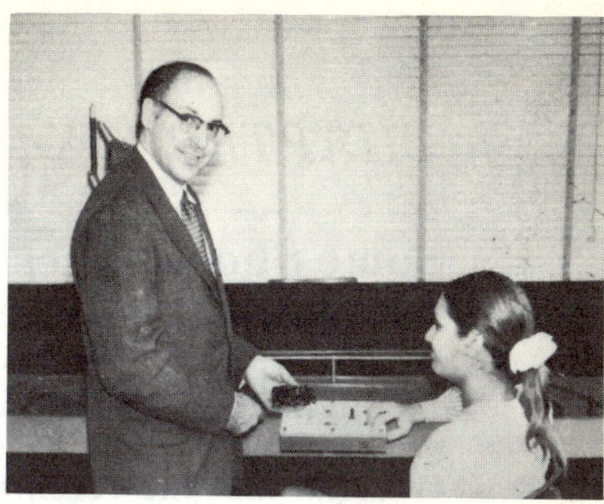

Doctor saves marriages with electric trains! Here I am (on the left) sampling his technique, and Dr. Ravich is shown above.

I sat in on a "poetry therapy" session with an unwed pregnant teenager, part of a government-sponsored project administered by Dr. Jack J. Leedy.

CHAPTER XIX

Some Short Takes About Life...
And A Most Tragic Death

By highlighting just one dominant difference, ordinary people can become distinguishably intriguing and interesting. But more often than not, it is an unusual set of circumstances that creates that difference. The common cop who walks his beat, day in and day out, leads a most uneventful life. That is, until by chance a hold-up occurs and he heroically shoots it out with the perpetrators.

Thus, this chapter will be a potpourri of such actual case histories where average people were nobodys, until Providence decided to make them somebodys.

In June '66, nobody outside of the residents in Miami Beach ever heard of seventy-nine-year-old Sophie Katz. And many who eventually did, especially those not collecting social security checks, couldn't have cared less. Miami Beach is a heartless haven for the naive elderly who flock to the southern resort spot as if it was indeed "the Promised Land" — while in reality it's a menacing mecca for the mended masses. Heartlessly, the precious savings of the geriatric sick are methodically taken from them, all legally and properly. And when the elderly become critically ill, for many of them forget the limitations of age and exceed their own limits, the inept specialists fail conveniently to display their "best" medical efforts to save them.

I know all too tragically well. In march '75, my dad died, neglected in one of their fine "showcase" hospitals. He was processed for death. "If your dad doesn't show any great improvement at the end of this week," the cold, calculating internist said to me, "I'm afraid I'll have to throw him in a nursing home. Can't keep these beds tied up for too long. If I don't make room, quickly, the hospital won't let my other patients be admitted here. You know. I'm sure you understand." I kept a written record of all that transpired there and reported the doctor to the hospital's chief administrator, who wasn't any better. He apologized and upon learning I was a reporter, totally ignored my father's critical condition and began promoting the accomplishments of the hospital. "This is the finest, most advanced hospital in the United States," he said proudly, making sure I would take every quote down, which I did, hoping it would insure preferential treatment for my dad. "We even manufacture nuclear materials here, in our basement," he added. "But we have to pay for our nursing and educational expenses," he began to cry on my shoulder, hoping my written words would bring a flood of public support to change his financial dilemma.

Most of the doctors who staffed this hospital maintained private practices along Alton Road, minutes away. And even further down Alton was the thriving funeral parlor business that offered the bereaved a chance to get out of the eighty-eight degree heat into the bone-chilling thirty-nine degrees of their morbid sanctuary. Like selecting a car from a showroom, an asexual clerk offered a complete selection of caskets — "the most modern," he said. He was even kind enough to fly my father to New York for burial, but not before he received a check from me for $2,441.00 that same night, only four hours after I affixed my signature to his lengthy contract. The memorial chapel, intentionally or otherwise, neglected to honor certain requested and prescribed procedures that were in strict accordance with our religion.

The tragedy of thousands who come to Miami Beach looms as America's "next" major scandal. It is far more heinous and corrupt than the exposé of New York's barbaric nursing homes. Like ducks flying South for the winter, older people arrive at this favorite spot under the sun to rest, rejuvenate and escape the wrath of northern winters, only to find their dream end unnecessarily — in death!

I had intended to visit the managing editor of the *Miami Herald,* a forthright newspaper known to champion justice and initiate reform. While my dad was alive, I feared repercussions might be exacted against him. It's so simple to "accidentally" detach a vital oxygen tube or turn it off entirely. For while one physician was examining him, I noticed that an attendant had disconnected the valve to the air-producing apparatus. When I brought it to the medic's attention, he put on a show of force and screamed at her, probably apologizing later.

In my possession, I had documented evidence of flagrant hospital violations; licensed practical nurses had the unmistakable smell of vodka on their breath. And one such "nurse" assigned to my father would bring her five assorted wigs to work so that a knowledgeable male attendant on the floor could restyle them, free of charge. She was more at the front desk chatting with her friends than beside my dad's bed. Primping was practical for these ladies of leisure. Work was a curse, to be avoided.

On the fatal weekend in February when my dad died, his breathing became increasingly labored. I sensed imminent danger. When I asked the head nurse to look in on him, she said: "Listen, Mr. Bernard. Your father is getting the finest care. I can't be running in every minute to look at him."

Two minutes later, a hospital nurse blurted

out: "This man is dying. Look at his hands." We had been in the room for two-and-a-half hours and this was the first indication the hospital had given my mom and me that the end was near. Over the ill-fated weekend, only a skeleton staff was on duty; even the resident who was in charge of my father's case was off!

Suddenly, my father opened his eyes that had been shut and his breathing stopped. I dashed out to the front desk and pulled the head nurse by the arm and into the room. More than fourteen nurses, doctors and attendants came in and out of the room in the next sixty-one minutes. Their efforts to revive him failed.

We left instructions for where the body was to be forwarded and I took my mother to the emergency room as her blood pressure was at a critical level. Before we got off the floor, the nurse who had been grooming herself those three weeks on the case wouldn't let me leave until I had paid up all the nurses who were owed anything, and that was less than $75. "I'll mail it to you," I said. "No, you'll pay it now."

Where was the internist who had been attending my dad from the day he arrived at the hospital? Dressed in golf clothes, he arrived after my dad had stopped breathing, having known full well in advance of his deteriorating condition.

Everything about that hospital was inferior, including their help. When certain ill-trained, compassionless, undedicated groups get a foothold in a hospital, better to check into a funeral parlor from the start, especially if you're considered elderly.

Miami's elderly should receive priority consideration in their hospitals. For if not for these senior citizens supporting the city, the resort town would surely shrivel up and die in the hotter months of the year. Putting gambling casinos along Collins Avenue has been suggested to put

261

Miami Beach back into the black, but all efforts to push the bill through have failed miserably. The fear is that with the influx of gamblers comes the gangsters.

But returning to the plight of Sophie Katz in Miami Beach who, after getting her weekly vitamin shot and feeling "like a spring chicken," decided to walk home from the hospital. But shortly afterward, the lovely lady was carried by a stretcher back to the same hospital for a twelve-week stay because she had been dumped by an open drawbridge. The *Enquirer* thought this was bizarre enough to look into.

On March 12, '66, I visited Sophie after catching a few hours of a scorching Miami sun. She had been hobbling around the place on crutches, but felt more comfortable in a wheelchair, which she was confined to most of the time.

Sophie told me that normally she would ride home in a cab. This had been the first time she had dared to walk across the bridge, and it was her last time.

The accident took place on December 4, '65 after Mrs. Katz left the outpatient clinic of St. Francis Hospital in Miami Beach and started across the Indian Creek drawbridge. She was actually a little more than past the mid-point of the fifty-foot span when it began rising to let a boat through.

Sophie was too slow to run and attempt a dive for the safety railing where she might have been able to hold on, if her strength would have permitted. Like a boulder cascading down a mountain, Sophie tumbled down the rising pedestrian walk and crashed onto the fixed portion of the bridge.

The man who had been operating the bridge for thirteen years without one mishap, so he claimed, ruined his perfect record. The operator said he wasn't aware of the accident until the bridge was lowered and he saw two men crouching over Mrs. Katz. Then an ambulance rushed her back to St. Francis Hospital. She had deep cuts and other lacerations, including a severely broken leg. Then Sophie did the only thing available to her. She sued the city of Miami. Thank God! I'm sure that this sentiment was shared by *Enquirer* readers when my article broke on June 26, '66: "WOMAN IS DUMPED BY OPENING DRAWBRIDGE AND BREAKS LEG."

Seeing Sophie strain in pain for the energy needed to just get from the kitchen to the bathroom was a pathetic sight. Approaching eighty years young, Sophie would not recover as quickly as a twenty-five-year-old. If only Texas businessman Malcolm Jackson had been around a year earlier to help the poor Miami resident.

For the thirty-eight-year-old resident of Greenville, Texas had revolutionized the old crutch. Called "Hydro Crutches," they took five years of research and cost $100,000 to develop. The device worked from battery power and could effectively raise and lower a handicapped person, like Sophie Katz, in a few effortless seconds. For Mrs. Katz, like so many others in her predicament, modern science wasn't programmed for the few, but for the many, and came too late.

Jackson revealed to me that initially he would market the crutches for about $400, but was striving to get the price down — "so that every one of the eight million crippled Americans could afford a pair." The battery-powered crutches had passed a solid year of intensive evaluation and testing at the Veteran's Administration in New York and received the seal of approval for V.A. hospitals throughout the country.

While the first reports of the revolutionary crutches were running in the *Enquirer's* April 23, '67 issue, I recalled my November 27, '66 report of another obscure individual who was attempting to help others. Cleveland's Mike Shepp was getting honest jobs for murderers, muggers, arsonists, burglars and two-bit crooks who had paid their debt to society and wanted to go straight.

Strangely enough, Shepp didn't charge his grateful customers a fee for his service. Mike was running a *free* employment agency for ex-cons. And he was best suited for the job of founder and director of Con's Way Unlimited — because he was an ex-con. In fact, his agency was the only one of its kind in the U.S. and television star Steve Allen was the honorary president of Shepp's firm. But the bulk of the big bundle of money it took to run this unusual employment agency came directly from Shepp's savings.

But Mike was having better success placing his former "pen" pals in Cleveland than Norman Thurber was having in Washington, D.C. finding a job.

Thurber, a resident of Indianapolis, Indiana, didn't get the job he was applying for because he flunked a lie-detector test which was administered to him when he applied for a bus driver's job. Thurber was turned down by the machine for withholding information about a theft from another bus company he had worked for. So the twenty-eight-year-old Thurber kicked in the glass door of the bus office one night where he had failed the test. He smashed the polygraph "truth" machine and with a hammer he found in a cabinet, broke everything in sight. Every desk was turned over, mirrors were smashed, tape recorders damaged beyond repair and file cabinets kicked over.

When it was ascertained that Thurber's only willful intentions were to destroy and not steal, the charges were reduced to a misdemeanor of trespassing. He was fined $100 and sentenced to thirty days, but his fine and twenty-seven days were suspended if he repaid the damage within a year's time.

On October 9, '66, Norman Thurber's true story of how he "wrecked" the employment agency ran in the *Enquirer*. My photos of the office that looked as if a herd of buffalo had stamped through, accompanied the piece along with a serious head shot of "thoughtless" Thurber.

As Mike Shepp was trying to find work for ex-cons, a medical genius was laboring to save lives in the operating room by taking from the dead and giving to those barely living.

In the January 28, '68 *Enquirer* edition, Dr. Christiaan Barnard, the man who performed the world's first heart transplant on a human, told me: "I MAY HAVE TO GIVE UP MY WORK AS A SURGEON." Dr. Barnard revealed that his hands, which performed the amazing heart transplant on Louis Washkansky — the first person to live with another person's heart — were pain-racked and crippled by rheumatoid arthritis.

Dr. Barnard confessed he even encountered the knifing agony in his fingers during the operation on Washkansky. "It was great enough to make me stop on one occasion," he added. The noted surgeon said that even at the moment of our interview, he was in pain. "But I'm not going to worry about it," he laughed, then gritted his teeth as the pain continued. "I won't become so distraught about my problem that I'd walk into a car and get killed. If that happened, who would be here to continue my work?"

Posing as a British journalist who was wired from South Africa to update the doctor's visit to America, I first asked the customary throw-away questions about his reactions to Radio City, the Empire State Building and other tourist landmarks. Then, after he was at ease, I asked him to confirm my *Enquirer* tip, which he did.

Iain, another chieftain at *The Inc.,* loved the

exposé, but felt the article was incomplete. "George," he said, "see if you can go back and get some good pictures of the doctor's rheumatoid-ridden operating hand. We'll pay you extra."

That next day, Mayor John Lindsay was honoring the Cape Town heart surgeon at Gracie Mansion. The forty-four-year-old physician had not as yet arrived when I flashed my press card before one of "New York's Finest" and was admitted to the stately mansion.

After five minutes, Christiaan appeared with his matronly-looking wife, whom he would later divorce for a girl half his age. I double-checked my camera. There could be no mistakes. The article had already been laid out, less a space for the doctor's million-dollar hands.

I wondered how he could ever perform a delicate heart operation when the man was as jittery as a jumping bean. He couldn't sit still for a moment. And he had a hand in one pocket with the other tucked by his side.

Exasperated, I bluntly asked him to hold up the gifted hands that were making medical history. But before I could step back to refocus, he took on a stupid sense of modesty and dropped his hands to his side.

I did manage to capture several hand gestures while he was conferring with the Mayor. And I rushed the roll to *The Inc*.

When the story ran, so did a photo of the surgeon and his hands — only one of them. My pictures came out, but in one, his movement produced what looked like six fingers on one hand. And in another, he had nine or ten. The *Enquirer* used a photo rushed to America by special jet from South Africa, and showed Barnard using chalk and a blackboard, demonstrating how he performed his delicate heart operation — despite the fact his hands were occasionally crippled with arthritis.

266

Can you imagine, George Bernard interviewing Christiaan Barnard? After the article ran, the *Enquirer* thought the two similar-sounding names might confuse their readers. "It would have been better if we called you 'Joe Screwup' ... for not getting the pictures," a sarcastic editor said.

The Inc. may have frowned on my inability to photograph moving fingers, but when it came to Concetta Ann Ingolia, they learned I was not all thumbs. In fact, I interviewed the Brooklyn-born star on two separate occasions for the *Enquirer.* And, on each occasion, my interview ran in *The Inc.*

The first time I met this bright-eyed, blonde actress was at a cocktail party in March '65. Reggie and I used our "Radio Caroline" cover to infiltrate the performer's confidence. A few weeks later, she told *Enquirer* readers: "I DON'T WANT TO BE A GOOD GIRL."

Her recordings included: "Kookie, Kookie, Lend Me Your Comb," "What Did You Make Me Cry For?" and "Sixteen Reasons." She made these movies: *Drag Strip Riot, Parrish, Crusoe A-Go-Go.* She was the female star of TV's long-running "Hawaiian Eye" and also appeared on the tube in "Wendy and Me." Her biggest show-biz break, however, came on September 17, '74 when she portrayed a Marilyn Monroe-type character in the controversial, critically-acclaimed ABC-TV special, "The Sex Symbol." Columnists reported that she was even featured in a nude scene during the overseas version of the broadcast. Millions have undoubtedly seen her as the enticing, enterprising spokeswoman for Ace Hardware. It is even speculated that she was selected for the lucrative network commercial after her "sex symbol" ABC-TV portrayal popped the peepers of the sponsor.

Our mystery woman was born August 8, '38

and she married a man who had lost twice in marriage, who was hardly worthy of her genuine goodness and beauty.

Of course, I'm talking about Connie Stevens!

In the summer of '67, Connie was playing the role of a kooky blonde in the hit musical comedy "The Star Spangled Girl." She was also engaged to marry cry-baby crooner Eddie Fisher who had left Debbie Reynolds and two children for Liz Taylor — who subsequently dumped him.

After the Broadway curtain saluted Connie four times to thunderous ovations, Connie made her way to the dressing room. I was waiting by the door, and before I could introduce myself, she said to me: "Oh, I know you. You're with that 'pirate' station. Bernard Shaw, or something like that."

"George Bernard. And the 'pirate' station has been torpedoed. It's no longer afloat," I explained.

"Well, come on in and tell me what brings you here," she said hospitably, leading me to a seat in her dressing room as she scrubbed off her make-up. It was apparent Connie had not seen my *Enquirer* story of '65, and even if she had, it was a flattering piece — not a hatchet job! All she had revealed in that earlier *Enquirer* scoop was her desire for different, demanding roles, rather than the bubble gummy, gooey garbage she was getting. I have no way of knowing if her fairy godmother was an *Enquirer* subscriber, because Connie's wish did come true. She was hardly a Mary Poppins for long.

In her "Star Spangled" dressing room, Connie told T.A.F., the front I employed, that she was good for Eddie. Fisher was practically a kid when she had first met him, she confessed — "but now I'm straightening him out," she added, indicating that she was now restoring to the distraught entertainer the confidence Eddie lost after his two marriages collapsed.

Connie was down on the press for giving Eddie a "terrible beating" when he was getting out of his marriages. The versatile verteran insisted she would turn Eddie into a man — "a tougher man" — whom everyone would respect. "Eddie will never be stepped on, ever again," she vowed.

Miss Stevens was thoroughly convinced she wouldn't become the third consecutive divorce disaster for her dear beloved Eddie. "This marriage will work. It isn't any ordinary romance. I treat Eddie for what he is — a fine, warm-hearted person who needs to love and be loved."

Connie felt Liz had never given any meaning to marriage with Eddie, but treated him like "a confused boy." Debbie had never understood him, she said, explaining that Miss Reynolds probably wasn't mature enough at the time to handle Eddie — "who was extremely sensitive," Connie said. "But I'm mature. I've been married once, and like Eddie, I've really learned from my mistakes," or so she thought naively at the time of my interview.

She said that she would be married to Eddie "right now," except that her fiance thought he still was legally married to Liz, and didn't want to take an unnecessary chance until it was official. In the meantime, Connie was still wearing the large five-carat diamond ring Eddie had surprised her with at one of his recording sessions a few months earlier.

The innocent-minded actress who resented playing the dumb, kooky blonde, seriously believed that Eddie would never stray to another woman — that their marriage was going to be Eddie's last. With an air of confidence, she told me that Eddie's days of wandering and loneliness were over for good. She added that for the first time in the virile vocalist's life — and he must have had something sexual to interest

three beautiful women — he was really living —
as a man.

On October 29, '67, Connie and Eddie had a
child together. The New York Public Library's
reference service apologizes for the fact that
there is no available date recorded for their
marriage. It was speculated that they secretly
tied the knot — after Connie had already con-
ceived. And, on June 12, '69, Connie and Eddie
were divorced.

On July 25, '75, columnist Earl Wilson, still
going stronger than ever, and approaching seventy, interviewed the equally-energetic Fisher
who was attempting to stage another of his famous comebacks from the tombs of entertainment's forgotten. Naturally, Fisher was starting
in the Catskills. Wilson asked Eddie to comment
on what he would do if two free hours were made
available to him — which of his ex-wives would he
want to see. Concerning Debbie, Fisher said:
"She's a great entertainer, but I don't care for
her as a person. She's fooling the world for too
long." Of Liz, Eddie confessed she was the "love
of his life — but I never thought of her as a
performer!" About Connie, he was the kindest: "I
don't care what kind of reviews she gets. I'd
rather see Connie. She's my best girl friend."

While everyone's entitled to an opinion —
especially of celebrities in show business — I've
always wondered what Eddie Fisher ever had.
When he lost Connie, I knew for sure — total
zero!

In the *Enquirer's* April 6, '76 edition, Eddie
openly discussed another girl friend, a 21-year-
old college beauty queen, Terry Richard — who
had come and gone as the crusading crooner's
wife number four. "The 26-year age difference
was too much," admitted Fisher of his four-
month marriage. Eddie, how predictable you are.

It was also obvious that Maria Magdalena von

Losch, sixty-four when we met, was entertainment's enigma. Her legs were alluringly timeless and she even had the pleasure of seeing them banned from posters in Paris subways. It was too demoralizing for the customers, in spite of fearless French liberty.

Marlene Dietrich, as you guessed, was talking to me during a Plaza Hotel press conference to kick off a one-woman show of songs at the Lunt-Fontanne Theatre on Broadway.

Attempting to get an "exclusive" interview at a news conference attended by rival reporters, is like trying to walk on one's nose across a tight rope. Impossible! So, as soon as everyone completed their questions, I took her by the arm and to the side. Two reporters rushed over, but I bravely barked at them: "Please, can't you give Miss Dietrich a chance to get her breath!" I said it with authority, and they backed off.

"You've got some nerve," she said. "Are all Americans like you are?" she asked, knowing full well after having lived here that I was not representative of "all Americans." And to further complicate matters, "Easy" Ed Finklestein, a layout man at the *Enquirer*, and a friend, was standing over my shoulder. On occasion, Pope would allow his staff to do stories. And this was one of those "on occasion" instances.

I couldn't shrug Ed, as I didn't want to blow my cool, and show it! So I allowed him to stay. He heard my questions and her replies while I was privy to her reactions to the queries. When the story ran on December 10, '67, we wound up splitting the fee.

When Dietrich came to America in '30, she was billed by Paramount as the studio's answer to MGM's Garbo. Dietrich remained in the United States during World War II, and was still regarded by many in her home, *Deutschland,* as a traitor — especially after the American newsreels smuggled into Germany revealed she was actually campaigning courageously in Hollywood for the country to put their money into war bonds instead of booze or other luxuries.

"Would you ever play in Germany?" I asked.

"Do you think I'm totally crazy? I'm not a masochist!" she said firmly, trying to demonstrate her continued loyalty to the people of America who supported her cinema career. But the answer to my question was still an open one in my mind.

In Dietrich's popular-selling A'B'C's book, under "G", she writes: "Germany ... The tears I have shed over Germany have dried ... " For "K," Dietrich declares, "Kisses ... Don't waste them. But don't count them." And for "S": "Sex ... In America an obsession. In other parts of the world a fact."

I couldn't take my eyes off her fabulous face, figure and, of course, those luscious legs. Judgment could not be passed on her neck as it was concealed smartly by a beige, high turtle-neck blouse that matched her skirt. The late Mike Todd called Marlene, "The world's greatest showwoman." And long-time friend, Ernest Hemingway, said of her: "Brave, beautiful, loyal, generous ... I value her opinion more than professors."

Our interview shifted to television, and magnificent Marlene insisted she wouldn't be caught dead on the tube — "unless it's on one of my old films. I'm too old to risk television." Of her age, she opined, the cameras were "too probing" for her. "All the make-up in the world won't hide the blemishes of age and make me look young again. TV close-ups would kill me, so I'll stick to the stage — where I can have personal contact with my audience without getting so close to them that all the tell-tale signs of age show up."

How could Dietrich ever know that just a few

years later — while even further up in years —
her London stage appearance would be televised
in America? And not only were her lovely legs
fantastically youthful, but her face was vib-
rantly alive, agelessly — reminiscent of her *Blue
Angel* days. She had withstood so well the searching cameras of television that had so frightened
her.

"They say that *Blue Angel* was one of my finest
efforts, that it would give me immortality. As far
as I'm concerned, the film was just so-so, certainly not great." The ageless beauty confessed
that *Judgment at Nuremberg* brought her critical
acclaim, but she didn't particularly enjoy making the film, nor did she feel her best performance was registered. There was only one redeeming value to *Judgment* she said — Spencer Tracy,
whom she considered a great star, and was proud
to have played opposite. Marlene considered
Tracy to be a real man. "There hasn't been anyone like him before and there never will again.
He brought great personal dignity to every part
he played because he was that kind of man."

The dazzling Dietrich was convinced that her
remaining show-biz career would be solely restricted to singing on the stage. Movies were *ver-
boten!* "I won't make anymore motion pictures,"
she assured us. Rising at dawn, working twelve
hours a day on the set, was sure to dissipate her
energies, she reasoned. "I want to preserve
whatever I've got left, if that's anything," she
said philosophically. Whatever the mysterious
Marlene did have, turned on a super-charged reporter two-and-a-half times her junior.

The next time I met "Easy" Ed Finklestein
was in February '75, at Miami Beach, seven
years after I had left the *Enquirer*. Ed had married a girl I had been seeing, for in those days, I
was seeing them all. The girl's theatrical name
was Lisa Di Milo and if anyone was ever a Sophia

Loren look-alike, this tall Roman beauty was it.

Ed and Lisa had packed up and moved to Arizona. The arid climate was the doctor's prescription for her acute asthma condition and an opportunity for "The Fink," as he was called by former staffer Arnie Goldstein, to join the reporting staff of a local newspaper, "and learn how to really write."

But when I saw Ed years later, he was glum. He had split up with his wife and she had left with all his savings, he claimed. To boot, the memories of Arizona and a marriage he called "hell" were so morbid, he had packed up and moved in temporarily with his mother in Miami Beach.

Ed had contacted the *Enquirer* at Lantana to report he was now back in circulation and open for assignment. So they assigned him to interview George Raft at the Eden Roc Hotel in Miami Beach.

"Hello, Mr. Raft," Ed said on the phone. "I'm a reporter and I'd like to interview you on your new book, regarding that memorable car ride you took with Sylvia Sidney in one of your movies..."

"Sure, I'll give you an interview. But where'd you say you're from?" Raft requested.

"The *National Enquirer*," Ed admitted.

"Oh, no. Anything but that," he said, slamming the phone down.

Is it any wonder Raft was raging? Look at the Enquirer record: On April 5, '64, *The Inc.* had reported: "I SHOULD HAVE STAYED A GANGSTER ... Says George Raft ... As An Actor, I'm the Loneliest Guy In The World ... I'm what you call an ex-big shot. I'm in the same class with Sonny Liston and Floyd Patterson, and nobody likes a loser. ..." Under his photo caption was a further indictment of the former box-office biggie: "Has-been movie star George Raft wants to get back into movies, but he says he's a forgotten man."

June 12, '68, cover story: "GEORGE RAFT REVEALS: I'M BROKE. I'VE BEEN EVICTED FROM MY BEVERLY HILLS HOME."

So "Easy" Ed had just cause for being depressed. But he didn't miss his "Mrs." as much as losing the story. The night I had scheduled to meet Ed for a drink at the Holiday Inn, was the day my dad had died. Since then, I have not spoken to Ed and am not aware if the *Enquirer* took him on full-time, or dropped him for "failing" to torpedo the Raft and send the body of the "exclusive" story floating down to Pope's catch basins at Lantana. Certainly, losing Raft was not as much Ed's fault as it was *The Inc.'s* shabby treatment of the rough n' tough actor.

Eight years earlier, Jason Robards, Jr. was having a rough time with his marriage of six years to Humphrey Bogart's widow, Lauren Bacall. It was common knowledge in the entertainment industry that Robards resented the constant comparison to Bogart but not to the unbearably sickening degree I uncovered for the *Enquirer.* Bill gave me the option of interviewing Lauren alone on how she compared Jason to Humphrey, or Robards separately on his innermost feelings about living with Bogart's ghost — or both together.

Celebrity Register refers to Lauren as "the sloe-eyed, Johnny Walker-voiced queen of Broadway smashes," and I was well aware that her dynamic stage presence was matched only by her off-stage temper. She was to be avoided, if at all possible.

Take the time that Galella rapped on her dressing room door to give her a set of photos he was submitting to several leading magazines. In that way, the considerate cameraman developed a devoted and sympathetic following of celebrities who, to show their appreciation, would give him exclusive shooting sessions to the exclusion of other free-lance photographers.

"Yes, what is it?" she said angrily, opening the door.

"I'm Ron Galella and I'd like you to have these," he said meekly, frightened by her overwhelming, dominant presence. Ron was so shook up he didn't even take the photos out of the envelope they were in, but handed her the package. For all Lauren might have guessed, he could have been delivering a box of candy or two BLT's.

"Thank you," she said brusquely, then slammed the door in his face.

There was no percentage attempting to interview the husband and wife together. Either she'd clip me on the chin for prying into their marriage, or Jason might sock me in the chest to show he was like Bogey, and more so.

So when I found them at a New York night spot having drinks together, I waited patiently, one-hour-and-fifty-three-minutes to be exact, for them to separate. Robards went to the men's room and I followed.

Of all places to conduct an interview. Robards was losing high octane fluids into a urinal and I was combing my hair two feet away.

I saw my opening: "Isn't it a shame," I said, concerned, "that people won't let poor Bogey rest in peace? They keep resurrecting him."

"Yes, it is a damn shame," he responded. "But who are you?"

"George Bernard, Trans-Atlantic Features," I said. "I'm just covering this party and I thought this was as good a place as any, to speak with you on the subject. I don't think it would go over too big with Lauren, do you?"

"Hardly," he confessed.

I bent down and looked for legs and dropped trousers in the toilet stalls, but we were the only ones in the men's room. If there was a lock on the door, I would have bolted the room off from any intruding patrons. I could only hope that my ingenuity would keep Robards talking before we were interrupted.

"Why can't people, all people, stop pulling the nails out of Bogart's coffin and let the poor man lie in peace?" said an exasperated Jason Robards, Jr. to this *Enquirer* reporter. Jason started soaping up his hands. "After all, he wasn't God. Why should he be 'resurrected' which is the word, I believe, you used. He's been dead for ten years now and I haven't had real peace of mind since I married Lauren."

Jealous Jason said that the Bogey revival was making him sick, and considered the giant posters, buttons and sweat shirts capitalizing on Bogart's name to be "immoral."

Robards revealed that wife Lauren still received letters from all over the world offering sympathy—asking questions about what was life really like with Bogart. "Some of the letters make it plain," Robards noted, "that some people don't know, or won't accept, the fact that he's dead. Some people even ask me what he was like. How am I supposed to know? I never met him. People just assume that I took over from Bogart when I married Lauren. I didn't. I never tried to step into his shoes—and Lauren didn't ask me to," ranted Robards, the "cadaverous-looking" actor who concedes publicly that he looks "stepped on".

The Chicago-born performer was distraught that "just about everybody seems to have put me in Bogart's shoes. Now, do I resemble Bogey?" he said. "Do I?" Ten months earlier, Edward G. Robinson, standing before his hotel room mirror, had asked me if he looked like himself—"Little Caesar." Why was my opinion so valued?

"There is a *bit* of a resemblance," he insisted, "and because of it, nobody will ever let me forget the name Bogart."

Robards praised Bogart's many acting skills, but was thoroughly convinced that Hollywood and commercial interests " will never allow him to die," even though he was medically pronounced dead in '57.

Jason felt that Bogart's Hollywood image made him worth as much dead as alive. But that's not what bothered the sensitive spouse. He was tormented not so much with what Hollywood was doing with Bogey's memory, as much as Humphrey's haunting his life with Lauren.

It was reported in the press that following Bogart's death, more than $1 million was left to Lauren and her two children. But Robards didn't deny that Bogey was a "great, considerate husband" to Lauren and was able to provide handsomely for her and the children. "It's just that I simply want the public to remember that he's dead and I'm alive. And I want them to remember that I'm married to Lauren Bacall now."

The men's room door suddenly opened—of all times. And a little man entered and walked over to the urinal. I was afraid my interview was over, but Jason just looked at the ceiling as we both waited what seemed to be three minutes before the man finally felt relieved. I was sure he had a wooden leg and if I wasn't atop a bigger story, I would have investigated the odd off-beat for G.P.

Robards continued: "Lauren is completely reconciled to Bogey's death. Why can't everybody else accept it?" he asked rhetorically.

"Look, I've been away from the table long enough. I'll just tell you one more thing, and you can print it: there's only room for one man in the Robards household, and that man is me."

I stayed behind and double-checked my notes quickly after shaking Robards's hand for his generous time.

My story ran in *The Inc.* on December 24, '67,

but the toilet locale was substituted by the more elegant table setting. G.P. became sickened reading my first-person account of crawling through a New York sewer, and toilets weren't any more appealing to him.

On September 11, '69, two years after my interview, their marriage of eight years ended in divorce. Many believed, knowing Robards's resentment of Bogey, that the wedlock woes would eventually bring on the inevitable marital ending to their fabeled relationship. For Jason, his house with Lauren was anything but a blissful home. If anything, it was a Hollywood museum perpetually paying tribute to Bogey, in one way or the other. Some considered their home even haunted, by you know whom.

After Bogey passed on, Lauren was quoted as saying: "I'll miss Hollywood. Of the twenty friends I thought I had, I'll miss the six I really did have. But it was quicksand for me." Lauren then fled to New York, went "legit," and married Jason Robards, Jr. "Well, there's nothing to say about *that* except that it's over. Period."

CHAPTER XX

GP—"The High Priest Of Low Brow"

My profound gratitude to the *Miami Herald*, the erudite journalism revue known as *MORE*, to *Newsweek, Time, Editor & Publisher, CBS News'* *"60 Minutes"* and the many other news sources that provided me with additional background and reference material to orchestrate this chapter. Incidentally, "The High Priest of Low Brow," which is the title of this in-depth, investigative chapter, is a literary loan from the January 14 '73 *Miami Herald's* slick Sunday supplement, "Tropic." Not surprisingly, when I attempted to order a back copy, I was informed that "There's not a damn one left. They went like hot dogs at a barbecue." Is it conceivable that Gene Pope, the titan of the tabloids, could generate such reader interest? Or, are there facts contained in the *Herald's* in-depth article which might prove embarrassing to the *Enquirer?* Gene, let me ask you a serious question. Did you buy up all the papers?

Generoso "Gene" Pope, Jr. was the third son of Generoso Papa, an Italian immigrant who landed a pauper in New York City at age twelve. From there, the enterprising Papa got his first job as a waterboy in a piano factory. Destined for greater business heights, he shunned mediocrity, and opted for enormous wealth which he eventually realized as owner of both the Colonial Sand and Stone Company in Port Washington, N.Y., and the Italian-language newspaper *Il Progresso*. And in the process, the father changed his last name to Pope. It was a startling rags-to-riches Horatio Alger story, but for one exception. Horatio did it *solely* on his own.

According to William R. Amlong of the *Miami Herald* staff, before Gene purchased the *Enquirer*, he went to M.I.T., not because anyone twisted his arm, but because engineering fascinated him. From college, he went into the sand and gravel business. "It didn't intrigue me," he told the *Herald* reporter. Then it was on to Washington. D.C. where he joined the Central Intelligence Agency, working in the division that blueprints propaganda. The C.I.A. didn't appeal to Pope either. "I really got fed up with the government bureaucracy. You'd spend weeks trying to get things done, and then you couldn't do it," he recalled with frustration.

Pope grabbed his bags and hopped on the first transportation — a train — back to New York. Planes scared Pope to death, so he made sure never to take them. Then, by chance, he heard somebody in a bar say that the widow of William Griffin was putting on the selling block the *New York Enquirer*, a paper that was originally started by William Randolph Hearst in 1926 "to fill the gap between Sunday morning and Monday morning, and which gave the publisher a paper on which to try out experimental ideas."

But Gene's dad, by then extremely wealthy, wouldn't loan his son the money, not believing in inherited wealth. So Gene scrambled to raise the bread to buy the paper he was convinced could make him a millionaire — in time.

Pope said to reporter Amlong that when he hopped a cab to his lawyer's Wall Street office, he didn't have the money to pay the driver. "I had a lucky silver dollar, so I paid the cab with it and went up to close the deal — more on nerve than anything else." And so Pope took over the paper in '52 for $75,000 — $20,000 down, and started out with one full-time employee and about $75,000 in debt notes. "He had something special from the start, though: the heartfelt backing of racketeer

281

Frank Costello," according to Frank Greeve's article in *MORE* which is an incisive, articulate, probing publication that comes up with sound conclusions. It really gives you *more*.

The paper was a week away from bankruptcy — mental and fiscal. At the time, the *Enquirer* had such a reputation for faking stories, that when in Pope's first issue he scooped the nation on a major story, other newspapers and wire services laughed, and wouldn't touch it. The historic day was April 7, '52, and the story read:

"Gen. Matthew B. Ridgeway has been recommended to succeed Gen. Dwight D. Eisenhower as Commander-in-Chief, Supreme Headquarters, Allied Powers, in Europe, it was learned on excellent authority today. The National Security Council, which settled upon Ridgeway to take over the defense of Western Europe against the threat of Communist aggression, also proposed Gen. Mark Clark to replace Ridgeway in Tokyo and Korea."

While the credibility of the *Enquirer* has been growing in the consumer audience progressively since '52, it was only in '75 that the other news media finally came around to believing in Pope's miracles as truth! Pope's coup came in April '75, when he personally masterminded the reunion of Russian "love child" Viktoriya Fyodorova and the ailing American father she had never seen — Admiral Jackson R. Tate. Viktoriya was the product of the Admiral's World War II romance with actress Zoya Fyodorova in '45 in Moscow when he was an American liason officer stationed there. But after Joseph Stalin got wind of their affair, he ordered Tate out of the country and Zoya was jailed for eight years.

And when the intriguing, human-interest story first broke of Viktoriya's driving desire to meet the man who could give her legitimacy, two of Pope's Moscow-based editors tracked her down and then rushed back to Pope in the United States with a letter, tapes and photographs which the proud publisher turned over to Admiral Tate.

Pope made a generous offer to pick up *all* the daughter's travel expenses and provide a "secret" Florida hideaway where they could inconspicuously be united — away from the "other" news media. So, escorted out of the U.S.S.R. in wig and dark glasses, she arrived in Miami only to be whisked off to her rendezvous. And to throw rival news hounds off the scent, Pope dropped misleading bones along both Florida coasts so expertly and deftly that the *Miami Herald* fell for one of them in print. Had G.P. remained with the C.I.A., I'm sure he would be running it today. The man is an unequivocal genius!

Then, Pope scooped the entire news media by running a four-page spread on the reunion ... and all the other newspapers, magazines and broadcast stations could do was quote the *Enquirer*. But few gave *The Inc.* any attribution, which must have angered G.P. immensely.

On the heels of the Russian reunion, Pope followed with another. The rumors were out that Viktoriya was planning to remain in the United States and marry an American — airline pilot Frederick Pouy. And while reporters from around the world were converging on Lantana, Pope used his C.I.A. *intelligence* to deceive them again. Then, pop comes the *Enquirer's* "exclusive" wedding pictures. One editor joked to me: "I wouldn't be at all surprised if Pope himself came up with the guy to keep her in the U.S. and get a front-pager for the *Enquirer*. He'll do anything for a story."

How true! In May '76, Zoya Fyodorova, who flew 4,665 miles from Moscow to be at Viktoriya's side for the birth of her grandchild, was, according to a statement made by Frederick Pouy to the

New York Daily News, "tricked into the meeting with retired Admiral Jackson R. Tate by a magazine reporter." The dispatch added, "it was learned that the weekly tabloid involved was the *National Enquirer.*"

After an *Enquirer* reporter was flatly refused exclusive rights to Zoya's American visit for a substantial sum of money, the correspondent used another ploy on Frederick Pouy. Pope's representative called again and offered to take Zoya to New York City, which included a sightseeing trip around landmarks as the Empire State Building and a lunch at the world-renowned Four Seasons restaurant. Pouy agreed. On the way to Manhattan, however, the car turned towards the airport and the *Enquirer* reporter convinced Zoya that Tate was "very sick and might not be able to wait." The newspaper account states that the *Enquirer* reporter produced two airline tickets, which he assured the confused woman that Tate had paid for, which Tate later denied.

When Zoya attempted to call her son-in-law before leaving for Florida to explain the change of schedule, the *Enquirer* reporter took her by the arm "and rushed her on the plane, saying there was no time." Zoya, who had planned to see Admiral Tate *after* the birth of the child and *only* with her family, returned in time for the birth of Christopher Alexander Fyodor-Pouy. How far will Gene's gang go for a scoop?

But in the *Enquirer's* July 29, '75 "operation trash" edition, G.P.'s collection of garbage accomplished for him the greatest scoop in his twenty-three years at the reins of the *N.E.* And for one week, the entire news media was buzzing while Secretary of State Henry Kissinger was fuming. In the precious article, *Enquirer's* "richest" story asked its readers this question: "What type of information could a foreign agent or assassin glean from the household garbage of an important cabinet member?"

That was precisely what Pope wanted answered when he assigned one of his trusty reporters to collect a week's accumulation of garbage from the home of Kissinger. Oddly enough, getting the trash was easy, but getting away with it posed another problem. The ambitious reporter was stopped by Secret Service agents who ordered him to "return the garbage!" The *Enquirer* reported that when their reporter refused to remove the five plastic bags of refuse from the trunk of his car, an agent asked if he was ever in an "insane asylum." Another Secret Service agent complained that he'd been trained to cope with assassins, but not garbage-grabbers. And so he called for his supervisor.

The supervisor spent considerable time interrogating the *Enquirer* reporter. Then, the agent took the *N.E.* reporter's photograph and told the spunky snooper he was free to go — with the garbage. As it turned out, Henry's household trash contained "hundreds of Secret Service documents" which would be of vital interest to any assassin. One document, for example, disclosed that the Secret Service was testing a new coded light signal system for all its limousines. And yet another document, which was a handwritten note on the back of an activity report, revealed the number and type of arms and ammunition supply carried in "each Secret Service limousine." And there were considerably more golden goodies, even special code plans of the Secretary's itinerary, which obviously, after *Enquirer* publication, were discarded for future use.

Two weeks later, the *Enquirer* followed up the Kissinger collection with this story: "Secret Service admits ... Confidential Documents That ENQUIRER Found in Kissinger's Trash Was a 'Breach of Security'."

The article said, in part: "The Secret Service admits the *Enquirer's* discovery of sensitive papers in Henry Kissinger's garbage has exposed a breach of security procedures — and the agency is asking for the documents' return ... 'the documents should not have been in the trash,' admitted Secret Service spokesman Jack Warner, assistant to Director H. Stuart Knight ... In a letter to the *Enquirer*, Warner made an official request for the return of the items and added, 'Your policy not to publish the specific contents of these documents is appreciated.' The *Enquirer* will return the papers as requested ..."

The *Enquirer* didn't stop there. They went to the "loyal opposition" — the Democrats — to vilify Republican Kissinger and praise the *Enquirer*. Sen. Lee Metcalf (D.-Mont.) praised the paper for bringing the security breach to the public's attention — and ostracized Kissinger for "unconscionable disposal of sensitive documents." He went on to say, "You fellows did a good job."

But super-sleuth Steve Mitchell, a handsome, mustached reporter on the *Palm Beach Post*, did an even better job. In fact, a day after *The Inc.'s* first article appeared on the heist of Henry's hunks of heaping rubbish, Mitchell made a daylight raid on the *Enquirer* bins. In the following edition, Mitchell printed the *Enquirer's* garbage, which consisted of "secret" G.P. memos to his staff which the embarrassed editorial entrepreneur would have liked to have burned before discarding.

Photographer John Freeman drove the getaway car for Mitchell, who recalled: "My goal was the same as the *Enquirer* reporter's — to sort through old bills and any other documents for a story. If apprehended, my defense would be the same as the *Enquirer's*: trash and garbage, once discarded, belong to anybody who has the stomach to go through it.

"Precisely at 1:57 p.m. we arrived at the narrow, twisting road leading to the *Enquirer* building . . . I spotted a cluster of Dempsey dumpsters and told Freeman to park the car and be ready for a quick getaway . . . I examined the first dumpster. It was full: a computer print-out of *Enquirer* stories, thick manila folders bulging with rejected stories and correspondence . . . a veritable trove of trash.

"With mounting excitement, I began stuffing the trash into the black plastic bag I had brought along for the purpose. I rejected the ruins of pizza and the gnawed hulk of what had once been the pride of Colonel Sanders.

"The bag was nearly three-quarters full and getting heavy. As a former police reporter, I knew that our chances of apprehension were increasing sharply with every passing second.

" 'Let's go, John, we've more than enough,' I said. We drove away exchanging smiles of triumph."

The two snoopers were extremely successful. For when they got back to the *Post* and began rummaging through their rubbish, they uncovered the secret of the *Enquirer's* success — a memo to the editorial staff from Generoso Pope, Jr. himself!

The memo, dated August 17, '73, told the reporters, writers and editors how to write stories "packed with color and emotion" to "make our readers react."

The two daredevil delvers should have received journalism's Medal of Honor for going above and beyond the normal call of a correspondent's duty. Instead of rubbish, they found rubies. Other gems included: "We should touch our readers' souls," Pope said. "Cause them to smile, to get lumps in their throats, to break down and cry. We want the *Enquirer* filled with stories like the classic 'Yes, Virginia, there is a Santa Claus' . . . We need quotes that tug at the heart.

"Prod, push and probe the main characters in the story. Help them *frame* their answers. For example: How did it feel? I don't know, it just hurt. Was it a sharp pain? No. Was it more like a toothache? No.

"Have you ever felt anything like it before? Not really, but it was something like an electrical shock. Where did you feel it? It hit me in the back of the neck and went down my spine. Did you scream? I couldn't."

According to Pope, at this point, the *Enquirer* reporter is ready to proceed: "Let's see if I've got this straight. You said 'The pain hit me. It was like an electrical shock that started in my neck and shot down my spine. I wanted to scream but I couldn't. I've never felt anything like it.' Yes, that's it."

G.P. even exhorted his trusty troop of reporters to ask "leading questions" such as: "Do you ever go to the corner and cry?" "What do you pray for?" "Has God forsaken you?" As for "quotes", Pope stated that they "should not only be appropriate but believable. A Japanese carpenter should not sound like Ernest Hemingway, or vice versa."

Mitchell mentioned: "Although emotion is important, Pope cautioned that 'the story cannot be all emotions, all high points. You set the reader up and then smash! You hit him in the pit of the stomach. In the right context and in the proper setting, such a simple word as "yes" can have a powerful impact.'"

About changing quotes, G.P. issued a cautionary note: "Take the story about the mother who had the flag that covered her son's coffin stolen. The writer wrote, 'I wish they'd bring it back.' But it was changed to 'If they don't bring it back,

God help them.'"

G.P., aren't you ashamed of yourself, after I've said all those nice things about you? Shame, shame. When I wrote for you there was none of that malarkey.

In summing up, publisher Pope urged his staff to "try to resolve our personal likes and dislikes in a way that works for the story and the paper. There should be some exciting and interesting times ahead for us all," he concluded cryptically.

But no one has ever turned up a memo, directive or other document from G.P. to "fake an article." I defy anyone to ever produce such a document ... that is legitimate. It will never happen. But something equally catastrophic occurred on March 7 '76 which sorely rocked the *Enquirer's* credibility before a massive, "prime time," network television audience. The bomb of devastation was delicately detonated by CBS News correspondent Mike Wallace, a newsman's newsman and probably the most proficient in electronic journalism. For during a highly informative, fourteen-minute segment of "60 MINUTES" devoted to the phenomenon of the *Enquirer,* investigative reporter Wallace uncovered, unequivocally, "shoddy reporting," which set *The Inc.'s* believability back to the year '52, when Pope purchased the paper known for faking fact.

Pope's right-hand man, Iain Calder, took the brunt of Wallace's battering. The network newsman questioned the *Enquirer's* September 23, '75 article which stated that colleague Walter Cronkite was not only TV's highest paid newscaster, but made three-quarters of a million dollars a year.

Wallace: "It's not true. If I can prove it to you, will you retract it?"

Calder: "Depends on what kind of proof you give me."

Through a pre-taped interview with Walter on that specific issue, Wallace called on Cronkite to corroborate, or deny, the *Enquirer* story.

Cronkite: "Mike, not half that do I earn . . . that's *not* the way it is!"

Directing Calder's attention to the *Enquirer's* February 18, '76 front page story, Wallace, like a pugilist mixing his punches, set up *The Inc.'s* boyish-looking executive for an even harder, many times more embarrassing, fall. The article under Wallace's scrutiny concerned a *picture* of Raquel Welch and Freddie (Chico) Prinze. And, according to the *Enquirer*, Welch said, so Wallace reported, "I love him. He makes me feel like I'm 20 again." This from the thirty-four-year-old sex goddess. From Freddie, twenty years old, "This is it, man."

"True story?" Wallace asked.

Calder avoided a direct answer, apologetically replying: "But it is true they did go out together."

Wallace: "Well, we checked that one out, too . . . with Hollywood columnist Rona Barrett."

Barrett: "Everything they wrote is totally false. They are totally made-up quotes, so said Raquel Welch to me."

Wallace: "Were these two people in the same place, at the same time standing side by side when this picture was taken?"

Calder: "No!"

Wallace: "Why would you go to the bother of doctoring this picture to put them together this way if you couldn't get a picture of them together legitimately?"

Calder: "Actually, it's the first and only time we've ever done that and we probably won't do it again, to be quite honest. Because it did cause us a little bit of a problem."

Wallace: "You're a little embarrassed, Iain Calder. I get the impression that you believe *now* that Walter Cronkite *does not* make three quarters of a million dollars a year. I get the impression that you feel a little bit ashamed for having doctored the picture of Raquel Welch and Freddie Prinze . . . and you've said that you wouldn't do it again . . . "

Calder: "Yeah, you're right. Yes."

Gene, has the drive for the dollar become more important than the accuracy you once strived for?

Going back in time, Gene had "other" problems after he became a publisher. G.P. recalled, according to Amlong: "I ended up owing about $250,000 — I don't know how. It was all on nerve, since there was no collateral. The printer would not take checks. The employees wouldn't take checks. Everything had to be in cash. I'd be carrying $10,000 in my pocket to pay the printer, but I couldn't pay the rent.

"I was getting dispossess notices from my apartment every month. The process servers used to wait in the lobby. When my first son was born, I had to go out that night and borrow money to get him out of the hospital."

Gene had to work fast. He started running gory accident pictures in his paper. "That's when the circulation started to climb," Pope remembers. "We decided to go ahead and see where we'd level off. With that formula, we got up to a million copies."

It was no secret around the paper that G.P. despised the sight of blood, especially the kind that curdled — and primarily his own. When a photograph required a slight retouch to highlight the gush of blood, Pope always managed to disappear. And each time he might stumble by the scene of an accident, he'd walk away quickly so as to avoid throwing up. "It bothered the hell out of me running that kind of paper, but it was paying the bills and after all those lean years, it was a good feeling to have some money in the bank."

Languishing in the prestige of being a real live publisher, Pope began to take full advantage of his significant station by moving in Tammany Hall circles. He even told the *Herald* he used to have breakfast at Gracie Mansion occasionally with then-New York Mayor Bill O'Dwyer, and even claims he went to the White House to visit the President. Knowing about the Pope's powers, it is possible.

"I knew everybody in New York who was famous," he further told the *Herald* — including hoodlum Albert Anastasia, who gave him "one helluva story" about a corrupt Brooklyn judge who was trying to run for mayor. Anastasia, however, wasn't the only hoodlum Pope remembers. G.P. said he didn't realize until years afterwards whom he had met — face-to-face — when a friend told him "there's a guy in Brooklyn who owns an olive-oil business and he wants to see you!"

According to the *Herald's* account of what actually transpired, it was reported that "Pope went to Brooklyn, climbed four flights of stairs and found a shriveled old man behind a desk. They went to lunch at a nearby Italian restaurant, then by a church where the priest told Pope what a good man his host was. Then it was off to the old man's house for a drink. 'I kept asking myself, what am I doing here?' Pope recalls. 'Then he said: "The Mayor wants you to see him. As a personal favor to me, will you go see him?" I said, 'Sure, but I'd go see him if he had just called me up himself.'"

Not another word was exchanged between the two, Pope remembers as if it was just yesterday. So Pope promptly went to see Mayor Vincent Impellitteri, an opposition partly member he had been attacking editorially. Frank Greve reported in *MORE* that when Gene had left the C.I.A. he had "inherited" from his dad a coveted Honorary Deputy Police Commissioner Badge and was subsequently appointed by then-Mayor O'Dwyer to the city's Board of Education—"moves widely interpreted as godfatherly assists from Costello." But the tables of political pleasures would soon turn against Pope. For when O'Dwyer in '50 suddenly "resigned," the new Mayor, Impellitteri, who had no fondness for G.P., would attempt to gain a just retribution. Almost immediately, G.P. lost his salutes from policemen. Even a further assault on his ego and self-esteem, Pope was also deprived of his parking privileges on the contention he was an "emissary for Costello." While Pope was being stripped of his city privileges, he did manage, however, to salvage his higher education post — but only after he kept his word to the man in Brooklyn. G.P. and Impellitteri struck a truce at their meeting in the famed New York Athletic Club. The shriveled olive oil merchant just happened to be the mighty underworld *capo* Joe Profacci. "But it was Costello to whom Pope had allegedly turned after he bought the *Enquirer*," notes *MORE*.

"Each week, Costello would loan him ten thousand dollars to meet operating expenses," wrote Leonard Katz, the *New York Post's* underworld expert, in his Costello biography *Uncle Frank*. "Pope would repay the loan promptly the following week in two five-thousand-dollar installments as revenue from newsstand sales rolled in. Costello continued to loan Pope money for his payroll even when he was in jail, (May '56 to April '57). Bobbie (Costello's wife) or Big Jim O'Connor (his doorman) would deliver the cash." With time out for the period Costello was in jail, according to Katz, Pope, Costello, Bobbie and *Enquirer* columnist John Miller and his wife dined together an average of twice a week. Asked about the relationship, Pope refused comment beyond saying that "Frank Costello never bankrolled the *Enquirer*." It is known that as the *Enquirer* prospered and Costello floundered amidst declining influence and rising notoriety, Pope cut his connection.

By the end of '57, a pulsating potpourri of celebrity revelations, off-beat court actions and human-interest articles shot the circulation to the quarter-million mark. By '62, the paper known as the *New York Enquire*—until June 16, '57, was selling a million copies a week.

In '66, Pope promptly discovered that he had saturated the gore market. He told then *Wall Street Journal* reporter A. Kent MacDougall: "I decided to clean up the *Enquirer* and turn it into a condensed version of *The Reader's Digest*." A second reason for converting the paper was the decline of newsstands in the wake of New York's newspaper strikes, and the growth of supermarkets, drug stores and convenience stores as outlets for magazines.

"I wanted to get away from sex and gore," Pope told Newton H. Fulbright at *Editor & Publisher*. "We had never gone in too much for sex—gore was ours. But we wanted to get away from it. People were getting away from it — everywhere. There are only so many libertines and neurotics. I didn't want to be with that crowd. I wanted to put out a paper a woman, say, at the supermarket, would pick up and take home, expecting to find something in it that would mean something — that would be of some practical or educational value to her in this life of decency most of us are trying to live."

Pope admitted drastically losing circulation during the conversion period — from under a million to 775,000. "It stayed down a few months," he said, "and then began to rise. We lost our old readers but we started picking up new ones, and we have gone on gaining, week by week."

How true, Gene. How true. For as Mike Wallace aptly noted: "What's the largest selling news weekly in America? It isn't *Newsweek!* It isn't even *Time* anymore. In first place is the self-proclaimed *newsweekly*, the *National Enquirer*. Now of course, *Time* and *Newsweek* would take issue at being in the same bag with the *Enquirer*. They'd say — 'The *Enquirer* really doesn't deal in news,' and they'd be right! 'O.K.,' says the *National Enquirer*. 'Just call us a magazine. We sell more copies per month than *People*, *Penthouse* and *Playboy* put together.'" In fact, Pope projected the *Enquirer's* '76 gross at $50 million. How much of that would be profit? "Pope wouldn't say," reported Wallace.

When G.P. makes his mind up, there's no turning back. But his biggest problem was trying to get his writers and editors to make the change with him. Reporters who had written eloquently about sex and crime couldn't write with clarity about finance, automobiles and household needs. So, he told one reporter, he found it absolutely necessary to "discharge some people" and hire new ones. But that's a laugh, for G.P. was always known for firing people, and it wasn't any new procedure in his regimented routine. If he didn't like the way you combed your hair, provided you had hair to comb, or your tie, or your shoes, you could be on the unemployment line.

CBS's Wallace also reported during the broadcast that Pope's wrath *is* to be taken seriously, especially by those who work for him: "His employees call him an unpredictable tyrant who can fire as quickly as he hires . . . Pope affably waves off the charges."

Though mighty Mike Wallace and his producer for the *Enquirer* installment, Harry Moses, couldn't establish a present-day mob connection

with the *Enquirer*, the CBS newsman, nevertheless, took great liberties in referring to Gene as
the "Godfather of this magazine, journal, newspaper" . . . "he rules it *like* the Godfather," and in
questions like, "You knew Frank Costello,
Joseph Profacci, Albert Anastasia?" Pope replied
a disconsolate "Yes!"

And so while instituting a drastic shift in editorial policy, Gene, in '67, moved his cramped and
congested offices from Manhattan's Madison
Avenue to rustic, picturesque Englewood Cliffs
in New Jersey — a veritable home in the country.
"No need working in some grubby, crowded place
when you can have this," Pope said.

To effectively discern what the public *really*
wanted to read, Pope properly sent skilled reporters around the country. And through a
series of panel discussions — during which editors would feed the panel moderators questions
from behind a one-way mirror — G.P. discovered,
among other findings, that Americans didn't
want to read any more about Vietnam. It was an
unpopular subject. They did want to read about
UFO's, the occult, about medicine, success
stories and human interest reports. And the public did want to read *happy news*.

Gore was gradually gone. Instead of showing
decapitated heads, broken arms and mutilated
limbs bloodying up the paper, Pope phased out
the mutilations by substituting "off-beat" crime
capers, many coming from the backyard of "My
Man Chu in China."

The conversion of the *Enquirer* was now taking
shape. And the paper's *new* image was gaining
new readers as well as attention in the press.
Then, feeling he was too big for Englewood Cliffs
after only four years of editorial residence there,
Pope in '71 picked up his staff, those he wanted to
go with him, and moved south to Lantana,
Florida.

In search of respectability, G.P. hired William Hall, a young St. Louis supermarket executive, who was thoroughly convinced he could sell the *Enquirer* faster in supermarkets than anyone could sell Heinz's 57 varieties. Hall felt that *The Inc.'s* competition was not *Midnight,* or the *National Tattler*, but display space competitors like *TV Guide, Women's Day* and *Family Circle*. In August '75, I learned that Hall had outlived his usefulness to G.P. and had been released.

Also a key figure in establishing the supermarket as the major sales spot for the *Enquirer* was G.P.'s long-time friend, New York public relations specialist Henry Dormann — then *The Inc.'s* board chairman. Dormann was instrumental in converting the *Enquirer's* political neutrality into an asset and made Lanstana a stopping-place for the likes of Ed Nixon and Melvin Laird. "When conventioneering supermarket executives toured backstairs at the White House in '74 at the *Enquirer's* invitation, Laird was the guide," *MORE* noted.

The *Enquirer's* main offices are set in seven-and-one-half acres of beautifully-landscaped gardens in Lantana. An editorial staff of one hundred-fifty gives the paper world-wide coverage. The printing plant is in nearby Pompano Beach, and G.P. lives with his wife and children only five minutes from the office.

The *Enquirer*, which according to a recent demographic survey G.P. authorized, discovered that their typical reader was female, between 25 and 49 with a family income under ten thousand dollars a year. In terms of over-the-counter sales, the *Enquirer* only lags behind *TV Guide*. But the entire thrust of the *Enquirer* comes from the spacious, teak-paneled office of Pope, a man who rules his tabloid as a monarchy. "I don't believe you can run a paper by committee," he was quoted as saying in the *Herald*.

But as the *Miami Herald* reporter noted: "Unlike a monarchy, no succession has been established." If G.P. should drown in his own bathtub today, nobody — not his reporters or his editors — would have any idea of who would take over the paper. Even he has not voiced his choice of a definite replacement.

"Right now," Pope says, "my executives are instructed that if anything happens to me, they are to sell it and set up trust funds for my family. Of course, the employees would have first option to buy it, since nobody in the family could run it," he told the *Herald* reporter.

It was reported that Pope's son, Generoso III, in his mid-twenties, has no interest in the multi-million-dollar business. And the only person who is involved in the slightest is his wife, who is one of the paper's sharpest critics.

G.P., his wife and their children live in an opulent fourteen-room house, said to cost in excess of $500,000. Three nights a week, they manage to be alone in the chic breakfast room of their mansion atop a natural sand dune on four acres of oceanfront land in Manalapan. "Basically, this is when I tell her my pipe dreams and she pulls me back to earth," said G.P. to the *Herald* of his wife.

Pope is the *only* individual among those connected with the editorial content of the paper who makes decisions. He is the one — the only one — who OK's stories after reading religiously through nine hundred story-idea memos a week. And a proof of every single page of the paper goes to his desk before it is molded into metal and put on the presses.

Pope lives for his work, and even takes unfinished editorial business with him whenever he leaves from the office for a day or two. He told the *Herald*: "One thing I've been accused of is having an unnatural drive. A good friend of mine, who is a psychiatrist, told me that. I think he was trying to sell me some sessions. I said to him: 'So what's wrong with it? It's working!' "

G.P. has even gone on record, stating that if his paper was up to the twenty-million sales mark each week, he could stop the narcotics flow into the country: "How? Pressure. Enough pressure on Congress, plus our own good staff out in the field exposing it. It's almost an open secret how they smuggle the stuff. And there's a tremendous rivalry among law-enforcement agencies. Instead of fighting crime, they're competing with one another."

And after stopping dope? "My real goal is world-wide circulation, second to none. My individual opinion is that there's no country that can straighten out all its problems. If I can reach the common people . . . I don't care what kind of government is in a country, it has to respond to the wishes of the people, even if it's a totalitarian government. And you've got to force the governments to help. I guess I'm saying what we're trying to do is what the United Nations hasn't been able to," he further told the Miami paper.

While I was an *Enquirer* reporter, I was forbidden from suggesting an article involving the underworld. I never saw an article in the *Enquirer* mention organized crime — except on one occasion, and it was favorable to the mob. The January 16, '66 *Enquirer* featured the following headline: UNDERWORLD REPAYS OLD WIDOW'S KINDNESS—THEY CAPTURE HER KILLER FOR COPS". This story is worthy of mention, so let me quote from the opening paragraph: "Gangster Horst Bessmens bludgeoned a helpless old widow to death when she refused to give him a cash loan. Then he fled to underworld friends, seeking a hideout. His gangland buddies were deeply sympathetic — but not with the fugitive killer. For instead of hiding him, they turned him over to the police — because the woman he murdered was known in gangland as a crook's best friend."

The West German police told the *Enquirer*: "The underworld crooks took the case right out of our hands by capturing Bessmens themselves. And they had him all for us — tied up like a present."

While mob stories were taboo, Gene Pope, since the death of J.F.K., did not give the Kennedy family a moment's peace—in print. Look at some of the recent *Enquirer* headline facts:

September 28, '69: "PSYCHIATRISTS REVEAL TEDDY'S 'DEATH WISH' ... Joan Kennedy Deeply Hurt and Humiliated."

October 19, '69: "PETER LAWFORD, FORMER BROTHER-IN-LAW, SAYS: 'I'D BE A JERK IF I SAID I BELIEVED TED'S WHOLE STORY.' " This blistering indictment of the Massachusetts Senator was preceded in the *Enquirer* by the glaring statement that "Ted becomes 'keeper' of the Kennedy flame — until doused in the waters of Chappaquiddick Island."

November 16, '69: "ETHEL PLANS TO REMARRY BECAUSE OF TED ... Ethel Kennedy plans to remarry for the sake of her 11 children because Teddy Kennedy let her down as a substitute father."

December 7, '69: "Teddy Breaks 119-Year U.S. Senate Tradition."

December 14, '69: "JACKIE ORDERS 2 SECRET SERVICE AGENTS TO GET ME ... Says Photographer Who Was Hauled Into Criminal Court For Taking Her Picture."

Pope may have had to answer to Senator Edward Kennedy for the aforementioned unfavorable articles, were it not for the July 1, '75 *Enquirer* story.

Hardly out of conscience for his treacherous attacks on the Kennedys, and acting as the Pope himself conducting a medieval Inquisition, G.P.

in his July 1, '75 edition, attempted to make peace with all the Kennedys — through Ted — who just might become, someday soon, the President of the United States. Surely Pope was well aware of the Chief Executive's "special" powers, like sending special agents, even from the C.I.A., to even scores. And of all people, Pope knew just how tough it might be for him.

Note the headline: "EXCLUSIVE — SCIENTIFIC EVIDENCE PROVES: TED TOLD THE TRUTH ABOUT CHAPPAQUIDDICK." William Dick, a staff reporter who survived the canning factory, and whom I knew personally during my tabloid tenure, wrote the article. Dick interviewed Charles McQuiston, a former U.S. intelligence expert who used, as the paper emphasized, an "amazing new 'truth detector' to analyze tape recordings of statements Kennedy made about the tragic accident that killed Mary Jo Kopechne."

McQuiston analyzed more than one thousand feet of Senator Edward Kennedy's tape recordings, meticulously breaking down each word into syllables, looking for the revealing signs of stress. The forty-nine-year-old former Army major used an incredible nine hundred-fifty feet of graph paper analyzing just one of the senator's speeches.

The "truth detector," called the Psychological Stress Evaluator (P.S.E.), the *Enquirer* reported, is being used by one hundred fifty-nine law-enforcement agencies in the United States, and is "so accurate its results have been admitted as evidence by courts in at least five states."

Gene, what you're saying is that the P.S.E. has probably been admitted in "five states" — no need for "in at least." Further, you don't tell the readers how successful the "truth detector" has proven to be *after* being admitted as evidence.

"And I know now Kennedy was telling the

truth about Chappaquiddick — the absolute truth," McQuiston says. Gene Pope is a most complex individual.

One day you can be his best friend in print. The next, you can be hounded, derided and ridiculed through the enormous power of his penetrating press. Is his motivation to sell more papers, or is it the enjoyment he derives from the throne of his *Enquirer* empire?

CHAPTER XXI

The End of "The Inc."— And How Elvis's Doll Brought Me Back

"After eight years of working for the *Enquirer* I have decided to leave — so I can earn a living. The drastic cutting of story rates was, of course, the final nail in my personal financial coffin; but the matter is far deeper than that."

These were the actual opening bars of termination orchestrated by a fellow reporter for *The Inc.* whose initials are D.P. His letter of February 27, '68, made available to me, was directed to Nat, who was then top dog — but who recently has been embarrassingly demoted to second-in-command.

D.P.'s missive adds: "Since the new order, there is no more real writing. The last story I did, 'Graphology,' was 90% digging, or reporting, and only 10% writing. My writing ability no longer matters — any reporter can now do the work I have been doing."

Dick — his first name — resented turning in "notes" instead of the polished finished pieces he was accustomed to preparing. "With G.P.'s current demand for 'special stories,' " Dick continued, "I am forced to either lie or be sued. If I don't tell psychiatrists, doctors etc. where a story is going to appear, they will object and threaten to sue when they read it in the *Enquirer*. If I do tell them, they refuse to cooperate — so no story. I will not go on writing stories with the knowledge that I may be sued. So far I have been threatened legally by four professionals (psychiatrists, etc.), although I very carefully quoted each of them correctly.

"To put it very simply, I will not work for the new low rates. Is it any wonder that I've just signed a contract to write a book?

"I have no argument with J.D.," he continued, "and my decision has nothing to do with him. He is simply trying to run the paper on his own basis of efficiency, and I wish him well. But I will not be part of a low budget system."

On the same day Dick tendered his formal written resignation, he sent me this note: "Dear George: After a great deal of thought, I disagree with your advice not to quit. I agree with your point that the only way to win fair payment is to stop writing for the paper. This I have done. Enclosed find my letters to J.D. and Nat.

"If you can take the gradual death they are handing out, that's up to you. I cannot and will not . . . Lot's of luck in the torture factory. I simply won't take it any longer — D.P."

Dick went on to write his book and became a top television writer. "J.D.," to whom he referred, was another reporter working undercover who competed with D.P. and myself. Invariably, I would beat both out on "page one" stories, and other choice sections of the paper. So instead of continuing to take a financial bath, J.D. sold G.P. a bill of goods — which the illustrious publisher bought — for a while, before canning him.

J.D. functioned as a combination efficiency expert-editorial taskmaster. His special office, established like T.A.F. solely to service the *Enquirer*, piled Dick and myself with ample assignments. But instead of getting the customary rate for fast, efficient service, the fees became a quarter and a fifth of what they were.

And through his short-lived reign, J.D. was reported pulling in no less than $1800 each week — for all the money he was saving G.P. from reporters like Dick and myself.

Things finally reached the point where I had to

confront the terrible truth. The great days of gore, grime, exposé were winding down to extinction. The paper, to sum it up, was becoming "the pussycat of the tabloids!" The adrenalin that would flow furiously through my veins was all tapped out. I was becoming bored interviewing shrinks on matters and issues they were not qualified to decide . . . and people on the street for insignificant *Enquirer* polls. The challenge, the excitement and the enlightenment were all gone. And so was the monetary incentive. Better to be back in broadcasting, I reasoned. At least there my salary would be steady and the work relatively redeeming — or so I thought, and hoped.

On September 17, '68, I became the Manager of Press Services for the Columbia Broadcasting System's radio network. I had been the successful nineteenth, and last applicant interviewed for the responsible post. To account for a chunk of five years in my working career, I was forced to reveal my *Enquirer* exploits to the radio division vice president. Intrigued, impressed and flabbergasted, W.T. Dawson, one of the most professional, genuinely honest men I've ever worked with, made this unforgettable statement before he hired me: "Anyone who could tackle all those 'impossible' stories, must be the man for us. You'll have to employ all your writing skills, *Enquirer* drive and determination to restore radio's prominence as a news-making and entertainment medium."

Dawson, who asked to be called Tom, outlined the duties I was to perform, which included press representation and "direct" contact with such notables of the network as Walter Cronkite, Mike Wallace, Roger Mudd, Dan Rather, Daniel Schorr, Abigail Van Buren, Arthur Godfrey, and others. I was even required to fly with Godfrey in a helicopter to promote his network shows.

And when CBS News broke a "world exclusive"

on the radio network, I was expected to write and disseminate the scoop to the "other" news media for CBS attribution. When Mike Wallace extracted the first account of American atrocities in South Vietnam from former P.F.C. Paul Meadlo, I wrote the "first" story of the infamous My Lai Massacre for the media. I vividly recall phoning *The New York Times* and instructing the editor to "hold up" their first edition. While a secretary was frantically transcribing the recorded atrocity accounts, I was busy batting out the article. Racing through the newsroom to the lobby and into the street, I hailed a cab that sped through three red lights before we reached the *Times* Building on West 43rd Street. Though my byline never appeared in any story for the Columbia Broadcasting System, "CBS Radio" most assuredly did. In fact, my article on My Lai, which appeared on the Tuesday, November 25, '69 front page of *The New York Times* crediting the "CBS Radio Network" for first breaking the story, aggravated Walter Cronkite's T.V. unit to the point of establishing a serious rift between the radio and television divisions. Cronkite's staff, who broke an abbreviated version of the exposé minutes later, wanted "all" the credit. Weren't the TV boys aware that radio also thrived on the ratings?

The story of My Lai was one of the most terrifying revelations of American history. It raised questions for the conscience of a nation. While the Watergate scandal came to light as a result of an eighty-dollar-a-week guard, My Lai and the morality of America came under shocking scrutiny by the world when an Army private blew the whistle. P.F.C. Meadlo, who had lost a foot in a land-mine explosion the day after the My Lai sweep, told how, on what he claimed were orders from Lieutenant Calley, he had emptied four clips — sixty to seventy shots — into forty to forty-five "men, women and children" at My Lai and "might have killed ten or fifteen of them . . . I see the women and children in my sleep." Mr. Meadlo said, "Some days . . . some nights, I can't even sleep. I just lay there thinking about it."

Like a doctor, or an *Enquirer* reporter, I was on call twenty-four hours a day. My home was equipped with sophisticated taping and transcribing equipment so that I could convert news bulletins into major news breaks in the nation's newspapers and magazines. And when former President Nixon visited China and the Soviet Union, I was one of the few at CBS who, to coordinate the coverage, was privy to his top-secret itinerary. All the Apollo manned space flights, including the historic moon missions, fell under my area of responsibility.

The CBS hierarchy entrusted me with many of their deepest, darkest secrets. And at all times, I respected the confidential nature of my position. I wondered, however, why they demonstrated such deep faith in a former *Enquirer* reporter who had the calculating capacity to perform — for the public's enlightenment and possibly entertainment—a brutal autopsy on CBS television eye and radio ear.

After four years and one day, I resigned from the network. I felt I had more than justified W.T. Dawson's confidence in my abilities to write and generate press for CBS. I wanted to join the sporting world — World Team Tennis and the World Football League. I became vice-president and general manager of the New York Sets (the name I coined), and for the gridiron group, I was head of press information at the New York franchise. At the time, both leagues were financially tottering and faced a most uncertain future.

While there was considerable speculation about expanding professional sports in a recession and a dwindling-dollar market, the brilliant future of the *Enquirer* as a dominant force in publishing was becoming considerably obvious.

I was always resolved to someday make publicly known the memoirs of my past with the paper. More than a decade had passed since my first article for *The Inc.* ran, and I was solidly convinced that the timing was right for such an undertaking. My decision was not solely made on any inherent nostalgic significance, but basically because it placed the phenomenal growth of the paper in fascinating, factual perspective.

Then, as if by predestination, I received a phone call from a guy nicknamed "The Horse," a label he carried because of his uncanny equestrian imitations. According to "reliable sources," he once whinnied to a police horse in Puerto Rico. The animal neighed and then charged him, throwing his rider to the ground.

"The Horse" told me that he had attended a private cocktail party for an actress at the Plaza Hotel earlier in the day. But while leaving the affair, he noticed that another event was just starting in the next suite. "It's for the *Enquirer*," he reported. "They're having a Christmas party on the second floor. Thought you'd like to see some of your old buddies. There's some pretty good-looking chicks there, too," he added.

"The Horse," now in his mid-forties, has become a living legend in Manhattan for pursuing parties, and he has a penchant for busty broads and fabulous food. Often, when he reveals his real name to young girls and requests their phone number, he is told: "It's the same number as it was twenty years ago — when you picked my mother up and tried to screw her!"

He was one of the very few who knew of my *Enquirer* connection. "The Horse" would read *The Inc.* religiously, even framing the gruesome greats that tickled his fancy. I would later learn why: "They were the greatest conversation pieces. They were so distracting that before the broad knew it, I was pulling her panties off!"

Christmas '74 for the *Enquirer* at the Plaza was the dullest, dreariest, dumpiest soiree I ever looked in on. I didn't recognize a face in the crowd, and not even "The Horse" was roaming about. Could Pope's guillotine have changed the entire face of the editorial staff? Many of the guests were either with their wives or girlfriends, and many appeared three-quarters crocked. I quickly walked through one door of the suite and out the other. I was not interested in sharing their liquor, sampling their lovelies or singing their lullabies. Many of the *Enquirer* staff had been brought over from the United Kingdom by Pope who contended "these were the best workers in the world." But I was not at all fascinated by their lifestyle, especially when they got together over booze and broads at a Christmas party.

I was intent on snooping for scraps of papers, documents, memos and any other interesting inside information that might be scattered about. Yuletide bashes are hardly ever a 100% expression of the boss's altruism. Aside from the benefits of maintaining office morale and holiday cheer, actual good will is often superceded by a subtle recruitment procedure to sell media people. And in the case of G.P., he was obviously courting the key people at the ad agencies whom he was hoping to convert to disciples of the *Enquirer*. But at *The Inc.*'s staid and stolid supper buffet, aside from the foot-high pile of ravaged spare ribs and chicken bones, there wasn't a morsel of meaningful material I could glean from their great celebration.

Definitely dejected at not having dug anything up, and my curiosity now satisfied, I was preparing to leave the hotel when I was suddenly attracted to two knockouts — a voluptuous brunette and a sensuous blonde. I was sure I had seen the brown-eyed blonde before, but where? Could they possibly have been checking into the hotel — for the *Enquirer's* Christmas party?

"You're really beautiful," I said to the blonde who was standing by the front desk. "Haven't I seen you before?"

"I hope you aren't trying to pick us up?" said the brunette beauty.

"Who me?" I said naively. "I just think I've seen your girl friend's face before. That's all!"

"You probably have. She's Elvis's girl, Linda Thompson. I'm Jeanne LeMay, and we're here in New York for a few days Christmas shopping, compliments of Mr. Presley."

Can you imagine that one flight directly above, the *Enquirer* was missing out on a scoop that G.P. would have severed his left arm to have? If any of the Enquirerites knew that the hottest story was below them, they would have dropped their drinks and dames and stampeded like a pack of wild wolves down the side corridor stairway for this precious prey. They didn't know, and I was not about to let them in on my secret.

After gaining the confidence of the two girls, I promised to do an in-depth article on Elvis's girl. As an added inducement, I offered to throw in Ron Galella's candid, spontaneous photography to accompany the article. Elvis's envoy, I resolved, would be the vehicle that would return me to reporting — but on a higher level than at the *Enquirer*.

So I scheduled lunch for the next day at the Plaza's famed Palm Court where Jeanne LeMay joined Linda. Galella, whom I had not worked with professionally in seven years, was also present. Aside from being the most proficient paparazzo in America, he was now the most controversial. In addition to a camera confrontation with Jackie Onassis, Marlon Brando, totally un-provoked by the photographer, had caught Galella off-guard and smashed his fist into Ron's chin, busting his jaw. Two years earlier, off the set of *Hammersmith Is Out* in Cuernavaca, Mexico, Richard Burton and Liz Taylor's bodyguards caught the imaginative Galella photographing them from the cover of a cave adjacent to a pool with his 300mm telephoto lens. Before he left Mexico, he was minus fifteen rolls of "exclusive" film of the Burtons, was kicked, stomped and tortured, and then was thrown into jail, Galella told me after returning to New York. I furnished Earl Wilson with the item at the time it occurred. The next day, the Burtons' publicist, John Springer, issued a general denial.

I asked Linda if she would instruct the switchboard not to give out their room number. Also, I wanted her unrecognizable, so I loaned her my dark sunglasses, hoping to avoid other reporters canvassing the hotels for stars and falling upon this catch.

On January 8, '75, Elvis would turn forty. No one was able to corner Elvis for an interview and finding Linda Thompson was next best to chatting with the rock idol. Especially since she had been living with him for the past two-and-a-half years.

"Elvis is second only to one in my life, and that one is God! He's like an angel on earth," revealed the twenty-four-year-old Linda, the '72 Miss Tennessee-Universe. Girl friend Jeanne LeMay met Linda at the same pageant when she was the representative from Rhode Island.

Elegantly attired in a smashing $500 black leather Gucci outfit, the Memphis model was the recipient of no less than nineteen different beauty awards — and was, unquestionably, the envy of millions who had religiously followed, and worshipped, the unprecedented career of

Presley.

My interview with Linda was her very first. It was also her initial exposure before the lens of a paparazzo, without Elvis. Our combined efforts led to the January 13, '75 *PEOPLE* magazine cover story which generated considerable reader attention, and sales, for the Time, Inc. publication.

While lovely Linda was thrilled with all the attention that she was directing to Elvis's accomplishments . . . and her dedication to the rock idol, it would ultimately work against her and lead to her dethroning as Presley's "live-in" girl. An unnecessary description *PEOPLE* employed in a photo caption provoked the wrath not only of Ms. Thompson, but of Elvis, too.

Linda's intentions were honorable, but Presley misinterpreted them as promotion for herself. It is said that Linda, unknowingly, played into the hands of those who resented her being "too close" to Presley and used the magazine exposure to her disadvantage.

She did, however, jump to "girl friend" status on July 6, '72, the day she met Elvis. At the time, Linda was Miss Tennessee. "'To what do I owe the honor?' I said to Elvis as he sat down beside me at the table. I was absolutely certain he was married. I had never dated a married man and Mr. Presley was not going to be the exception. That is, until he said he was *legally* separated. I attacked him on the spot. A week later, Elvis filed for divorce."

For a little more than two-and-a-half years, which Linda called "bliss," she lived with Elvis in a posh eighteen-room house on a sprawling thirteen-acre estate called Graceland on Elvis Presley Boulevard in Memphis. Her parents lived just around the corner, less than a few minutes away where they had moved to be close to their daughter.

But after the *PEOPLE* article appeared, Linda's pleasure became her poison. I do not believe that Ms. Thompson was in any way capitalizing on the Presley name. If anything, she was doing one helluva public relations job on Presley, who was in desperate need of having the record set straight!

When I asked Linda a difficult, provocative question, she fielded the curve like a professional: "Inasmuch as you and Elvis are of strong religious convictions, how do face the moral issue of living together — not as husband and wife?"

"Elvis is not a John Doe," she replied. "It is a special situation. As for morality, this situation cannot be compared to anything else. So, morality is not applicable.

"The fact of the matter is that Elvis has so much. He just wants to share it. He believes his wealth is really from God, too. He's a good man. He doesn't smoke or drink.

"And I would go on record saying that Elvis is the most considerate, most generous man in the world. Four months ago, he purchased twenty of the most expensive automobiles. And he gave them all away — even to some he didn't know. There were Mark IV's, Cadillacs and Pontiacs. The maids and the friends of the maids whom Elvis never met, all received cars. Why did he do it? Again, Elvis has so much, he just wants to share it."

"What was your reaction to seeing this massive expenditure?" I asked.

"I loved it. Between the cars and the houses ..."

"The houses?" I asked.

"Yes, there were houses ... and jewelry. In all, Elvis gave away more than half-a-million dollars of merchandise.

"On a recent 747 flight, Elvis gave a stewardess an expensive ring he was wearing. He had never met her before, nor had Elvis known the steward he presented with a beautiful made-to-order watch."

I was charged again, doing what I did best. Reporting was my bag and I knew my life was finally getting back on the right groove. I wondered, though, if Elvis's generosity was in any way related to tax advantages. "Elvis doesn't take tax deductions and he isn't interested in tax shelters. He loves America and doesn't want to cheat her."

Linda revealed that Elvis had better protection than the President of the United States. "His security is so tight you can't get a button, or a thread, from his garments."

Brushing back her sun-streaked, long-flowing hair, Linda condemned the press for printing "heartless, vicious rumors" about Elvis taking drugs. "He's so energetic, so spectacular and so exhilarated by the excitement of performing that there are those who would trace his energies to drugs. And were you aware," she added, "Elvis is a federal narcotics officer? Three years ago, former President Richard M. Nixon issued Elvis a federal narcotics badge which means he has the authority to make an arrest. Elvis is actually on the police force of more than thirty-five states, and all his badges are legitimate. He wouldn't accept an honorary one. See, here's one," she proudly displayed a shield from the Kansas City police force of which Elvis is a bona fide member. "Elvis is dead against drugs," she added. "He feels that your body is the temple and you shouldn't abuse it. It's all part of his Christian way of life."

Does this sound like someone who's out to use another for self-gain —if only to ingratiate herself even more with Presley?

Linda revealed that Elvis held an eighth-degree Black Belt, which is a Masters of the art.

Then the part-Cherokee model removed a pair of keys from her matching black leather purse. "Elvis told me to hold car keys between my fingers, like this," The Presley method, "and to slash muggers, like this." The Presley procedure appeared to be most menacing, even from a girl. "You know, you can't be oblivious to those around you—to those who might want to do you harm. Elvis has even taught me the basic moves of karate. He wants me to be aware!"

On the heels of my *PEOPLE* piece on Presley, the *Enquirer* ran an "exclusive" interview with Linda Thompson on their back page. I thought it strange, especially in light of Elvis's disdain for the *Enquirer* and her promise she wouldn't speak elsewhere.

"George, that *Enquirer* article is pure fabrication. Imagine the *Enquirer* saying that I said Elvis teaches me karate to keep the wolves away. That's ridiculous. How can they get away with such things anyway? And they even said we always kept a pot roast on the stove. I'm going to write the paper and give them a piece of my mind."

What I suspect is that the *Enquirer* got caught printing a *phoney* piece from a stringer. Taking the reporter's word, Pope went eagerly to press. For that very reason, many of the more prestigious papers in the country do not take outside work. But once in the existence of every news organization in America, a paper, magazine, radio or TV station gets caught with a dud.

It's no secret that the *Enquirer* is hated by Presley. Examine some of *The Inc.'s* raunchiest:

May 17, '64: Hollywood Keyhole by Gene Carter — "Presley Falls for Gal. Then Gets Floored By Her Boyfriend."

November 1, '64: cover story — "IT'S A MIRACLE ELVIS IS A STAR . . . Says Teacher Who Knew Him When." The *Enquirer* interviewed

Mildred Scrivener, who was the history and homeroom teacher at Humes H.S. in Memphis, Tenn. "Elvis wasn't a good student ... I've never stopped wondering how Elvis Presley became a world-famous entertainer ... I don't know whether he ever dated."

April 4, '65: cover story — "TIRED OF BEING A BACHELOR, ELVIS PRESLEY, NOW 30, MOANS — I'M LOOKING FOR A WIFE ... But I Can't Find Anyone."

March 14, '65: Hollywood Keyhole by Gene Carter — "Presley Pulverizes Pal For Playing Dice At Home."

June 4, '67: "Leading Psychiatrist Explains — WHY ELVIS PRESLEY WAITED SO LONG TO MARRY." *The Inc.* said, "He may have been slow in maturing mentally and therefore was reluctant to accept the adult possibility of caring for a wife. He probably had a deep fear of being 'taken' financially by a wife — by having to make huge alimony payments if she ever left him."

August 25, '68: back page: "ELVIS IS FADING, SAYS PRODUCER ... But He'll Come Back Like Sinatra, Bigger Than Ever."

November 19, '74: "Elvis at 40 — Paunchy, Depressed and Living In Fear. Middle age has put a paunchy roll around rock n' roll king Elvis Presley." First of all, the Pelvis wouldn't turn "forty" until January the following year. G.P., I'm surprised at you!

July 27, '75: "ELVIS FINDS A NEW LOVE." According to the *Enquirer*, Sheila Ryan, twenty-two, was Elvis' "new" girl.

When Elvis did actually turn forty, I was the *only* reporter to write about what *actually* happened. My "exclusive" interview appeared in *TV Radio Mirror* magazine, while the second U.S. rights to my initial interview with Ms. Thompson, almost 7,200 words, ran with little cutting in Pat Seller's *Motion Picture* magazine.

When Elvis was suddenly rushed to Baptist Memorial Hospital in February for suspected stomach blockage and overweight, Galella cut short his West Coast stay and arrived on the 10th.

Recalls Galella: "I wrote a letter to Linda who was said to be at Elvis's bedside, requesting photographs of them together. The next day when I got through to Linda on the phone, her words from Elvis were 'no way!' But she did agree to let me photograph her — on the floor and in front of the hospital. While I was there for three days, *Enquirer* reporters were splitting round-the-clock shifts. 'I will not consent to be interviewed by them,' she said, pointing her finger in rage at the *Enquirer* reporters in the distance. 'Elvis doesn't give interviews, and if he ever decided to, it would never be to the *Enquirer*,' she said to me."

Galella recalls an *Enquirer* reporter telling him that there were "thirty-two" exits out of the hospital.

"It was impossible to figure out which escape route he would select. But, a day later, after I was back in New York, I learned that he left undetected. What really astounds me," noted Ron, "is that the *Enquirer* reporters stayed two blocks away — and even if they were threatened with loitering, how can you cover a big star like Elvis from that distance?"

Linda Thompson no longer lives at Graceland. Many editors thought she was *totally* out. But on July 14 and 15, '75 she met Elvis at the Hartford Hilton where he stayed in Connecticut while performing in Springfield, Mass. Earlier, Elvis purchased a $52,000 home for Linda in Memphis, just a half mile away from his sprawling estate.

Instead of being "the" girl friend of Elvis, lovely Linda is now "one" of Presley's pretty "girlfriends," and probably the most congenial he's ever known, or lived with.

Obviously forbidden to further discuss Elvis's state of health, even in the form of a slick, protective whitewash, Linda remained obediently silent after the rock king, on August 20, '75 was suddenly rushed from the third day of his Las Vegas engagement to the Memphis hospital. Reportedly, it was the fourth time Presley had been hospitalized for indefinite, vague medical reasons since the fall of '74.

"I guess it must be his weight or stomach blockage problems again?" Galella inquired of Cliff Ayres Ostermeyer in New York three days later.

"No, not at all. It's much more serious. Elvis has cirrhosis of the liver. And all the junk food and 'other' things he's been abusing his system with over the years hasn't helped his condition," said the publisher of the *Music City Entertainer* in Nashville.

Not too long ago, Ostermeyer was personally praised by Presley for a glowing piece the publisher ran on the millionaire entertainer.

"I'm really worried about Elvis," the Memphis man added. "I don't want to write his epitaph so early in his brilliant career."

Linda Thompson and much of the world pray it doesn't come to that, "so early."

Sensuous Linda Thompson, Elvis Presley's girlfriend for more than two years, gave me an exclusive on the fabulous rock idol. *(Ron Galella)*

CHAPTER XXII
Jackie O, Mr. Wonderful, Patty Hearst, Tiny Tim and John Glenn

Having spoken personally with Bobby and Teddy Kennedy, it was understandable why a person of my determined nature had to interview Jacqueline Kennedy Onassis. When I wrote for *The Inc.* the *closest* I ever came to the former First Lady was through psychiatrist Milford Blackwell's erudite evaluation of why she was under the constant threat of death.

Ironically, Milford's well-chosen words of caution continue to hold true a decade later. Blackwell, a member of the American Medical Association, the American Psychiatric Association, the New York County Medical Society and the American Board of Psychiatry and Neurology told me: "Jackie is definitely a target for the mentally deranged. For although she no longer lives in the White House, she is still considered to be the 'First Lady' by thousands of citizens.

"The urge of some disturbed individual to kill Mrs. Kennedy can be compared to a candle fly that will dash into a flame and die in order to achieve one split-second of ecstasy in its life. For there are many mentally deranged people who will do almost anything — to anyone — to gain world-wide publicity and front-page coverage."

And while Galella was chasing Jackie around the globe, I was firmly entrenched in broadcasting. But I did manage to keep track of the former First Lady's escapades through the news media.

Then shortly before Ari's death in March '75, came the chance I had so long awaited. In fact, a foreigh publication which purchased my mini-interview confirmed it was the first of its kind "ever granted to anyone" since the assassination of J.F.K.

In part, here's what happened in February '75:

"Mrs. Onassis. My name is George Bernard. I'm a journalist. I would like to interview you."

Undaunted by my brash invitation, the former First Lady's face was expressionless. Then she smiled politely, looked me in the eye — both of them —and turned towards the exit.

"Yes, I would like to interview you," I reiterated.

Jackie stopped. A broad smile now captured her face. I had touched a vital cord. "If you can figure out a way, you're a genius!" she said, now bursting into uncontrollable laughter that only matched her sexy style of speaking.

Mrs. Aristotle Onassis, accompanied by sister Lee Radziwill, was leaving a festive charity function on Manhattan's East Side. We were in the vestibule together at the Lenox Hill Neighborhood Association, amid the crunch of the crowd and the blinding strobes of fifteen photographers. On this same hallowed spot, twenty minutes earlier, a British press agent for the benefit was barking nervously at Ron Galella.

"You're not on the guest list. And if you won't leave," he emphasized, energetically exercising undue authority in quest of moral support from his glum associates, "I'll have the police force you to."

Ron, the undisputed dean of all paparazzo and a true friend to all press agents, dejectedly left, his press credentials proving ineffectual while other less accomplished photographers gained easy entry. And so into the night, Galella sped away in his fiery T-bird.

But that was twenty minutes earlier, before Jackie arrived. Now she and Lee were practically out the door. No time to claim my winter worsted overcoat, so I attempted to continue my interview on the run, jogging along with Jackie.

She was now on the street with Lee. They turned right and started walking towards Second Avenue.

"Mrs. Onassis. That is a very beautiful coat you are wearing." I said, at a loss for something more original. Can you imagine, after all those years, here I was with my "impossible dream" and I was acting as if in a stupor.

"Ooooooh," she replied, matching the wit of my comment, as if to say: George Bernard, as a journalist, you can do better than that!

I guess I could have done better, especially after I had complimented her on the "spring coat" she was wearing in eighteen-degree weather.

"It's really cold, extremely cold tonight," I continued, convincing myself I was lounging by the pool at the El San Juan. "Don't you have a limousine waiting for both of you?"

"No. There's no limousine," she laughed. "For some reason we didn't call one. We're going to get a taxi at the corner," she admitted in her baby-like voice.

"I hope so," was my reply.

The blinding photographic flashes continued.

"Aren't these photographers something? They don't seem to let up for a second," I said.

"That's nothing unusual," she remarked matter-of-factly.

Jackie's eye seemed to be caught by Galella's protege, free-lancer Paul Schmulbach, who has become amazingly adept at shooting subjects on the dead run, backwards. Graceful as a swan, he moves in reverse like a ballerina on tiptoes. Definitely, if there's ever going to be another Galella on the scene, Schmulbach is the likely candidate. His pictures are candid, crisp and calculatingly controversial. But he remembers the smashed chin Galella got from Brando. "I hope my international fame comes not through punches, but pictures," says the frail, featherweight Schmulbach, holding his fragile chin and cherishing it.

For no amount of money, not even the $40,000 Galella would later receive in October '75 from Brando in an out-of-court settlement, could sway the dollar-dreaming Paul S. to stray unnecessarily close to his subjects. The spunky Schmulbach's flash-popping has, on more than one occasion at show biz bashes, dramatically encountered the wrath of actor Paul Newman who he has caught, *off-guard* . . . guzzling beer. And while Newman has screamed for assistance, practical Paul S. was forced—out of dire need for self-preservation—to quickly head for the hills of shelter, far from the onrush of ushers. On February 24, '76, Schmulbach's agility would again be tested, and put to good use, in the true Galella tradition. Paul's press credentials, though bona fide, could not gain him admittance to a Bloomingdales' department store charity benefit, featuring the mystifyingly-beautiful Marisa Berenson. Turning seeming defeat into instant success, Schmulbach crouched low, and comically like the speedy *Road Runner* cartoon character, eluded security . . . and up a *moving* down escalator he sped, and into the party.

Meanwhile, back on the East Side, the pace suddenly picked up as we approached the corner of Second Avenue. Jackie stopped for a few moments and whispered into Lee's ear. Then they continued on, now only twenty-five feet from the curb where two men from the party had rushed ahead to hail a cab. No, they weren't her escorts, nor were they security—governmental or private. As the wife of a fallen President of the United States, Jackie is no longer accorded protection from the Secret Service. And she is definitely not immune from muggers and other would-be-assailants, noted Dr. Blackwell. Anyone, even I, could have been a threat.

Four occupied cabs whizzed by. I couldn't recall
a single reported instance when Jackie was ever
without a male escort during evening hours in
New York, or failed to have a limousine waiting
brief steps away. Had there been one, certainly
my mini-interview never would have developed.

Suddenly a cab screeched to a full stop. "These
are not the most advantageous conditions for an
interview. May I get a letter to your apartment
tomorrow concerning my credentials, and what I
would like further of you," I asked as Lee entered
the cab first.

"Yes, that would be fine," she said before step-
ping into the yellow cab. As the taxi pulled away
from the curb, I all but kicked myself for not asking if I might join the dynamic duo — whatever
their destination. Certainly, the conditions were
atypical, and the chances of such an opportunity
arising again were infinitesimal. The unbridled
nerve I had as a fearless *Enquirer* reporter had not
been, as yet, fully restored. But I was bridging the
guts gap!

My letter was delivered to Jackie's Fifth Avenue apartment the next morning. I waited almost forty-eight hours for a reply, but none was
forthcoming.

I phoned Jackie's press agent, Nancy Tucker-
man, an affable gal at Olympic Airways: "Yes, she
read your letter. Definitely. She hasn't given interviews ever since I've been with her when she
came to New York in '64. She's a person who would
like to have as much privacy as possible. She has a
lot of friends who are newspaper people, too, and
they get the same reply. Even those whom she has
dinner with are told the same, so I think it's pretty
definite."

"Have you ever been the subject of an interview?" I queried.

"I don't give interviews either."

"You *can't* give interviews?" I pressed.

"Well, I work with her very closely and I'm with her a lot."

"May I do a profile on you?"

"Afraid not. Same thing!"

Following Ari's death, Jacqueline withdrew emotionally, but only briefly, re-emerging at press conferences to preserve a New York landmark threatened with demolition. And while jogging in Central Park, she even spoke with a reporter from *The Enquirer*. It is conceivable that if the reporter had flashed his real credentials, (which seems inconceivable), she might have sped away or trampled over the courageous correspondent.

being known as "Mrs. J.F. Kennedy," will become an emissary of peace and understanding for the nation—a role she has been criticized for not assuming after the assassination. Others contend that the former First Lady is making a truly conscientious effort to end her self-exile and reestablish lines of communication with the so-called "real" world. She has, in fact joined the staff of a New York publishing firm, called press conferences to preserve a Manhattan Landmark, and in July, '76 appeared at the Democratic Convention and travelled to Russia on a cultural mission.

While Jackie O. continued to generate headline news, Sammy Davis, Jr. couldn't shrug the highly-publicized shadow of Richard M. Nixon which seemed to hound and haunt the versatile entertainer — everywhere he went. The Watergate scandal bugged him — and for good reason. In the presidential campaign of '72, the outspoken entertainer openly endorsed Nixon for re-election, and his "total commitment" even prompted him to pose with the incumbent President in an honest, impromptu embrace before a plethora of photographers.

"I regret hugging Nixon now. I thought I was

doing something for 'the cause,' " Davis said in February '75, during a rare interview with a TV reporter from a black news program in the Miami area. On that show, he explained his mistake in judgment — an error that has prompted many blacks in America to brand the well-intentioned Davis as an "Uncle Tom."

"There were others, too, who supported Nixon. I was not at the end of that line alone," Sammy countered, without drawing reference to such fellow celebrities as Mickey Mantle, Sam Huff, Charlton Heston, John Wayne, Jimmy Stewart and former Rat-Packer Frank Sinatra, all of whom came out for Nixon, pledging their allegiance to the President's platitudinous, plankless platform.

"Now, if you don't like Sammy Davis, Jr., then don't come and see him," he bristled. "Remember, no black man and no white man ever lost a job because of Sammy Davis, Jr. Again, if you don't like me — for any reason —then don't come and see me in my act. That's the way you can effectively respond to me."

The Nixon nostalgia nauseates Davis, and the old mutual admiration society is but a lingering, painful memory. Davis has reportedly moved the dozens of framed letters from the President that once occupied a place of prominence, and has installed them in an obscure spot off his den in the six-figure Beverly Hills home he shares with his third wife, Altovise.

In '73, Davis, at the personal request of President Nixon, entertained returning POW's in Washington. Davis has also gone on record in the press, stating that prior to his endorsement of Nixon, the President promised reform towards blacks, but never specified what form that change would take.

And so, brimming with undue hostility, as volatile as a chemical cocktail, Molotov fashion,

Davis barricaded himself inside a posh penthouse suite provided by the management of the Diplomat Resort and Country Club in Hollywood, Florida. There, presidential-style, protected from frenetic fans and the rest of the outside world — and possibly himself — Davis was guarded by no less than six round-the-clock private security officers.

While in Florida, Davis accepted no calls, with one exception: Shirley Rhodes, the wife of Sammy's musical director. Shirley screens *all* calls and relays messages.

Which leads me to my involvement with Super Sammy. While I was in Miami for three weeks in February '75, *In The Know* magazine contacted me from New York to interview Davis. The publication, a replica of *People,* first heard of me from the Presley piece and was eager to obtain my writing-reporting services.

Mel Shestack, a veritable Santa Claus to all in appearance and actions, learned of my dad's sudden hospitalization from a fellow writer in New York. Shestack, the editor, considerate and sympathetic, suggested that if my father's condition should stabilize, *In The Know* was interested in having Davis discuss Nixon. "Keep close tabs on the doctors there," Mel cautioned. "I had a personal tragedy in Miami that I'd rather not talk about — it might frighten you," he said compassionately and ominously. You couldn't help but feel a fondness for Mel.

When the time was right, I placed a call to Davis. I assumed getting the interview would be a snap. I had interviewed Sammy while he was in "Golden Boy," and assumed he would be appreciative and extremely grateful for my "praiseworthy" article.

But getting through was impossible. "Even Frank Sinatra?" I queried the hotel operator. "Well, I can't recall Mr. Sinatra calling Mr.

Davis, and I've been here a while. But all calls *must* go through Mrs. Rhodes while Mr. Davis is here," the Southern belle informed me.

Approximately three minutes before show time, Davis was escorted hurriedly through a rear elevator to the lobby that leads to the famed Crystal Room where he would arrive precisely on the hour to do two, back-to-back performances.

The performer is said to sleep until three in the afternoon and to watch personally-selected motion pictures that are flown to his suite. On occasion, while relaxing, he will permit close friends—and their friends—to visit him. But he makes it a firm practice never to venture to the Diplomat pool and cabana area.

A local stripper, her possessive "live-in" girlfriend and a tag-a-long acquaintance visited Sammy while I was in Miami Beach. They stayed for about an hour—after spending another hour passing through security. The tag-a-long, formerly a dancer who switched over to become an X-ray technician in Baltimore and was on vacation, told me that Sammy was edgy and easily irritated by some harmless statements she had made. At one point, she said, Sammy threatened to throw her out the door if she didn't "cool it!"

Davis's deppression was compounded by a caustic opening night review from the *Miami Herald's* entertainment editor, a man named John Huddy, who was anyone but a buddy to Sammy. Davis, who thrives on accolades, was blasted by Huddy for indifference and not giving his act enough of the professional touch; for resting on his laurels, when an audience should be treated to the best, at all times.

It was no wonder that Sammy's short fuse blew when he was asked in Florida about his conversion to Judaism. "I am a black Jew," Davis roared. "But why do you ask me about my faith? Do you know what religion James Brown is, or

Jim Brown or Aretha Franklin?" The reporter, a black man, was speechless. "Then don't ask me. Leave me alone." Later, Davis went on record stating: "The religion of blackness connects us!"

Sammy's secretary, Shirley, got back to me — but only after I had left fourteen call-back messages with the switchboard. "Sammy said no," she reported. "Yes, I told Sammy that you did that article on him and why you were down in Florida, but he said *no*. I'm sorry," she added, "I even said you only wanted fifteen minutes with him. But once he says *no*, that's it!"

This wasn't the Sammy I once knew. He had really messed himself up in the past ten years. He was black, a Jew and a former Nixon supporter. His guest appearance on Archie "The Bigot" Bunker's "All in the Family" made some mighty waves in the black community and his theological conversion may have alienated certain influential groups. For eight years, many of them stormy, Sammy had been married to a white girl.

And then the icing on his crumbling cake came when, under the Nixon Administration, he was appointed to the National Advisory Council on Economic Opportunity; a year later, in '72, the Presidential Commission on Drugs. But when the tide turned for Nixon, it turned for Sammy too. He was not forgotten for his connection with "Celebrities for Nixon."

In November, '64, Sammy was playing to a S.R.O. crowd in the Broadway production of "Golden Boy." He was everyone's favorite. Sammy loved the world, and in turn, everyone adored Sammy.

It was at one of those late afternoon celebrity discotheque parties, less popular today, that I had first met Sammy. The bright spot was the Disc-Au-Go-Go, which is no longer in existence, like so many others that folded in Manhattan's show-biz section of the city.

"Mr. Davis," I said, "my name is George Bernard, and I'm on assignment from a national magazine. I cannot go back without interviewing you." Compassionately, Sammy patted me on the shoulder. "Stay loose. When I leave for the show, you'll be leaving with me." An hour-and-twenty-minutes elapsed before Sammy glanced at the bar clock and indicated that I should follow him out the front door.

Comic Alan King rushed past me to usher Davis to his waiting Rolls, while Jack Carter vied for the honor with a double-parked black sedan.

"No thanks," said Sammy. "I'm going with my man, George," Davis declared to the totally dismayed King and Carter who appeared, at that fleeting moment, to be immediate candidates for cardiac arrest.

Instead, Sammy hailed a cab. And as fortune would have it, we were tied up in twenty-minute traffic jam. At the time, Davis was said to have stepped out of loving favor with Sinatra, who had supposedly told the black entertainer he was a fool to expose himself to the acid comments of the New York critics, even for $10,000 a week—a record for the time.

It was typical of Davis just to grin back at Sinatra: "That's what life is all about." But Frank didn't think it was funny, especially when Sammy's "Mr. Wonderful" on Broadway was panned for the egotism of a one-man show. One newspaper critic even asked, "Mr. Who?" Still, it had been a hit.

I was trying to probe into their feud, but I found only a Sammy-Frank mutual admiration society. Sinatra, after all, had used his prestige to launch Sammy into major motion pictures such as *Ocean's Eleven* in '61 and *Robin and the Seven Hoods* in '64, among others.

"I'd quit show business tomorrow if Frank told me to. Frank's the boss. When he gives orders, I obey," said Davis — in the *Enquirer*. He added that everything he had achieved in life, he owed to Sinatra: "My career, my success, my marriage, my family. If it wasn't for Frank, I wouldn't be where I am today. That's why I'd do anything he wanted me to do!" Davis was delighted that I was providing the forum for his impressive indebtedness to the man New York disc jockey William B. Williams called "The Chairman of the Bored." The black entertainer added that Frank had guided him throughout his career, providing encouragement and advice. "He'd never make the wrong move for me," noted Davis. Of "Golden Boy," Sammy said: "This show is a hit, but if Frank told me to quit, I'd hand in my notice. Frank is the boss, but he's also my best friend."

When we finally arrived under the theatre marquee, Sammy, against my wishes, picked up the taxi tab. He then shook my hand, wished me good luck with the story, and asked I send him a tear sheet of my story. Then he darted through the open stage-door entrance.

I mailed a copy of the article to Davis in care of the theatre, but I never received confirmation that he had even received it. Then again, possibly he was too busy.

I question whether I will ever be able to forgive Davis for his refusal to see me in Florida. For even after I was turned down on the phone, I made the trip to the Diplomat in Hollywood, about an hour's drive. The answer there was the same, and neither the hotel's public relations gal nor one of the managers I knew in the executive office, could, or would, attempt to help me.

Today, Sammy is less cherubic and more discerning. He defers and denies those who would deprive him of his time. He thrives on privacy and simply wants no more than to do his own thing, alone, or with whomever he chooses. Thus, he joins the expanding ranks of entertainers like

Paul Newman, Robert Redford, Marlene Dietrich, and of course, Frank Sinatra, who avoid the probing press.

There are those close to Davis who contend that Sammy's willful withdrawal and aggravated attitude are the result of more than his Nixon blunder. Noted the entertainment director of a Miami Beach hotel: "Sammy is inexplicably caught in the middle of a mess, of which he is not totally at fault. He must be so many things, so many times, to so many people, he can't ever be the real Sammy to himself. And Nixon didn't help things either."

The account of Davis in Florida appeared in my June '75 *In The Know* article, entitled: "SHERIFF SAMMY DAVIS, JR. RENOUNCES NIXON." The article said, in part: "Davis is still, however, a firm advocate of Law and Order, the slogan of the first Nixon administration. Davis has just been sworn in as the Chief of Police of Langston, Oklahoma, an all-black university town of four hundred souls which has no police force to begin with. Like its sister black villages of Foley and Taft, where Redd Foxx and Flip Wilson are the honorary sheriffs, Langston now has an international celebrity to keep the peace, wear bell-bottom trousers, and tote a six-gun." Men may make guns — but guns don't necessarily make men, Sammy.

My stories on Elvis and Sammy began to pave a smooth comeback trail for me. The *National Star, The Inc.'s* closest competitor, was interested in me now. But practically before I could get started, J.D. from the old *Enquirer* moved in as news editor. When he saw me, he turned red with rage. To assert his authority over his subordinates, he summarily fired a receptionist, two secretaries, the photo editor and anyone else who didn't fit his specifications. He even tried to fire me, but how could he? I didn't work for the paper. But when he tried to mess with the *Star's* ace columnist, Steve Dunleavy, he got knocked out of the box—definitely the wrong guy to tangle with. And, in the end, J.D. was out on the street again. Dunleavy, an Australian, like Rupert Murdoch, publisher of the *Star* and a chain of other newspapers, "could do no wrong." In fact, besides being Murdoch's "favorite," he is one helluva journalist. In his caustic column, Dunleavy throws boulders at the Rolling Stones and urges liberals to take their lives before pulling American society into the shit pile.

Murdoch, a genius like G.P., is less frentic and, in many ways, more imaginative. According to Dunleavy, his boss will not only continue to run full-color covers, but will even splash their centerfolds with color photos. "Something Gene Pope is not capable of doing," Steve swears.

At the *Star,* the staff is not subjected to the daily threats of being canned for spilling "a cup of coffee on the boss' rug" — a story said to have happened at the *Enquirer.* Prior to Liz and Richard Burton's divorce, the second time around together, the *Enquirer's* Sept. 9, '75 issue showed the couple reunited in sharp black and white while the *Star's* color shot, also on the front cover of the feuding couple, seemed to suggest that it was just a matter of time before Murdoch surpassed Pope. In the April 21, '75, edition of *Newsweek,* Pope said he was unflustered by the possibility that a "competitor" would beat him out. Pope dismissed *People* magazine as "a little too high-brow" and the *Star* as "an imitator". But in the old days, the *Enquirer* was a follower, too!

In June, '75, I interviewed Joey Heatherton, who was Cher's summer replacement on CBS. She was headlining a variety show at the Waldorf's famed Empire Room, before flying to the West Coast to tape a month's programs for the network. Though she seemed to have everything going for her, no one ever thought of this blonde powder keg in the same breath as Raquel Welch, Claudia Cardinale, Marilyn Monroe or Liz Taylor. In fact, the only headline on Joey that had stirred any excitement with me was Gene Carter's January '64 column in the *Enquirer:* "Bette Davis hits starlet (Joey Heatherton) for calling her a fading beauty . . ." Apparently, the blow came after a remark about Joey's low-cut dress.

If you saw Joey perform from a table that was practically on the stage, as I did with Ron Galella, you would know instantly that she has it, and more. But when I attempted to do an interview in her suite following the performance, there were too many distractions. Carol Lynley was in town for one of the leads in Broadway's "Absurd Person Singular," and when Ron popped a picture of the sullen-faced actress and her male escort, the gent took noticeable exception to Ron's roving camera. Prudence then dictated that it was best to leave and come back the next day.

When I rang her room from the lobby, a less than hospitable Joey came to the phone.

"But I told you to call *first* before coming to the hotel!" she said in an angry, drowsy voice.

"What's the difference, I'm here?" I said, annoyed.

"O.K. I'm practicing my music right now, so why don't you come up in twenty minutes."

Joey greeted me in jeans and a rumpled sweat shirt. I did one of those movie double-takes. But then I realized there probably wasn't an actress in the world who looked ravishing after rolling out of bed.

Having lived, on-and-off, with a beautiful Broadway actress named Barbara for three years during my *Enquirer* days, I knew all too well the stark realities of waking up to a make-up-less physiognomy. When you're accustomed to perceiving a goddess of grooviness before hitting the sack, only to be confronted by a drab Dora the morning after, it makes you wonder why you've been hanging around for so long. Another Barbra, who spelled her name differently, once told me: "Any woman who allows herself to be seen without make-up is a fool. Life is an illusion, one giant game where we make our own rules and play it out until death. So why not wear the best mask you can find to get the most attractive partners to play the game?" Barbra, by the way, slept, showered, skinny-dipped, went to the toilet and made seductions in her make-up. How her pores avoided suffocation is a wonder. I guess she knew what she was doing, though — her phone never stopped ringing.

The blue-eyed, blonde Joey apologized for her unglamorous appearance, only after I loaded my camera with Kodak's Tri-X pan film and was about to click off a few frames. "No, no, no! I didn't think you were going to shoot me," she said holding her arms across her face and turning away from my camera. "An interview, yes. But no pictures."

"I haven't had the hit movie, nor the golden record to become a superstar. But I know if I'm *ever* going to make it, television will either do it for me, or my career will go on as it's been going —nowhere great!

"I've just cleaned house," she went on. "I had a real *bad* manager who took me on as a hobby. He's no more now. I just kicked him out," the 5'3" performer went on.

It was more than ten years since I had seen Joey. The last time was at a motion picture premiere while I was covering a film's opening, and she was squinting her eyes before the blinding television floodlights. So, from out of my camera bag I pulled out a photo of that nostalgic moment.

"Gee, is that me?" she exclaimed. "Look how

long my hair was then." She stared in amazement at the glossy.

Joey was about to play a subdued Cher-type to her dad, actor Ray Heatherton, whom the *National Star* compared to "Sonny." Ms. Heatherton was no fool. She knew the value of imitation, especially following the successful formula that worked so well for the Bonos while they were performing together. "I'm good friends with Cher," Joey volunteered. "Cher and I even bought the *same* black leather outfit at Gucci's a few Christmases ago," she noted. Obviously different sizes.

"When I was performing in Las Vegas's Riviera, Sonny and I went out. We're just friends—that's all!"

I accused Joey of "belting" out her songs, instead of "singing" them.

"You know something, George. Nobody's *ever* had the nerve to tell me that," she said, pausing to reflect. "Yep, I'm going to look into that. Hey, you may have something there," she said, and then repeated herself.

Sure enough, though, when Joey premiered on CBS with her doting dad, she wasn't belting out songs Ethel Merman-style. Instead, she came across super-slick and sophisticated, vocalizing sultry songs and ballads.

Deborah Raffin was another woman who was making news for her role in *Once Is Not Enough*. So when publicist Myrna Post set up a "special" shooting session with Ron in July at the Plaza, I decided to come along with my recorder. At the time, I never imagined my machine would explode with the hottest, most bitter Hollywood feud since Otto Preminger kicked Robert Mitchum off his *Rosebud* set in Africa, replacing the allegedly intoxicated actor with Peter O'Toole.

Preminger was as violent as he appeared. I

recall reading John J. Miller's June 13, '65 column in the *Enquirer:* "Otto Preminger walloped a gate crasher who was bothering Olivia de Havilland at a party. Preminger's power-packed punch gashed the wise guy's face and four stitches were needed to close the wound."

If it ever came to blows between Mitch and Otto, I'd put my money on rugged Robert. What a bruiser! But as it turned out, Otto did Robert a considerable favor: the motion picture Rosebud, about a modern-day international kidnapping, set the film industry back in the dark ages.

The two separate occasions I interviewed Preminger proved to be editorially uninteresting. Every other word out of his egotistical mouth was preceded by "I," and when I tried to sort out the pearls from all the pebbles he was dropping, or sift diamonds from his dust, I wound up with hot air!

But enough of Otto and back to Deborah.

The caption under a photo accompanying my article in the *National Star* asked the question: "Kirk and Deborah smile on camera — but are their teeth clenched?" My story stated that the pair are portrayed as lovers in *Once Is Not Enough,* but that off-screen, Kirk and Deborah are about as friendly as two roosters in a cock fight. Deb's camp claimed the trouble stemmed from the fact that Kirk was annoyed because at 5'8½" she was too tall to play opposite him. Kirk's camp claimed the charge was ridiculous and that Deborah was "an excitable newcomer."

But Deborah told me on tape, before Ron and her husband-manager Michael Viner: "Let's say that working with Kirk Douglas was an experience that I'm pleased to have behind me."

The big blast, however, came from Michael, who said, "I just feel that Douglas is so hung up over his personal inadequacies that he wants to prove his masculinity.

"His shortness is one thing that worried him. Deborah had to do the whole movie in ballet shoes and he had to stand on his tiptoes so it would work out.

"He resented the height situation terribly and I think this is part of the reason he resented Deborah."

Viner also claimed that the fifty-eight-year-old Douglas expected Deborah to do a nude scene but her contract specifically barred it. Deborah told me that she is not against nude scenes in movies, as long as she's not involved!

In the film, which is the biggest crictical bomb of all time, Deborah plays the part of January Wayne who falls in love with a considerably older man.

The *Star* printed the reaction of Douglas's press people to Viner's theory that the height difference precipitated the feud: "As for the height, he is over six feet. How could there be any height problem?" But other sources put the actor's height at considerably less than six feet.

Deborah's hubby, also a West Coast record producer, claimed that Douglas was unnecessarily rough with actor David Janssen during a fight scene in the film. "Douglas hit Janssen so hard he caused the door to break that Janssen fell into. Misplaced aggression," Viner snorted.

The twenty-two-year-old "young Grace Kelly-type," a former model with three movies completed and a brilliant screen career ahead of her, was as professionally cool before Ron's clicking camera as she was on the set of *Once Is Not Enough*. Deborah said that whenever there was any trouble she never said a word. "I just walked off the set." Asked for his reaction to Douglas's reported treatment of his wife, Viner said: "I felt like slugging him. But then I remembered he was once a professional boxer and he'd probably beat the hell out of me. Discretion was the better part of valor."

I couldn't say I blamed Viner either. In fact, an out-of-town model I was dating told me over lunch at Sardis she could empathize with Viner's position. "You can't knock over a speeding locomotive just because it blows hot steam every time it goes past your property, can you?"

On the few occasions I dined at Sardi's, film-maker Bob Roberts was always about. But this time he was nowhere in sight. Roberts was always into projects that made for intriguing listening and while my date was intelligent and occasionally amusing, she was basically a bore.

Then, as if by magic, Roberts was making his way towards my table, extending his hand in a vigorous handshake. "Georgie boy. Haven't seen ya around for a while. What you into lately?" he said.

"The *National Star, In The Know* and a few other publications," I said. "I've even written a screenplay or two."

"Great going, Bernie," he said. "But talking about movies, I'm going to have 'Patty' on the set tomorrow."

"Patty Hearst?" I asked jokingly.

"Well, her father's a millionaire and she was kidnapped and she attended a university, and no one's been able to find her."

"Then you are doing the story of Patty Hearst?"

"Well, I'm not doing Mickey Mouse." Roberts laughed. "Let's play it safe and say my film is *inspired* by the bizarre and continuing story of America's first political abduction and I call my motion picture 'Patty'," Roberts revealed.

"The more I hear, the more I like. I think the *National Star* would like this one. How about I meet you on the set tomorrow? If there's a story there, I'll continue on until the film is in the can."

"You have a deal," Roberts said, writing out the address of the shooting.

"We start at 6:00 a.m.," he said, trying to frighten me.

"I'll meet you for coffee at 5:30 a.m." I said. Didn't he realize that as a former *Enquirer* reporter I've not only been up before the crack of dawn, but have gone on extended assignments without sleeping for seventy-two hours?

I was so impressed with the script that Roberts had written, his direction and the capable cast, that I stayed on until the filming was completed. My photos and copy made three-quarters of a page in the *Star* and eight pages in *Film International. New Times, Swank, Viva, In The Know, Bunte* of Germany, the *London Telegraph,* more and others carried my on-location feature articles which were replete with graphic photos simulating the dramatic events surrounding the kidnapping of the heiress-turned-revolutionary.

Roberts was even employing actual shrinks to portray themselves in the film. The psychiatrists, through their experience with aggression and social alienation, were able to weave a psychological tapestry of the events that might have motivated Patty and her S.L.A. cohorts to commit their devastating deeds.

But for Roberts, as he explained, the primary problem was finding not only a girl who resembled Patty, but one who could act. "A New York casting agent, attempting to tackle the impossible," recalls Roberts, "telephoned me at my home and said to stop looking. 'The girl is found' were her exact words."

And not only was twenty-two-year-old Sarah Nicholson a look-alike for the twenty-one-year-old Patty, and could act, but in May '74 she was stopped and detained briefly by a New York City police officer who was, in Sarah's words, "dead certain he had snared the catch of his lifetime.

Fortunately, I just managed to have my birth certificate with me. Was he disappointed!"

The bank holdup Roberts staged for his Trans-World Attractions Corp. cameras was so realistic that a bank guard told me "It was more frightening than the real one we had here recently." In fact, the manager of the branch office became so apprehensive after seeing Robert's rogues, including a hulking black actor portraying "Cinque," that he double-checked the security system on the vault.

Roberts even went so far as to recruit Lenny Montana from the first of the two *Godfather* epic films to portray the character Lou, right-hand man to reputed mobster Mickey Cohen who was commissioned by Patty's dad to find his missing daughter.

I was excited beyond my wildest imagination. The adrenalin was once again flowing through my veins. For no longer would I be compelled to adopt a cover or hide behind a front. The *Enquirer* was behind me now.

And after nineteen months of successfully evading the law, Patty Hearst was finally apprehended on September 18, '75 by the F.B.I. and local authorities in San Francisco's rundown Mission District, within miles of the university town of Berkeley — where her "kidnapping" had taken place. Within a half hour of her capture, Roberts went into swift action, contacting his composer to alter the lyrics . . . and Patty look-alike, Sarah Nicholson. Then the resolute Roberts began writing the absolute final chapter to the sensational saga that he vowed would be kept up-to-date before theatrical release.

"I'll go back into production, if need be, to keep the screen story accurate," Roberts had stated earlier to the news media. It was as if the film-maker had a sixth sense about Patty's imminent capture, for the movie had been in the can a few weeks before her arraignment.

Ironically, on August 27, just three weeks before her surprising seizure, Roberts met with a local supervisor of the F.B.I., providing tapes and transcript material from his film to aid the Bureau in the co-ed's capture.

And, can you imagine how elated I was in late September '75 when the *New York Times* News Service contacted me to syndicate internationally my "Patty" photos and text!

While the real Patty Hearst clung defiantly to the underground's militant methods of changing society — and was less than a month away from capture — one Herbert Khaury was busy blueprinting his plans of reform for the country, which he hoped to personally implement as President of the United States.

Khaury, otherwise known as Tiny Tim, in a exclusive, entertaining interview, uttered a lot of sense, as well as what would be considered by most as total nonsense! In this respect, however, he was in the league of all politicians, but with one decided difference: T. T. was genuinely sincere. He was incapable of being any different.

Instinctively, people tend to mock and grow annoyed with a ukulele-strumming entertainer when he becomes serious about anything other than the musical instrument he is playing. For many years on CBS, super pitchman Arthur Godfrey preached the preservation of a deteriorating environment over his radio network broadcasts. Some of the affiliates became irritated at the redhead's reluctance to change. One station, in spite, aired his program before the roosters crowed. Network brass were boiling mad at Arthur, but where Godfrey was concerned, they trod on egg shells, lest their special talent become upset. After the damage was done, and the Administration acknowledged the ecological erosion of the environment, the conservation-minded Arthur was properly praised as being perceptively right.

When a considerably less articulate, white-faced, mop-haired, fluttering Tiny Tim plays the uke, his views, especially those political, are not initially taken any more seriously ... or appreciated.

So it was that Tiny revealed he'd like to have Senator John Glenn the hero astronaut, as his Vice-Presidential running mate in '76. That is, providing of course, he could muster up enough political support to run for the Presidency.

"I feel that John Glenn is a real American," observed Tiny. "And I support his views. I feel he would be the best of all running mates ... but I doubt he'd want to run with me."

Two leading magazines scoffed at the Tiny Tim interview, and one editor remarked sarcastically: "Glenn, just a nice guy, who's no one to get serious over as a Vice-President. Why, Tiny Tim would have better odds for the Presidency."

Ironically, a year later, Glenn was considered a strong favorite in a field of three to be Jimmy Carter's choice for the second spot on the Democratic Party ticket. The Sunday evening before the start of the party's convention, I accompanied paparazzi Galella and Schmulbach to one of the most elegant outdoor political celebrations ever hosted at the Rockefeller Center Promenade. The temperature was most comfortable and a mild breeze was blowing in our faces. It was in this relaxed, informal setting I first met the Ohio Senator. Beads of nervous sweat were pouring profusely from the head and neck of Glenn who continued not to count his drinks as the countless line of delegates and other well-wishers stopped to shake his hand and wish him luck.

When I humorously related Tiny's earlier preference for him as the '76 Democratic V.P.

candidate, Glenn burst into a king-sized grin. "How is Tiny?" he asked, as if they were best friends. "If you see him, please give him my best, would you?" A pensive look then played over Glenn's face as he pondered the absurdity of being on a ticket with Tiny Tim, yet he responded to the news as any politician surely would. Glenn continued to clutch his glass as our conversation was interrupted by a cluster of admirers who were serious about establishing ties with the youthful-looking senator.

Two days later however, the affable, soft-spoken and so-easy-to-like John Glenn apparently didn't take his speech before the Convention delegates and Jimmy Carter, watching the coverage on a television set in his hotel room, seriously enough. Many delegates had told me he was a shoe-in, and possibly Glenn believed the rumors too and stopped trying. All we will ever know is that after delivering a totally disappointing, low-key, dispirited speech, which was further diminished by that of Texas delegate Barbara Jordan, John Glenn was dropped from all Vice-Presidential consideration.

It is highly unlikely that there was ever a real connection between Tiny Tim and John Glenn, other than a possible mutual fascination, or respect of their apparent differences. How remote, however, is the possibility of a Tiny Tim ever becoming the President of the United States? If a tie salesman from Missouri can reach the highest plateau of politics, and a peanut farmer from Georgia capture the voting public's heart, then is it really so unlikely that Tiny Tim, if properly packaged, could capture the imagination of a nation and the Chief Executive's seat?

Consider Tiny's platform: "I would rid the country of crime, by getting to the root of poverty. *Everyone* in the poor and middle class, as soon as they are born, would get a monthly allotment

344

of up to $100 until the age of eighteen. At age twelve, children would be drafted, not into an army, but into fulltime work and would therefore bypass the wasteful lingering and loitering phase of their lives that could lead to crime. Poverty is caused, my friend, by the fear of being put into the streets, and that is why people commit crime. They can't pay their rent . . . ."

Tiny also advocates having "every" aspect of society represented in government, including prostitutes, criminals and beggars, among other seemingly undesirable groups. "It would seem healthy to have the people of this country see that we're all God's creatures. With such representation of all kinds of people, it would tend to make others more aware of what's going on in the world," he adds.

"I would have the government abolish all rent from the people of the middle class down, just like the Medicaid program. I would have the government use the taxes of the country to pay this rent. I believe we need taxes — to support our highways and our system. Taxes should take care of the people the way people are taking care of taxes."

If Tiny became President, he would impose controls on our over-consumption of food, the cause of heart attacks and other diseases, he contends, and model our eating habits after the French, whom he praises as being "frugal" in that respect. Tiny would also institute a massive food giveaway program to starving nations, "and we'd still be filled," he points out.

But Tiny, in the following respect, sounds like a practical politician when he says: "My ideas would not be good for a Congress who would vote against my programs. For what good is running for President if I couldn't accomplish my goals? One way to circumvent this problem," he observes, "is to only have men running with me who agreed with everything I said and voted *with* me, and not against." But isn't that every politician's unreachable dream? Indeed, good men with good people behind them, ushering in good times for the nation at best appears improbable.

Oddly enough, both an article on the film "Patty," in which producer Roberts practically pinpointed the reasons for, and the time of, her capture, and the Tiny Tim interview on John Glenn, were rejected by . . . the *National Enquirer*. "You lose some, you win some," Pope might say when confronted with the two that got away. Yet again, he might just deservedly create a lot of heat for the articles editor who rejected these two scoops of editorial cream.

Times are euphorically different for me now. I choose my own assignments, those that are devoid of unnecessary peril and the hazards involved with tempermental giants, ferocious wild animals, scummy sewers, filmdom's intoxicated idols and the unequivocally insane. My days at the *Enquirer* are far behind me — finally — with brighter days ahead.

After checking out the Plaza for celebrities, Galella and I
are about to speed off in the *paparazzi's* T-bird for other
choice star spots in Fun City. (*Paul Schmulbach*)

Dr. Milford Blackwell, a psychiatrist, contends that
Jackie's life is in constant
danger.

I waited ten years for an interview with the former First Lady, but she rebuffed my request. "If you can figure out a way, you're a genius!" she said.

Deborah Raffin, star of *Once Is Not Enough*, told me that once was enough playing opposite Kirk Douglas. *(Ron Galella)*

(Above) Sarah Nicholson poses as Tania-the-Outlaw for the motion picture, *Patty*, and (below) producer-director Robert Roberts holds a megaphone while Lenny Montana of *Godfather* fame, loads a pistol for a chase scene. (George Bernard)

Tiny Tim without his ukulele, and an eye focused on Galella's camera, told me that to "tiptoe through the tulips" was not as important as becoming President of the United States.

(Ron Galella)

Senator John Glenn, on the eve of the Democratic Convention, burst into a big smile after I told him Tiny Tim wanted the former astronaut as his Vice-Presidential running mate.
(Paul Schmulbach)

EPILOGUE

In retrospect, however, I view my days at the old *National Enquirer* as journalistic joys. I am profoundly grateful to Providence for the weird and wondrous road I traveled.

I am also thankful to have escaped the hazards of monotony, which is attendant on most jobs in America. For as the erudite shrink, Dr. Jack J. Leedy, noted in one of my articles for the *Enquirer:* "Boredom equals death. Research studies have shown conclusively that many hospital patients who experience boredom over prolonged periods, simply expire."

While I was an *Enquirer* reporter, Leedy's studies of how boredom destroyed human brain cells never frightened me. I was inspired and considered myself immune to the perils of tedium. *The Inc.* was on my dangerous drug list. The *Enquirer* was my constant upper and I was addicted to the paper's adventurous assignments.

Shortly, however, I found my appetite for new excitement rapidly growing and demanding a steady nourishment of the beastial, the bizarre and the biggest stars of Hollywood.

I discovered years later, after I was commissioned to compile my many memoirs of the old *Enquirer* days, that the vast reservoir of personal experiences had caused a gigantic overflow.

Celebrities like Barbra Streisand, Van Johnson, Shirley Booth, Gig Young and even Muhammed Ali, (who said of his fight with Sonny Liston he was praying the better man won, even if it wasn't him) would have to be reserved for another time, another place.

The excess even included the miracle of six-year-old Mayumi Suzuki, a beautiful Japanese girl. While 3,000 tons of coal crushed fifteen neighboring homes, Mayumi slept through the terrifying avalanche in the morning, emerged unscathed with no knowledge of just how close she had come to death.

And there was no space for Ricky Nelson's confession that his dad, the late Ozzie Nelson, was a tyrant as a father and boss of the long-running TV show "Ozzie & Harriet."

The same fate met another Ricky: cut out! Ricky Bolton of Washington, D.C. had to wear a football helmet to remain alive . . . after losing one-third of his brain in an auto accident.

In the further interests of condensing my contents, I deleted the caper of bystanders who kicked maimed cattle after an accident in Oklahoma City, Oklahoma. And I shelved the story of a woman who died at her own birthday party when her guests were overcome by furnace fumes. And how inhumane I felt after failing to include the heart warming story of a mother who feared cystic fibrosis would surely claim the life of her remaining child as it had her first two.

For more than a month, I tossed and turned in my sleep over a foreign intrigue chapter. In the end, this one, as others, was snipped in the interests of space. The true incidents involved contacting the Kremlin for an exclusive interview with Alexei Kosygin. Speaking personally to Gamul Abdul Nasser. Discovering that Fidel Castro was not in Cuba, but with the U.A.R. leader in Egypt. My phones were tapped continuously and the tightest surveillance, twenty-four-hours-a-day, surrounded my office and personal life.

Would I repeat my *Enquirer* past with the same frenzied determination? Most assuredly! There are no time machines known to modern science, but, as the song goes, "I can dream, can't I?"